Matthew Hale Smith

Mount Calvary, with Meditations in Sacred Places

Matthew Hale Smith

Mount Calvary, with Meditations in Sacred Places

ISBN/EAN: 9783337288754

Printed in Europe, USA, Canada, Australia, Japan

Cover: Foto ©Lupo / pixelio.de

More available books at **www.hansebooks.com**

Mount Calvary,

with

Meditations in Sacred Places.

By

Mathew Hale Smith,

AUTHOR OF "UNIVERSALISM NOT OF GOD," "COUNSELS TO YOUNG PERSONS," ETC.

NEW YORK:
CARLETON, PUBLISHER, 413 BROADWAY.
MDCCCLXVI.

Entered according to Act of Congress, in the year 1866,
By GEO. W. CARLETON,
In the Clerk's Office of the District Court of the United States for the Southern District of New York.

Dedication.

To

Zion's Friends

and

Mine.

CONTENTS.

	PAGE
I.—Mount Calvary and the Land of the Bible	7
II.—Calvary Identified	11
III.—Calvary in the early Time of the Patriarchs	18
IV.—Calvary in the Time of our Lord	23
V.—Calvary and the Incarnation	28
VI.—Calvary and the Divinity of Christ	37
VII.—Calvary, or Eight Days before the Crucifixion	46
VIII.—Calvary, and the Holy Prophets	79
IX.—Calvary, and the Holy Gospels	91
X.—Calvary, and the Church of God	95
XI.—Calvary, and the Sabbath of Eden	100
XII.—The Mountains of Nebo; or, the Death-Song of Moses	109
XIII.—Jericho; or, the Scarlet Line in the Window	112
XIV.—Vale of Sodom; or, the Testimony of Lot's Wife	120
XV.—Tomb of Rachel; or, the Death of Children	127
XVI.—The Field of Boaz; or, Consecrated Affection	135
XVII.—Joseph, a Type of Christ	141
XVIII.—A Festival for all the Family; or, the Home of Jesse	150
XIX.—The Vale of Elah; or, Home Preparation for Life's Duties	160
XX.—The Ark of God on a New Cart	169
XXI.—The Mount of Offense; or, Perils of Age	177
XXII.—The Plain of Zaanaim; or, Butter in a Lordly Dish	182
XXIII.—The Plain of Ono; or, Religious Strategy	188

CONTENTS.

	PAGE
XXIV.—The Pulpit of Wood; or, the Power of the Bible	198
XXV.—Palace Shushan; or, Business Integrity	204
XXVI.—The Black Tents of Idumea; or, Death not the Great Enemy	213
XXVII.—Five Smooth Stones from the Brook; or, Future Life and Retribution certain	222
XXVIII.—The City of Ephraim; or, a Cake not Turned	246
XXIX.—The Oaks of Ephraim; or, the Fruits of Bad Training	252
XXX.—The Crafty confounded in the Temple; or, Hard Things in the Bible	257
XXXI.—The Sea of Galilee; or, a Well-Instructed Scribe	264
XXXII.—Footsteps on the Mountains; or, Preaching considered as a Profession	273
XXXIII.—The Corinthian Revilers; or, the Guilt of Ignorance	281
XXXIV.—Mount Hermon; or, Christian Union	288
XXXV.—Hebron; or, the Mission of Childhood	293
XXXVI.—Nazareth; or, the Home of the Child Jesus	302
XXXVII.—Mount of Olives; or, Passages in the Life of our Lord	307
XXXVIII.—Gadara; or, the Perishing Classes	316
XXXIX.—Home of the Lordly: or, Hell a Reality	322
XL.—The Mount of Temptation; or, Warnings to Youth	328
XLI.—The Pinnacle of the Temple; or, Satan not a Fiction	334
XLII.—The City of David; or, the Night Interview with Christ	339
XLIII.—The Well of Sychar; or, Sectarianism Rebuked	352
XLIV.—The River-Side Prayer-Meeting	357
XLV.—The City of the Great King; or, the Coronation of Christ	367
XLVI.—Mount Carmel and the Sea	376
XLVII.—The First and Last Supper	385

MOUNT CALVARY,

WITH

MEDITATIONS IN SACRED PLACES.

───◆───

I.—MOUNT CALVARY AND THE LAND OF THE BIBLE.

> "I'll carve my passions on the bark,
>   And every wounded tree
> Shall drop and bear some mystic mark
>   That Jesus died for me.
> The swains shall wonder when they read,
>   Inscribed on all the grove,
> That Heaven itself came down to bleed,
>   And win a mortal's love."

The land of the Bible is not large, but famed above all the earth. Out of its dust Adam was formed. Here man sinned and fell, and the curse, like the mist from the valley, spread over all the world. It was the home of the Patriarchs, and their sepulchres remain to this day. Among the hills and vales of the Holy Land, David's lyre awoke the echoes of melody. Amid its kingly scenery, Solomon reigned in all his glory. Isaiah, rapt in vision, saw the Messiah's day, and spake of Him: God walked with men in the cool of the day. The mountains were vocal, and He rode the chariot of flame. Palestine was the home of the Redeemer. In the sweet vale of Ephratah angels heralded his coming, and sang celestial praises to the Most High God. The Word was here made flesh, and handled by the sons of men.

> "Over these acres walked those blessed feet
> Which eighteen hundred years ago
> Were nailed for our advantage to the bitter cross."

Here our Lord passed his youth, earned the bread that sustained his humanity, lived and loved and taught, carried blessing to many homes and hearts, scattered mercy on all sides, filled the cities and villages with joy as he passed; healed the sick, made the blind see, and the lame leap for joy; robbed the grave of its prey, and gave back the dead to the hearts that "believed not for joy, but wondered." Here he bound up himself with the sinful children of woe, bearing the sickness and pains of God's suffering ones; here he was tempted, tired, and cast down, being made like unto his brethren, that he might have compassion on men.

The Holy Land is still true to its ancient title of the "Unchanging East." It is now as in the olden time. Buried cities come forth to confirm the sacred record. Sodom's sullen lake holds the story of God's judgment among men. Moriah, though a waste, is marked as distinctly as when its summit was crowned with the glorious temple to which the thronging nation came thrice a year for worship. Hebron holds the tomb of Machpelah, within which is kept the sacred dust of Abraham and Sarah. The dew of Hermon has wet the banners of all nations, from Nebuchadnezzar to Napoleon. Nazareth, Bethlehem, Zion, Jehoshaphat, Olives, and Calvary, remain as really as do Rome or London. The dark road to Jericho is dark and perilous still. The shepherd can be seen on the hillside, in garb and appearance like the sons of Jacob, leading his sheep, who know his voice and follow him. Women go out to the well to draw water for the noon-tide meal, and will, if asked, give the weary traveler at the well-curb to drink from the pitcher. The ox treadeth out the grain. On the house-top the family assemble. Men in the morning take up their bed and walk. The pitcher at the fountain is often broken, and the bowl at the cistern is destroyed. In the earlier time, God held the land of Zion sacred to worship. It has been bound up with the great and endearing events of life. It is loved and honored, and holds the tears, and prayers, and hopes, of the best part of our race. In the changes, revolutions, convulsions of the earth that are to come, in the overthrow of dynasties, and the rise and fall of kingdoms, the march of freedom, truth, humanity, and the Kingdom of God, with the dawning of the millennium and the subjugation of the earth to Christ, the calling of the Redeemer blessed, this portion of the world will have much to do.

"Dear to the exile is the soil
That reared Jehovah's vine;
Dear to the wretched heir of toil,
Thy memory, Palestine.

Land of the Patriarchs, he recalls
　　The days of promise, when
The timbrel rang along the halls,
　　And God communed with men.

And hope still guides his thoughts afar·
　　It tells to all who roam,
That *He* who rode the cloudy car
　　Will guide His people home."

II.—CALVARY IDENTIFIED.

> Calvary's mournful mountain climb,
>   Thus adoring at His feet,
> Mark that miracle of time,
>   God's own Sacrifice complete:
> "It is finished," hear Him cry;
> Learn of Jesus Christ to die.

It would require a miracle to blot out the site on which the Redeemer died for man. Calvary, for many centuries, has been fragrant with precious memories to God's people. The Lord had done marvelous things for them, and the covenant made with their fathers grouped many of its most hallowed features around this summit. It was the custom of the children of Abraham, in their better days, to mark the location of God's visitation to them. National gratitude and religious faith bade them stud the highway of their pilgrimage with memorials of his presence. From Canaan to Egypt, and from Egypt to Canaan, a few hundred miles, covered all their journeyings. From sire to son, the sacred localities would be handed down with pious exactness. The Jews of this generation hold in reverence and buy the privilege of wailing near the old foundation-stones on which Solomon's temple once stood.

So in all ages we find the Jew hovering over the site of his ancient greatness, marking with intense fervor places celebrated in the history of his race.

To such a people, sacred localities would neither be lost nor unknown. No matter how long the time between Abel's sacrifice and the offerings of Isaac on this Mount; nor how desolate or uninhabited might be Moriah or Calvary, it is God that points out the sacred spot, and commands and guides his servant where to make the great offering. The foundations of Jerusalem herself, her brazen gates, massive walls, and altars of daily sacrifice, were not better known in the days of John the Baptist, than was Moriah, the Mount of Vision, from the hour of Adam's morning song, to the present. As students of the Bible, we know little of the Holy Land and of the localities of sacred story. The Bible was written amid the scenery, the social and kingly customs, the arts and trades, and among the people who dwelt in or near Palestine. Few readers of the Bible have any clear idea of the geography of sacred events. Dim, misty, and far-off to the popular mind, is the theatre of those stupendous transactions that compose the historic parts of the Word of God. The homes where lived and wrote those holy men, who spoke by the Holy Ghost, are to us as mythical as the dreams of childhood. The location of the great things God did among men is hidden from the common eye as is the tomb of Moses. The long procession of generations has trampled them out of sight. We do not study sacred, as we do profane history. With the map before us, we do not follow the march of God's people as we do the march of armies. Their encampments are not studied as we study great battles. Did we do so, we should find that sacred localities have been preserved with an accuracy almost as exact as sacred history itself. Crowded into a circuit of about fifty miles from the summit of Calvary, transpired nearly all the marked events of sacred history. Standing on the Mount of Olives, near the site where the Redeemer wept over the doomed Capital of David, the eye takes in the locality of nearly all the events, from Eden to the preaching fields of John, the mountains and vales, the seas and towns, celebrated in sacred story and in song. Calvary and Moriah stand before us, so near that we could hail the priest that offers sacrifice near the site where Abraham offered Isaac. Standing on that spot, we could have heard the death-cry of Abel as he fell beneath the fatal blow. The Mountain of Corruption and the accursed vale of Hinnom are near. Carmel rises in great beauty, bathing its feet in the blue Mediterranean. The hills of Nazareth, backed by the mountains of Samaria, are plainly seen. Hermon, with its dew still descending; Tabor, where Deborah fought, and Moses and Elias talked with Christ; Sychar, the tent-home of Jacob, whence Joseph went forth to a prison and a throne, and where, foot-sore and weary, the seed of Jacob, in later times, asked water from the well of his fathers. We can see the spot where Abraham pitched his tent, when he "departed out of Haran, having Bethel on the west and Hai on the east." Hebron is within our range, where the ashes of Sarah and Abraham repose, now celebrated as the birthplace of John, the forerunner of our Lord. The sea of Sodom is in view, whose sullen waters pay no tribute to the ocean, beneath which sleep the guilty cities of the plain. Bethlehem, where Rachel died, and Jacob "set a pillar upon her grave, whose sepulchre remains to this day;" where Ruth gleaned, and where David dwelt and drank water from the well of his fathers; and where, greater than all, his greater son was born, in the fullness of time. The threshing-floor of Boaz is near the field of blood. The honored grave of Isaac, and the dishonored tomb of Absalom, can be seen. The seat of Adonijah's treason, near the Hill of Evil Council. Bethel, where God appeared to Jacob in the night watches, near to Emmaus, where the Saviour appeared to his disciples, after he was raised from the dead. Nebo, from whose summit Moses saw the goodly land that he might not enter, whose grave was dug by the Almighty Hand, and where God "buried him in the land of Moab, over against Beth-peor, no man knowing of his sepulchre to this day." Kirjath Jearim, where the ark rested for many years, is near the vale where the grim and bloody rites of Moloch were celebrated. Gethsemane, with the old strong walls identified with the days of kingly glory—all this and more can be seen by the traveler on the summit of Olivet, grouping the acts, miracles, battles, victories, defeats, and judgments, from Moses to Eli—from David to Herod. Tradition alone would be sufficient to locate the transactions of the Bible. Only seven persons would be needed, if it rested on tradition alone, to bear down the locality of these wonderful events from Adam to Abraham. Methusaleh was a man of years before Adam died. From the lips of the first man with whom he conversed, Methuselah could have learned all that transpired, with the places on which the events were transacted—from the fall and the expulsion, to the death of Abel. He could learn where Abel's altars stood, and where Cain committed the bloody deed. Methuselah, who knew Adam, talked with Noah. To Noah he could have committed the history that came from Adam. Noah died only two years before Abraham was born. Shem, the son of Noah, knew Isaac. All the events preceding the flood, in which Noah bore a part, with the wickedness of the world, the scorn of men while the ark was building—where the keel of the ark was laid—whether at Joppa or elsewhere—with all the scenes attending that terrible judgment that swept away the ungodly, with the coming forth out of the ark, and the spot where the altar of Noah stood on the new creation, yet wet with the deluge—all could, and no doubt were, borne along to Abraham and his children by Noah and his sons. And thus, through the same holy and inspired men, by whom the Scriptures came in the olden time, tradition could have handed down, in the most reliable form, the site of Adam's altar and the story of his ruin—the mountain on which Abel offered the sacrifice, in connection with the thrilling and interesting facts, and the places on which they transpired.

In New England, a short time since, there resided a gentleman who was over ninety years old. He had an unclouded intellect and an unimpaired memory, which stretched back to his childhood. He knew Washington, and was familiar with the events that attended his assuming the command of the **Army** of the Revolution at Cambridge. He knew the tree under which the Father of his Country pronounced his Inaugural. He could point out the exact spot upon which Washington stood when he gave his first word of command. These events were fresh in his memory at his death as if they transpired yesterday. He told them to his children and to his children's children. The march of time and the sweep of events may obliterate these localities. History holds them dimly now. In coming time it may not only be interesting, but important, to mark the exact site at Cambridge where these interesting events transpired. Should a dispute arise in after times, and one of the great-grandchildren of this New England Patriarch—no further removed from his ancestor than was Noah from Adam—go to the spot and say, "My father took me to this place, and said, 'Here my grandfather stood when he pointed out this locality where General Washington stood when he took command of the Army of Independence,'" such testimony would be received at once. It would end strife and settle dispute. But such tradition would not equal the interview of Adam with Methuselah, nor of Methuselah with Noah, nor of Noah with Isaac, and through them to his children's children.

The site of Abraham's offering was marked distinctly by the command of God to David, "to offer burnt offerings on Mount Moriah;" and the order to raise the house of the Lord on that same sacred site. From that moment to the present there has been no time when Calvary could be hid from the eyes of the living.

It was a marked spot in the time of the Saviour. It was offensive and loathsome, and devoted to the vilest uses. After the Crucifixion, holy women kept watch and ward through the long hours of the three days and nights in which the Son of Man lay in the grave. It was so dear to the great Christian heart that Adrian, to insult the Church, polluted it and placed on it an image of his god Jupiter.

But these efforts only made Calvary more marked. The Jupiter of Adrian and the Chapel of Helena identify Calvary beyond a cavil, and sanctify it as holy ground to this day.

If Mounts Moriah and Olives, the Vales of Jehoshaphat and Hinnom, the Dead Sea and Galilee, the pools of Siloam and Bethesda, are identified, Calvary cannot be unknown or unmarked.

III.—CALVARY IN THE EARLY TIME OF THE PATRIARCHS.

CALVARY, Zion, and Moriah are parts of the same mountain, standing alone in the solitude of the land. The Mount of Vision, called "one of the Mountains of Moriah," reared its tall rocky peak in the center, and gave its name to the group. Its summit was crowned with a broad flat stone, which, in latter times, became the "chief foundation-stone of the temple." Mount Zion was one spur of the mountain and Mount Calvary another.

Since men first began to call on the Lord, Calvary has been sacred to worship. The spot selected, on which the Lamb slain from the foundation of the world should be put to death, had been long dedicated to Divine Service. Tradition has persistently affirmed that the great and memorable events before the flood transpired on or near this mountain. From the red soil of Moriah, Adam was made and named. When he poured out his morning song in the days of his innocence, it was amid the same mountain and vales that heard the death-cry of the Lamb of God. And near the spot where the angel of God barred the gates of Paradise against the guilty pair, the second Adam opened the gates of Paradise to the penitent thief on the cross. The altar on which Abel offered his more acceptable sacrifice and his blood that cried unto God was near the spot on which the precious blood of Jesus was spilt. At the base of the same mountain probably the blood that cried for revenge and that which "speaketh better things than the blood of Abel" mingled on the same sacred soil.

Long before Abraham sacrificed his son, this locality was holy unto the Lord. Here Melchisedek lived and reigned King of Salem and Priest of the Most High God. He was so great, that to him "even the Patriarch Abraham gave a tenth of his spoils." When Isaac was to be made a sacrifice, God appointed the place. He chose Moriah, Zion, and Calvary. Why that long journey to "one of the mountains that I will tell you of?"—why take the journey, the wood, the servants, the lad, traveling three days and looking up toward the Mount of Vision "afar off"—when the sacrifice could have been made at home? But if, as tradition asserts, on this group of mountains Adam worshiped and Abel sacrificed, then we know why Melchisedek ruled and reigned in Salem, and why Abraham made his long journey to the "Mount called Moriah;" for, in the purposes of heaven in the fullness of time, the Lamb of God must be sacrificed on the same hill-top in Judea, and thus the type and ante-type meet.

The foundations of the City of the Great King were laid in religious faith and service. From the sacrifice of Isaac to the time of the Saviour the mountain was a place of worship. Here the children of Abraham called on the God of their fathers. Rude tents were pitched to shelter the worshipers. Rude booths formed a more permanent habitation.

Dwellings were builded here and there to accommodate priest and people. Advancing civilization and strength extended the foundations around Moriah till Jerusalem became the home of the nation and the joy of the whole earth.

The land of the Bible is the cradle of law and government, as well as religion. On the summit of Moriah civil and religious service joined hands to begin their mission of blessing to the children of men. When David reigned in Hebron, Calvary was a waste, Moriah a threshing-floor, and Zion a walled city, which David took from the Jebusites. But he purchased Moriah as a holy place unto the Lord. "With money current with the merchants" he purchased it, and dedicated to God, as the spot where saints and patriarchs had worshiped from the early time. The Most High accepted the offering. And when the sweet-smelling savor went from that ancient place of worship, God sent down the healing power, and the plague was stayed in all the land.

The erection of the Temple on Moriah was by the express command of God. Solomon was ordered to "build the House of the Lord at Jerusalem, where the Lord appeared unto David his father, in the place that David had purchased in the threshing-floor of Ornan the Jebusite." And the mighty Temple builded by Solomon crowned the high top of the Mount of Vision, where Adam worshiped, Abel sacrificed, Abraham was tried, and David bowed in prayer. God accepted the house as his own, filled it with his glory, and called up the great nation to worship within its gates, to pour its full living tide with song and joy into the Temple to keep holy time. Then Moriah, Calvary, and Zion were not more sacred to Divine service, than they were in those hours of the world's infancy when men began to call on the Lord. God has ever had a seed to serve him and a place for the Altar of praise. All along the pathway of the Church he has marked and hallowed this locality, from the sacrifice of Abel to the hour when the only begotten Son was crucified, there making his soul an offering for sin.

Identified as Calvary is with civilization, the arts and sciences, it will be more precious to the Christian and memorable as the hill-top on which the Great Expiation was made. Around it cluster the mysteries of redemption, when mercy in rich drops of blood wet the ground and silenced the voice of blood that cried for revenge. The name Calvary, so sweet to the redeemed soul, is named but once in the Bible. It is associated with ignominy, shame, and terror. Yet not one base or infamous thing would the Church have blotted out. The blood-stained sword of the patriot who died for his nation is a precious relic in the eyes of his children's children. The rope, the chain, the gibbet, by which the noble ones of the earth have passed to their reward from earth are more precious than rubies.

The Christian holds the soil of Calvary in all reverence. Men of all sects and nationalities tread its sacred dust beneath their feet with reverence, bow in prayer under the great dome that covers the site where the Lord of Life and Glory was crucified between two thieves. There are millions who adore the Holy One whom men sought to dishonor on Calvary. And, as Napoleon said on the rock-ribbed Helena: "There are millions to-day that would die for the Son of God," who died for man.

IV.—CALVARY IN THE TIME OF OUR LORD.

When the Redeemer was among men, Calvary was the foulest spot in the sacred city. It was without the walls, and infamous. It was the Tyburn of Jerusalem, where the vilest men were crucified and buried. Crucifixion was a great disgrace. No Roman could be subject to it. It was the last mark of detestation on the most abandoned and base of men. The soil on the hillside was thin and scanty. Victims had a hasty burial, and from their scanty graves the limbs protruded; and often the bodies of the slain were unearthed by jackals and beasts of prey, and the ground strewed with the skulls and bones of dead men. The hill was popularly known as "Golgatha, the place of the skull."

As our Lord was to die the most ignominious of deaths, he must die in the place most infamous. So the councils of men decided. But, long before Herod, Pontius Pilate, or Caiaphas took counsel together, the death, the season, and the spot, were appointed, in that council in which the Lamb slain from the foundation of the world accepted the mission to save ungodly men. "Die man or justice must, unless for him some other, able as willing, pay the rigid satisfaction, death for death." Infamous in the eyes of men, Cavalry has hallowed all forms and hours of service, from the earlier days, till the blessings of God came to the house of Elisabeth, in the gift of a son, the "Forerunner of the Lord."

Steadily the Son of God placed his eye on Calvary, and toward it he directed his steps from his birth. He came not into the world to live. He came to die. He did live. He "grew in wisdom and in favor with God and man." He has "left us an example." But all this was incidental. Without Calvary, he would not have trodden the earth at all. Onward, with a steady step, from the manger, he moved to the Cross. He saw its summit from his home at Nazareth. Its shadows fell on his path, as he toiled beneath the hot sun of Nazareth. All his thought tended to this summit. Devout Greeks, at Jerusalem, sought out his disciples, to whom they said: "Sirs, we would see Jesus." Our Lord knew that only through Calvary could the door of mercy be opened to the Gentiles. "His soul was troubled" at the request. The agony of the Atonement pressed upon him. Visions of the death he must die caused him to exclaim: "Father, save me from this hour." The "corn of wheat must fall into the ground and die." The strengthening voice of God from heaven swept the agony from his serene brow, and, with uplifted eye, he exclaimed: "But for this cause came I unto this hour." A trembling penitent received from his lips the only words of blessed admonition and mercy that she ever heard. She had been an outcast among men, with the brand of infamy on her brow. He called her and said, "Go, and sin no more." Soon she came into the divine presence bearing precious ointment—the wages of infamy, probably. She poured out the costly perfume on his feet. She knew not how that gift agitated the heart of Jesus, and bore him onward to the hour of expiation. "She did it for my burial," said he; "let her alone."

Our Lord stood at the grave of him he loved, groaning in spirit, and shedding tears over Lazarus. "Behold how he loved him," said the Jews. What was death to him who held the keys of hell? Why shed he tears that Lazarus had laid in the grave four days, when with a word he could summon him from the tomb, bound hand and foot? He knew full well, that, in eight short days, the work for which he left the bosom of the Father would be done. His best friends would behold him in agony on the cross. They would bear him to his sepulcher. His cause seemed to be lost; hell would be exultant. Nor would the disciples remember, till many days after, his tender words to Martha: "I am the resurrection and the life."

Our Lord has left us no memorials of his birth. Scanty are the fragments of his childhood and youth. Little do we know of that interesting period between the time when he talked with the Doctors in the Temple and his appearance at the waters of Jordan, demanding baptism of John. No life could be richer in incident, or more precious to the Church. As a man, he left the poor home of Joseph, a few tools, and his daily work, to take up power, renown, and repute. At thirty years of age he made himself a name, and filled the world with his fame. The earth shook beneath his tread. People were awed with his divine utterances. The sea and the elements heard his voice, and obeyed him. Disease felt his healing touch and departed. Demons knew him, and fled abashed from his presence. The grave and corruption gave back their prey at his voice. His miraculous power was seen in all that he did. When men arrested him, he told them that he gave them that power—that it was by his permission that any man touched him. In that Senate, amid the fiendish mockeries and exultations of his judges, he could, if he would, have let them down to hell. He had only to speak, he said, and a "legion of angels" would appear for his deliverance. He was arrested, because he came into the world for that purpose. He laid down his life because he chose to do so; no man could take it from him. When he chose, he could take up his life again. Of all this no memorials are left.

But of Calvary marked mention is made. An institution commemorates the agony and infamy of crucifixion, that will remain while the sun and moon shall endure. "Ye do show forth my death"—"Do this in remembrance of me"—"Show forth my death till I come," are the commands. The bread and the wine are emblems of a broken body and spilled blood. "We take, and eat, in remembrance that Christ died for us, and feed on him in our hearts, by faith, with thanksgiving."

But where are the memorials of his teachings, his miracles, his compassion, or his mercy? Blessed be God, for all this in the incarnate Lamb of God. But, as the great purpose of his life was to make his soul an offering for sin, he could afford no memorials but such as should exalt that grace which led him, though rich, to become poor, that man, through that poverty, might be rich.

Our Lord received guests from his Father's mansion. Moses and Elias were the chosen ambassadors to visit the earth, and converse with God's well-beloved Son. Tabor, a solitary mountain in the centre of a great plain, was selected as the Audience Chamber. Our Lord robed himself with the garments of light, to give audience to his celestial visitants. We know the theme of their discourse. It was not the wonderful success of Jesus—the mighty miracles he wrought—nor the renown of the Son of God. Simple and impressive is the record: "Moses and Elias appeared in glory to Jesus, and spake of his decease, which he should accomplish at Jerusalem." Even heaven could not be silent on the great theme of Calvary. Angels still look on that little summit with wonder. Calvary will never pass away. When the heavens shall depart and there shall be no more sea—when the sun shall be turned to blood and the stars to dust—when the angels of God shall shout that "time shall no longer be"—Calvary, like a jewel from a crushed crown, will abide. Around it the redeemed before the throne shall meet and shout, in the presence of the Lamb, "Thou hast redeemed us to God with thy blood;" and he shall lead them to living fountains, and his own soft hand wipe tears from every eye.

V.—CALVARY AND THE INCARNATION.

> "The Word descending from above,
>   Though with the Father still on high,
> Went forth upon his work of love,
>   And soon to life's last hour drew nigh.
> At birth, our brother he became;
>   Ever himself as food he gives;
> To ransom us he died in shame,
>   As our reward, in bliss he lives."

"For your sake he became poor." The fullness and grace of this saying we learn only at the cross. The mystery of the Incarnation who can comprehend? "A virgin shall bear a Son!" "The holy thing that shall be born of thee shall be the Son of God!" The fullness of time came, numbered not to the birth of the Saviour, but to the time he should "be cut off," as if the birth and life were nothing; Bethlehem of no account, Calvary all! Living in the town of Nazareth was a woman named Anna, with Mary, her daughter. She was of the royal line of David. Had the kingly line been unbroken, Anna and her children would have dwelt in the places of kings. Visions of royal greatness did not disturb that humble but happy home. Beneath that lowly roof Mary dwelt. Her ambition seemed to be, to serve well the God of her fathers and be, among her kindred, "the joyful mother of children." She was affianced to a man of lowly calling, but one whom revelation pronounced a "just and an honorable man." To that cottage-home a celestial visitor came. It was Gabriel himself, who "stood in the presence of the Most High." A great personage must be expected on earth, to have called such a messenger from heaven. Her heart died within her as Mary received the salutation of the angel. She was bewildered that herself, an humble maiden of Judea, should be addressed as one "highly favored of God," to be "forever blessed among women." The great mission to which she was called was revealed to her. It involved disgrace, derision, agony, perhaps death. Who would credit the visit of Gabriel? How could she meet the eye of that just man, Joseph? She hesitated not one moment, but bowed her head, and, with heroic trust, exclaimed, "Behold the handmaid of the Lord!" "Be it unto me according to thy word." Her ecstatic song, one of the noblest and most heroic in the world, indicates her fear and courage—her self-distrust and abiding confidence in the God of her fathers.

Her great secret could not be borne alone. In whom could she confide? Not in Anna; not in Joseph. Far away from her own home on the hillside nestled the ancient and honorable City of Hebron, located in the plains of Mamre, sacred to the patriarchs. In that city dwelt a kinswoman of Mary, to whom she could unburden herself, and tell the great story that swelled and surged in her almost bursting heart. She would credit the story of Gabriel, and tell the maiden of Judea what these wonderful words meant—"that holy thing to be born of thee shall be called the Son of the Highest—he shall sit on the throne of his father, David, and reign over the house of Jacob forever." This home in Hebron was the residence of Zacharias and Elisabeth. Zacharias was a priest of God, walking blameless in the ordinances of the Lord. His home was childless. Beneath his roof an infant's smile had not shed gladness. The bosom of Elisabeth had not throbbed with maternal love. The wail of childhood had not rang through the dwelling of the priest of God. Eighty years had sobered the hope and whitened the hair of this holy couple. But no voice had called the sweet name of mother. Many a lonely home had been made happy by the birth of a child. In the quiet hillside-house of many a lowly matron in the vale of indigence, children had been sent as a gift from God. But the great boon of a child—so longed for—so prayed for—had been denied to this otherwise blessed and happy abode.

For three hundred years, God had held no direct and special communication with man. His temple crowned Moriah, as of old. The yearly convocations were held. The morning and evening incenses went up from the altar of daily sacrifice. Men waited for the coming of Shiloh. Public expectation was excited. The devout prayed, "Come, Elijah, and bring the promised Messiah." But the oracle was dumb. There was no prophet or angel sent to man. He who rode the cloudy car, and directed the column of fire, seemed to have withdrawn from his chosen people.

Sacred were the associations connected with Hebron. It was a location fragrant with the memories of God's covenant love and mercy. The Cave of Machpelah, where, side by side, lay the dust of Abraham and Sarah, was committed to its keeping. It commanded the site where the tent of the father of this nation stood when angels rested at noonday "beneath the tree that stood at the tent-door" of the Patriarch. The broad fields of Mamre recalled the home of Jacob, and the spot whence he set out for Egypt, to go down and see Joseph ere he died. It revived the glories of David's kingdom, for in Hebron he reigned seven years before he made Zion a glory and a praise. From his hillside-home Zacharias came up to Jerusalem, to hold his course in the temple as a priest. He stood one day in the place of appointed duty, at the time of evening sacrifice. He was alone, near the altar, where he had presented himself to burn incense. At the right side of the altar he beheld a person clothed with celestial brightness. Zacharias was alarmed, and fear fell upon him. It was no common visitor. It was Gabriel, the Prime Minister of the Lord of Glory, the same who was sent to Mary. "I am sent (said Gabriel) to speak glad tidings to thee. Thy prayer has been heard. Elisabeth shall bear thee a son. He shall be filled with the Holy Ghost from his mother's womb, and many of the children of Jacob shall he turn to the Lord their God." The revelation was too much for the priest of the Lord. He staggered at the promise of God. He could not believe for joy.

To such a home Mary would be welcome. On the aged bosom of Elisabeth she could press her aching head, and into her sympathetic ear pour the great secret which, to this hour, had probably been told to no one. The distance from Nazareth to Hebron was long. She must take the journey on foot. Agitated, wearied, and full of fear, this lonely maiden neared the dwelling of the aged saint to whom God had so signally displayed his mercy. The coming was known to the mother of John long before the virgin came to the city. Her salutation thrilled Mary's soul like the blast of an angel's trumpet. "Hail thou highly favored! Blessed art thou among women. Blessed is she that believed." The object of her journey was attained. Her condition was no longer a secret. She could meet the gaze of the world. She could bear the taunts and jeers of friends. Her heart was strong and light, for it was staid on God. In the house of Zacharias she broke out in that heroic song, so expressive of pious submission, and devout gratitude and trust in him who had "regarded her low estate, had done great things for her, and caused all generations to call her blessed."

It is quite clear that, before she made her visit to Elisabeth, she had breathed her condition to no one. The visit of Gabriel was the great secret lodged in the inmost chambers of her own heart. Her situation could no longer be concealed. She must meet the eye of Joseph. The espousal of a pair was held sacred as marriage. Its binding force could only be thrown off by the solemnities of divorce. Ready to acquiesce in the Divine will, to tread, without fear, the thorny way opening before her, Mary was now ready to meet her affianced husband, and tell him how God "had regarded the low estate of his handmaid;" that he "that is mighty had done great things for her;" and that the promise was fulfilled as it was written: "Blessed is she that believed; for there shall be a performance of those things which were told her from the Lord."

It is quite clear, from the sacred record, that Joseph, her husband, did not believe her story. He loved her in what he supposed was her degradation. "He was a just man," so the Gospel informs us, and "was not willing to make her a public example." He could have publicly accused her before the Elders, and had her stoned to death in the presence of the people. All his hopes were blighted, and bitter disappointment had settled on his prospects. He had sought, in the humble cottage of Anna, one who was to share with him the good and the woe of life. Mary's character was without a stain. She was distinguished for her humble piety, her filial consecration, her holy and devout life. Now she was clothed with shame, and brought sorrow upon the house and heart that trusted her and loved her the best. She had, no doubt, rehearsed in his ear the visit of Gabriel—all that he had said and promised, and how, "when she saw him, she was troubled at his saying, and cast in her mind what manner of salutation this should be;" how he had calmed her fears and assured her that she had "found favor with God;" that "she should bring forth a son, conceived of the Holy Ghost, who should be great and be called the Son of the Highest; that to him the Lord God should give the throne of his father David; that he should reign over the house of Jacob forever;" and how the angel had confirmed these tidings by assuring her that far off in the city of Hebron, to her "cousin Elisabeth" God had "shown great mercy," and that to her a son should be born in her old age. All this Joseph heard, but he believed it not. He could not take Mary to his heart, nor allow her to share his home. "He was minded to put her away." He treated her tenderly. He did all he could to avoid public disgrace, for he resolved to put her away "privately." All this Mary foresaw when she accepted, with holy resignation, the mission of shame and woe to which she was called. She cast all her care upon God, uttering her faith in these impressive words: "He that is mighty hath done to me great things, and holy is his name." She left the future with God, knowing that "He is his own interpreter, and he can make it plain."

Doomed to bitter disappointment, with his hopes blighted, and his affianced bride in deep disgrace, with gloomy thoughts in his heart, while he felt the heavy pressing hand of God on him, Joseph laid down on his couch to sleep. The same celestial messenger that "stood on the right side of the altar of incense," while Zacharias stood in the temple of the Lord; the same angel who announced to Mary the great honor conferred upon her, in that hereafter she should be "blessed among women;" in a dream communicated to Joseph all that was needful to confirm the story of Mary. His fears were dissipated. He threw the shield of his confidence and position over the virgin mother. He guarded, cherished, and protected her. And when the fullness of time had come he started with her from their lowly cottage in Nazareth toward Bethlehem, to fulfill, all unconsciously to themselves, the word of God spoken to their fathers many years before, that in Bethlehem Ephratah the King of Zion should be born.

Few scenes are more worthy of the pencil of the artist than the interview between Mary and Elisabeth. The one, a peasant maiden from the hills of Nazareth, scarcely known beyond the circle of her own relations; in the morning of her life, artless, spotless, and of unblenching piety; excited and alarmed at the strange visitation of the Prime Minister of Heaven; conscious of the taunts and jeers that must beset her pathway; resolving to visit her cousin, and ascertain for herself what God was doing in that Hebron home; alone, foot-sore and weary, traveling the whole distance between the two cities, yet fainting not, faltering not, till the blue smoke of Elisabeth's cottage was seen ascending toward the sky—the other, an aged woman, well stricken in years, to whom God had showed distinguished mercy. She, watching and waiting for Mary, who came in haste to her house, and, before the maiden had opened her lips, or had gained breath to utter the great secret that troubled her soul, saluted her as the "Mother of her Lord," and, with a loud voice, saying: "Blessed art thou among women, and blessed is the fruit of thy womb." Mary's burden was gone and her fears dissipated; with exultant spirit she could shout back, "My soul doth magnify the Lord. My spirit hath rejoiced in God my Saviour, for he hath regarded the low estate of his handmaiden, for behold from henceforth all generations shall call me blessed."

And when the time came that Jesus should become incarnate, Joseph, the just man, went with Mary into the City of David, and stood by her in her great agony, as she laid down upon the straw, that the Prince of Life might be born.

> "Cold on his cradle the dew-drops are shining:
> Low lies his head with the beasts of the stall;
> Angels adore him in slumber reclining—
> Maker, and Monarch, and Saviour of all."

VI.—CALVARY AND THE DIVINITY OF CHRIST.

"While Jews on their own law rely,
And Greeks of wisdom boast,
I love the incarnate mystery,
And there I fix my trust."

The divinity of Christ is the great fact of revelation. It is the central truth, around which the system of grace and mercy revolves. Into it angels desired to look. God manifest in the flesh is the mystery of godliness. No other than a divine being could atone for sins. Like all the great truths of revelation, there is no attempt to prove it in the Gospels. It is asserted, and the grand doctrines that grow out of it are assumed. There is no argument to prove the existence of God, the immortality of the soul, or a future judgment. To "come to God, we must believe that he is." "The spirit that goes to God" at death, and the germ that survives the decay of the body of the seed-corn, and the tenant that walks out of the house that is to be taken down or dissolved, are the scriptural illustrations of the undying nature of the soul. The judgment is simply asserted. Men are warned to flee from the wrath to come, for "after death is the judgment."

"We look at the name of Jesus, and find it to be the Mighty God and the Everlasting Father." It was He who stood in the presence of God when the deep foundations of the earth were laid, as the morning stars sang, and the sons of God shouted for joy. John looked on him, as he walked among men, and knew him as the "Word made flesh," by "whom all things were made," who in the "beginning was with God, and was God, without whom was not any thing made that was made." In the furnace he shielded his faithful ones, appearing to them, as to the king in "the form of the Son of God." Being neither a man nor an angel, but superior to both, he is represented as debating in which form he would come to earth, either being a humiliation, and either within his grasp. He chose the garb of the seed of Abraham, as the more debasing. When he made the choice he was in the form of God, and it was then no robbery to be equal with God. Yet to die on the cross it was needful that he should surrender his divine form, be born of a woman, and "be made in the likeness of sinful man."

We have no controversy with those who speak of Jesus as a man; who talk of his sonship and subordination; who tell us that he was cold, weary, hungry, houseless, and poor. We accept him as human. He dwelt among men, and was touched with all the infirmities of our nature when he took it on him. But, after this is admitted, what is to be done with that large class of texts that as really assert that he is divine? That ascribe to him the sacred name and attributes of God, call him "the creation of God," "the Builder of the universe," "God manifest in the flesh"? Which teach that the Jesus whom men loved and followed was the "true God and Eternal Life"? We find no difficulty here. We accept all that the Bible teaches of Jesus as a man, for he was human. We accept all it teaches of his Godhead, for he was divine.

Without the divinity of Christ, without a belief in the pre-existence of the Son of God, without a life before he was born of the Virgin, it is impossible to credit either the Saviour or the word of God. We are told that to become the Saviour of men he became poor; that he had wealth, and laid it down and accepted poverty, that sinners might be rich through his penury. But such was not the fact with Jesus as a man. He never was rich in this world. He had no wealth to lay down. He was born poor, lived poor, died poor.

"Borrowed was his cradle bed,
His tomb was borrowed, too!"

He had no wealth by gift, by inheritance, or acquisition. How, then, simply as the son of Joseph and Mary, did he become poor, that we through his poverty might be rich? But admit his Godhead, and all is plain. He was rich in heaven when he was exalted above angels, when he dwelt in the bosom of God: when amid principalities and powers he had a name above every name. He was rich in the wealth of the Godhead and in the inheritance of the skies; in the praise of heaven and the worship of angels. All this he surrendered. Of all his wealth he "emptied himself," and "humbled himself" to be "born of a woman," and "made himself of no reputation." You believe this, or you do not believe in the Son of God. You know this, or you do not "know the grace of our Lord Jesus Christ." He dwells in your heart by faith, or you are in the gall of bitterness. You accept this as the Word of God, or abandon the Book to its enemies.

We are told that in the incarnation the blessed Son of God "made himself of no reputation." Not in this life. In a previous one, or not at all. He could not as a man lay down his repute to be the Saviour of men, for, as a man, he never had repute to lay down. As men count repute, he was in ill repute from the cradle to the cross. The circumstances preceding his birth were such that Joseph, a holy and just man, resolved to put his mother away. He could have brought her into the presence of the Elders, and had her stoned to death. Our Lord was known as the son of a carpenter. Men taunted him as a dweller in Nazareth, from which no good could come. His disciples, chosen from the lowly trades of life, reflected no honor on his cause. Men knew them as unlearned, and spoke of them as a "dozen fishermen or sailors." He was accounted a madman because of the doctrines he preached. His death made him accursed in the eyes of men. Could one have less repute among men? Was there a lower depth than this? All this he had when there was no room for him in the inn. He kept it to the bitter end. How, then, as a man, as the son of Mary simply, did he "*make* himself of no reputation?"

St. Paul tells us, that Jesus was "in the form of God," and that he "humbled himself, and took on him the form of a servant." But, from the visit of angels to the hour of ascension, he had no form but that of a servant. When in this life, as a man, had he the form of God? And when laid he that form down to take on him the form of a servant? He must have possessed that form when "in the beginning he was with God," or not at all.

The phraseology of the Bible is peculiar. It does not assert simply that Christ was poor, but that he "*became*" so. Not that he had no reputation, but that he "*made* himself" so. Not that he was lowly, but that he "*humbled* himself." Not that he died, but that he "*laid* down" his life. Not that he was raised from the dead, but that he *took* up his own life. Not that he was a sample of men raised from the dead, but that he was himself the "resurrection and the life"—that he held the "keys of death and hell," and came forth as the jailer comes from the cell into which he has locked himself for a moment, as one whom it was "not *possible*" for the prison or grave to hold.

That Jesus was a teacher, men were not disposed to deny. That he was a prophet of God, most of the generation that saw him were disposed to allow. But he claimed more. He asserted that he was "divine," in a sense that the people accounted blasphemy. And on this the controversy turned. He understood the popular impression. He did not correct it. He deepened it. When our Lord told the people that their "father Abraham saw this day and was glad," they understood him literally, and replied: "Thou art not yet fifty years old, and hast thou seen Abraham?" He knew the impression he made. The people understood him to assert that he lived before and in the time of Abraham. He said: "Before Abraham was, I am;" and the indignant people attempted to stone him for blasphemy. At another time, he spake to the Jews and said: "I and my Father are one." They understood him to assert his equality with God, a great crime in their eyes. Seeing them enraged, and about to stone him, he said: "Many good works have I shown you from my Father; for which of these works do ye stone me?" The people answered: "For a good work we stone thee not; but for blasphemy, and because that thou, being a man, maketh thyself God." By a word he could have recalled the idea that his language conveyed. He could have disavowed the intention of making himself equal with God. He could have refuted the charge of blasphemy. He did no such thing. But exerted his omnipotent power to escape from their hands. The crime of blasphemy, in their minds, clung to him. He did not disavow his claim to be equal with, and to be, God. With better success they renewed the charge when he was on trial for his life, and Caiaphas gave judgment against him as a blasphemer—which he was, if he was not divine.

A greater difficulty presents itself, if we deny the divinity of the incarnate Lamb of God. We cannot defend the integrity of the Divine Word nor that of the Son of God. In this life he was never in the form of God, and could not *take* on him a lower nature. In this life he was never rich, and could not *become* poor. As a man he had no repute to lay down, and could not *assume*, as a humiliation, what always attached to his nature.

As a man, he did not humble himself at all. As the son of Mary, his course was an upward one. He made a name among men and gained repute. Each step of life, till arrested by the Roman band, was an exaltation. He did what thousands would be glad to do. He left an obscure home, a few tools, and, at thirty, filled the whole world with his fame. His miraculous power was not known till after his baptism by John. Before that he was a peasant of humble toil, dwelling in an obscure home, living and worshiping with his people, asking and receiving no attention. All he had among men he received after his public life began. What did he leave to be known as the Prophet of Nazareth? A few tools and daily work. What reputation did he lay down when he left the carpenter-shop of Joseph? What did he take up? Renown, repute, fame! Men doubted their senses as people trod on each other to hear him, and asked, "Is not this the carpenter, the son of Mary?" But does all this fulfill the word of God, that he made himself of no repute? Would you cite Mohammed as an example of humility and condescension? He began life poor. Five camels and an Ethiopian slave was his inheritance. He moved on to unlimited power, and made for himself an undying name. His followers have planted on the foundation-stone of Solomon's temple a mosque, which, for twelve hundred years, has ruled the Holy Land. Did he make himself of no repute?

Our Lord claimed pre-existence; he claimed to be more than a man. He took special pains to deepen the impression made by his general teachings on this point. On one occasion he asked the Pharisees, "What think ye of Christ? Whose son is he?" They say unto him, the son of David. "If David in the spirit call him Lord, how can he be his son?" was the knotty problem put to these unbelievers. How is the Creator of David David's son? They saw the point. Not one of them was able to answer him a word. "Neither durst any man, from that day forth, ask him any more." To John, on the Isle of Patmos, he uttered the same paradox—"I am the root and the offspring of David." I am the root from whence the tree David sprang; I am the fruit that hung from the boughs of the tree David, whose root I am. Such claim ran all along his ministry. He was understood to assert that when the High Priest rent his robes and shouted, "He hath spoken blasphemy. Ye have heard his blasphemy." This claim he kept to the last. He laid down his life, he said, no man taking it from him. He was divine, and so bore our sins in his own body on the tree; or he died for his own sins, being guilty of blasphemy, in " that he that was a man made himself God."

On Calvary we behold the Word made flesh giving his soul an offering for sin. He who was with the Father from the beginning was made flesh, and dwelt among men, full of grace and truth. He had the wealth of the Godhead, yet took on him the form of man, with the poverty, shame, and ruin of our common nature. He laid down the worship of angels, and took up the insult of men. He left the mansion of his Father to be a houseless and homeless wanderer on earth. He left the atmosphere of holiness and worship to dwell amid blasphemy and sin. He became poor, that we, through his poverty, might be rich. "Thine all the glory, man's the boundless bliss."

VII.—CALVARY, OR EIGHT DAYS BEFORE THE CRUCIFIXION.

> "Thou loving, all-atoning Lamb—
> Thee, by thy painful agony,
> Thy bloody sweat, thy grief and shame,
> Thy cross and passion on the tree,
> Thy precious death and life—I pray,
> Take all, take all my sins away."

THE period of time measured by the eight days before Jesus was lifted on the cross is called the "hour of darkness." It began with the raising of Lazarus, and was completed when darkness covered the earth, when, amid the exultations of hell, the death-cry of the Redeemer was heard in the three worlds. Interesting and momentous events were crowded into the last eight days of the life of Jesus. The Jews demanded a sign, saying to the Saviour: "Show us a sign, and we will believe." He worked many miracles, which they rejected. He gave them a crowning and final miracle. On the eastern slope of Olives, Bethany was situated. Here resided Lazarus, with his sisters, Mary and Martha. Under this hospitable roof our Lord often rested from the toils of the day, and found sweet repose in the society of this blessed household. The home of Bethany was peculiarly dear to the son of God. Mary, Martha, and Lazarus were his especial friends. He who had no home of his own was ever welcome beneath this humble cottage. The inmates of this family were well known to the Jews. Lazarus sickened while the Lord was in the city of Jerusalem, only two miles from Bethany. To him a messenger was immediately sent, saying: "He whom thou lovest is sick." But he came not. His heart was there, and, guided by its throbbings, he would have hastened to their door, and turned disease away with a word. But God's glory was dearer to him than human affection or life. The knowledge that Lazarus was dead did not remove him "from the same place where he was." Lazarus died, and his death was an open and notable fact. The Jews loved him, and the strong sympathies of the place were drawn out toward the afflicted sisters. The people knew of his sickness and of his death. They bore him to the grave, and four days he lay in the tomb, while Jesus came not. In that hot climate corruption had begun its work, and the grave-worm had hastened to its repast.

THE FIRST DAY. The day we call Friday we shall number as the first day of the hour of darkness, the day on which our Lord called Lazarus from the grave, "bound hand and foot with grave clothes, and his face bound with a napkin." On that day the Saviour passed out of the gate of Benjamin, and with his disciples trod the narrow path toward Bethany. He passed Jehoshaphat, where the mighty dead of his nation lay, and where, according to the faith of the Jews, the world would be gathered at the last, and be judged by the Son of David. The road ran near the inclosure of Gethsemane, where soon, in agony and in the bloody sweat, his final conflict with the Prince of this World would take place. Up the sides of Olivet, near the retreat where he had passed whole nights in prayer to God; crossing the Mount of Ascension, from which the bright cloud would bear him to his God; thence down the eastern slope of the mountain, following the slender path, till he came in sight of the home of the afflicted sisters. His blessed form was seen on the summit of the mountain. Anxiously had those inmates waited for his appearing. Even now, they thought there was a blessing in his divine presence. He—who held the keys of death and of hell—met death at the grave, and, in the presence of friends and foes, bade the dead "come forth." The dead came forth—to eat, to drink, and to live among men. This great miracle threw the foes of Jesus into despair. It called the Sanhedrim together, "who took counsel to put him to death." The public mind was intensely agitated, and from that hour our Lord slept not in the city of David.

The Second Day of the hour of darkness was the Jewish Sabbath. Our Lord passed it with the family at Bethany. That small town was more honored than the city of David.

> "It seemed an humble village, few its houses
> And few and poor its dwellers; cottage roofs,
> Except one simple turret, are they all.
> Yet, save the neighboring city, it were hard,
> If Palestine were searched, to find a spot
> In which the Christian traveler should muse
> With fonder interest than Bethany."

How blessed the privilege to have looked on this impressive group, and listened to the themes of conversation. How great the boon to have participated in the solemnities of that—the last—Sabbath of our Lord before his death. His sun was declining. Shadows were thickening o'er his path. The night was coming in which no man could work. No mortal hand may lift the veil that is drawn around that Sabbath.

THE THIRD DAY answers to the Christian Sabbath. Jesus came in from Bethany. On Olivet he paused, and looked upon the scene open to his eye. The wonderful works of God among his people, from Eden to the flood, from Abel to John, were within his range. He has an important mission to-day. Five hundred years before, prophets had foretold that the Messiah should make a triumphal entrance into his capital—that, amid rejoicings and shoutings, he should enter the City of the Great King as monarchs come. And on this day that Scripture was fulfilled.

> "From Olivet's sequestered seats
>   What sounds of transport spread?
> What concourse moves through Salem's streets
>   To Zion's holy head?
> Behold him there, in lowliest guise,
>   The Saviour of mankind!
> Triumphal shouts before him rise,
>   And shouts resound behind:
> And 'Strike,' they cry, 'your loudest string.
> He comes! Hosanna to our king!'"

His kingly entrance was not according to the notions of men. A peasant of Nazareth, of the humblest origin, with a home of no distinction, known as a common laborer, homeless and without repute, with a few attendants! And he the king of Zion! Guided by an impulse they knew not of, the common people spread their garments in the way. For want of more royal offerings, they threw branches of the trees in his path. Going before, and following after, the multitude shouted: "Hosanna in the highest," till even Jerusalem itself was moved. Little children, drawn from their pastimes in the Temple area, joined the acclaim, saying: "Hosanna to the Son of David," the first fruits of that mighty army of little ones who are to have a part in the song and in the mansion of the redeemed. Shout! ye little ones; the King of Zion is your Lord. On this eventful morning, when Zion's King, meek and lowly, entered into his capital, he wept over Jerusalem. The spot is still marked, and, as we stand on that site, the whole city is before us—its streets, its marble courts, its palaces, its thronging multitudes. Not one glorious thing would remain in a few short years, and not one stone of greatness be left. Jesus came to them as a Saviour, but they would not be saved. He went out to Bethany, and lodged there.

The Fourth Day corresponds to our Monday. The Saviour came in from Bethany with his disciples, and was an hungered. Drawing near to a fig-tree, and finding upon it nothing but leaves, he cursed it, and passed into the city. Four hundred years before, the prophets had foretold that the Lord whom Israel sought should suddenly come to his Temple, and come like a refiner's fire and a purifier. To the Temple the Lord now came, to assert his authority as the Lord of the Temple. Previous to the resurrection of Lazarus, the Jews knew the Saviour only in his assumed character of the Son of Man. He did "not cry, nor lift up, nor cause his voice to be heard in the street." He attracted only occasional attention. He trod noiselessly the pathway of blessing. With the few he was an impostor. With the many a harmless enthusiast. With his disciples the prophet of Nazareth. Now he appears in a new garb. Authority marks his utterance, and royalty his acts. He talks, and walks, and moves among men with regal dignity. As a sovereign he entered his capital. As God, he purged his temple. The men sold animals for sacrifice within the sacred inclosure. Money-changers and brokers waited upon worshipers that came from distant countries, and their money-tables were near the altar of daily sacrifice. Under the pretense of piety, mammon reigned in the house of the Lord. The place of prayer was a den of thieves. The Lord of the temple drove out both the buyers and the sellers, and overthrew the tables of the money-changers to the astonishment of men. Not a few saw in that act the purging of the sons of Levi that they "should offer unto the Lord an offering in righteousness."

The change in the Saviour's conduct and speech attracted attention. Men in authority and the multitude saw and felt it. The raising of Lazarus from the tomb was well known. The great heart of the people was touched. The sensation produced was universal. The awe in which the Scribes and Pharisees were held could not silence the public tongue. Their interest in Christ they did not care to conceal. "When Christ cometh, will he do more miracles than these which this man hath done?" they asked. The rulers and chief priests understood this murmuring. They saw to what it tended. They knew, if unchecked, "all men would believe on him." They attempted to hush these utterances, and exerted their authority to turn the rising affection and confidence from the Son of God. The Pharisees taunted the people, saying, "Thou art his disciples—as for this fellow, we know not whence he is." The people replied, "Since the world begun was it not heard that any man opened the eyes of one that was born blind."

It was needful to put an end to the ministry of Jesus. To do this he must be accused of crime—be arrested by the arm of the law—and sentenced to death. This was well known to the people, and only an opportunity was wanted. It is not probable that the dwelling-place of Jesus was publicly known. Since the excitement created by the resurrection of Lazarus, our Lord did not walk openly in Judea, and the wonder of the people was whether he would come up to the feast, and, if so, whether the rulers would take him and put him to death. He was safe with the people. To have publicly arrested him would have created a riot. He had touched the great national heart. His enemies saw, with gnashing of teeth, the confidence and affection that men had in him. They withered under the scorn he expressed, and his treatment of them in the presence of the nation maddened them. This fourth day ended, he rested for the night beneath the roof of Bethany.

THE FIFTH DAY corresponds to our Tuesday. Twenty-four hours before he had cursed the fig-tree in the presence of his disciples. They passed in from Bethany, and saw the fig-tree "dried up from the roots and withered away." Awe-struck they beheld! "Have faith in God," said the Master. Soon would they need it. During his absence from the city his enemies had been in consultation. Something must be done to silence and confound him. The Jews were divided into sects, clans, and parties. They hated each other—they hated Christ more. Pilate and Herod healed their feuds over his body; and the Pharisees, Sadducees, and Herodians, formed a coalition, and joined in a conspiracy to put out of the way their common enemy.

A plan had been devised to silence and confound the great teacher; to array the prejudices of the people against his teaching, and to bring him into collision with the government as a sower of sedition. To carry out the scheme, the great array met Jesus as he came in from Bethany. They first assaulted his credentials as a teacher, and demanded his authority for what he said and did. The men who made the demand were in the plot to destroy him. He had assumed kingly authority, and made a public entry into Jerusalem. As one having divine right over the Temple, he had cast out the traders from their accustomed place of traffic. He taught in the Temple like one authorized to sit in Moses' seat. Now the rulers demanded his authority for those things. They gave him no authority. The Sanhedrim alone could give the license, and from that body he had obtained no commission. The Saviour replied, by showing that John the Baptist had no license from the Sanhedrim. Had he no authority? Was his baptism from heaven or from men? and if it was not needful for John to have such human authority to make his acts divine, was it needful for the Messiah, whom John pointed out? Here was a dilemma. It would not do to say that John was not an inspired man, for all the people held he was a prophet, and it was the people the conspirators wanted to conciliate. If they allowed John to be a prophet, then the reply would be, why don't you receive him, believe what he said, and receive the Christ he baptized and proclaimed? So they refused to answer. Thus the coalition tripped at the start. In the presence of the people, who had gathered to look on the humiliation of the Son of God, Jesus uttered that withering rebuke contained in the parable of the two sons, one of whom said, " I go, sir," to the command: "Go work in my vineyard," but went not. He spared not the rulers of the people. He denounced them as a people whose doom was sealed, from whom God's vineyard should be taken and given to other husbandmen; that highways and hedges should be searched, that the poorest of God's people might keep the marriage supper; while the proud, lofty, and self-righteous, should be bound hand and foot and cast into outer darkness, with weeping and gnashing of teeth. Viler than publicans and harlots, they should enter the kingdom of God before them.

In his indignant rebukes he applied to them an old tradition, preserved in the writings of the fathers. The tradition was, that, in the building of the earlier temple, a peculiar stone, fitting nowhere, and apparently worthless, was cast out and rejected, till the moss of years gathered on its surface, and almost hid it from the eye of man. The temple was nearly done, but the chief stone was missing. At last it was found amid the tangled grass of many years' growth, and was put in its fitting place, and "became the head of the corner." So should he, the rejected Messiah, become, in after days, the headstone of the corner, and the glory of Israel.

The chief priests and Pharisees were not fools. "They perceived that he spake of them," and that the people knew it. Under his rebukes they withered. They had not done as much with the question of authority as they hoped. The man of Nazareth had clearly the advantage of them in that matter. No one single-handed, and no sect, alone, could cope with or entangle him. If entrapped, confounded, and ensnared; if the heart of the people was turned away from him, it must be by a combination of all the talent, and all the hate, and all sects in the city. The pious Pharisee, too holy to touch the unclean meat, must join hands with the infidel Sadducee; and these must unite with the unscrupulous Herodians, the trimming politicians of that day, and unitedly "entangle Jesus in his talk."

A conspiracy was formed, and the conspirators met

the Son of God in the temple. The place was worthy of the occasion. Jerusalem was profoundly agitated. The events of the past few days indicated that great things were at hand. One personage filled all thoughts. One name was on all tongues. The Roman Government was not indifferent to a personage whose influence over the popular mind was great and increasing; whom the people more than once would have crowned; who had allowed himself to be escorted by the rabble into the city as monarchs come; and who was accused by the Jewish authorities with an intention of overthrowing the government and making himself king. The Sanhedrim held nightly sessions, and consulted with their ablest men, how they might arrest him without danger to themselves, and how put him out of the way without creating an uproar among the people. It was the season of the great festivals of the nation. The city was crowded with strangers. Distinguished men from all parts of the world came to keep holy time. It was near the feast of the Atonement. The audience-room selected by the conspirators was the broad pavement of the temple, from which, a few days before the Saviour had driven out the traders. Here the anxious Romans, the indignant and frightened Chief Priests and Elders, the representatives of the different parties who had engaged to ensnare the Saviour, with the intensely interested and excited multitude, gathered to witness the assault, and enjoy the confusion and defeat of the son of Mary.

First came the Herodians, to lead the assault.

They represented the politicians. Their design was to bring the Saviour into conflict with the Roman authority. This done, the work of arrest would be easy. The sower of sedition, the stirrer up of civil strife, the agitator of the people against the government, would be called to Cæsar's judgment-seat to answer for his offense. If no conflict could be made with the government, it would be easy to bring him into collision with the people. If their regard for him as a prophet could be removed, if their protecting arm withdrawn, and they be made to believe that he was taking sides against them, the people would shout as earnestly for his death as they now defended his person and his claims. The questions with which the Herodians were charged were political. In their judgment, they would inevitably involve the Lord with the Roman government or with the Jewish people. In either case his destruction was sure. Under the Roman rule the Jews had many privileges. The hand of the government was light. They had their own rulers, priests, temple services, and festivals; and but for the presence of the Roman soldiers, whose swords and spurs clanked on the sacred pavement, and but for the odious tribute, hardly a vestige of their bondage would have appeared to the public eye. The payment of this tribute was a matter of conscience with some of the devout Jews. Being the free men of Abraham, as they boasted, and never in bondage to any man, the tax was a disgrace. In some parts of the land it could not be collected, except by armed men. Collectors were frequently waylaid and robbed ere they left the district. It was on

3*

this delicate and sensitive question between the Roman Government and the people, that the Council had decided to tempt our Lord. The Herodians came with a lie in their mouth. Pretending to be his friends, to acknowledge his claims, they expected by flattery to throw him off his guard. "Master," said they, "we know that thou art true, and teachest the way of God in truth, neither carest thou for any man; for thou regardest not the person of men." With such a character he would answer their question regardless of consequences, whether his answer involved him with the government, the people, or both. "What thinkest thou?" they say, "Is it lawful to give tribute unto Cæsar or not?" Our Lord perceived their drift, and laid bare their wickedness. "Ye hypocrites! Show me the tribute money." They brought unto him a penny. "There is an image on this penny: whose is it?" They say unto him, "Cæsar's." "Surrounding this image is a superscription: whose titles are these?" They say unto him, "Cæsar's." "Do not your Rabbis teach that, where a king's coin is current, his sovereignty is acknowledged? Do you not take Cæsar's money in payment for dues, and pay the same to others! Do you not admit Cæsar's sovereignty, when you take and pay Cæsar's coin, stamped with his image and his offices? Do you not admit your allegiance to Rome in all your business transactions? Render, therefore, unto Cæsar the things which are Cæsar's, and which you admit to be Cæsar's, and unto God the things that are God's." Confounded and overwhelmed in the audience of the people, the Herodians "heard these words, marveled, left him, and went their way."

The Sadducees came in turn. They were the infidels of the day, and expected to arouse the sectarianism of the Jews by assailing the common faith of a future life. The Sadducees received the five Books of Moses, but denied that they taught the resurrection of the dead, or the existence of angels or spirits. "The Pharisees confessed both." As in later times Paul divided his enemies by raising the question of a future life between the Pharisees and Sadducees, so the Council hoped that the multitude would be so divided that Jesus might be delivered into the hands of his enemies. To make the case honorable to themselves, they selected from the Books of Moses a statute involving the impossibility, in their judgment, of a future state. By the authority of the law, if a man died having no children, his brother could marry the widow. An instance was cited in which seven brethren married the same wife. The question was—"In the resurrection whose wife shall she be of the seven?" This was, no doubt, a favorite and successful weapon of the Sadducees in their contests with the Pharisees. Jesus approached this question with dignity and conscious strength. He grasped its supposed absurdity and hurled back confusion on his foes. "Ye know nothing of the Scriptures in which ye profess to trust," said he. "That the dead are raised, even Moses showed at the bush when he called the Lord, the God of Abraham, the God of Isaac, and the God of Jacob. God is not the God of the dead, but of the living. You know nothing of the power of God, who is able of the rocks to raise up children unto Abraham. You know nothing of the state of the dead. In the resurrection they neither marry nor are given in marriage, but are as the angels of God." The Sadducees were silenced. Out of their own sacred books they were confounded and confuted. Swift ran the messengers to tell the Pharisees that he had filled their allies with confusion, and that the people enjoyed the triumph. Abashed and mortified, the infidels fell back and made way for others.

The Pharisees now gathered together. With dismay, they saw the discomfiture of their friends. With great caution they proceeded. They obtained the aid of a lawyer, who, learned in the law, tempted Jesus with a question of great moment. Like both of the preceding topics, it seemed to peril Christ with the people, answer as he would. It was the great question of the day—"Is the law equal? Which of the commandments is the greater? Master, which is the great commandment in the law?" He replied, "The first command is great—Love the Lord thy God. The second is like unto it—Love thy neighbor as thyself. On these two commands hang all the Law and the Prophets. Keep these two and none others will be broken." The triumph of the Saviour was complete. The whole coalition was routed and dissolved. The lawyer was compelled to confess, "Well, Master, thou hast said the truth." He was almost converted, being not far from the Kingdom of God. The people were strengthened in their conviction that this was the Son of God. Having answered and routed the coalition, he was not through with the men who assembled to ensnare him. They came to confound him, and brought an eager crowd to look on his confusion. In the audience of the people he spake those scathing words which Matthew has recorded in the twenty-third and twenty-fourth chapters of his Gospel. He laid bare the hypocrisy and wickedness of the chief men of their nation. He held the people in awe-stricken attention, as when he scourged the thieves from the temple. He accused their rulers of hypocrisy and sin—of sitting in Moses' seat teaching the Word of God, and living shameless lives. He set forth how they bound heavy and grievous burdens on men; devoured widows' houses and the orphans' substance; sewing the law on their garments and dishonoring it in their lives; loving the uppermost rooms of feasts, and chief seats in the synagogues; seeking greetings in the markets, and shutting up the kingdom of heaven against men; blind guides making proselytes twofold more the children of hell than themselves; omitting the weightier matters of the law; but cleaning the outside of the cup and platter; and whitening the sepulchers full of dead men's bones; a nation of serpents, a generation of vipers, filling up the cup of iniquity to the brim, and hastening to the damnation of hell. Such were the words of one who that morning they expected to clothe with disgrace. So speaking, he departed from the temple.

But more solemn was the closing address. With men and angels the day must be ever memorable, for with it Jesus closed his public ministry with men, preached his last sermon, and gave his last warning.

From the temple he departed to the Mount of Olives, and to his disciples he discoursed on the coming doom of Jerusalem, and the signs that should precede and attend it. Thence he passed to the Judgment of the Great Day, of which the destruction of Jerusalem was a type. In the graphic and fearful language recorded in the twenty-fifth chapter of Matthew, the destiny of all nations is irrevocably fixed in everlasting punishment or life eternal. It was his last sermon to man; his last message of warning and entreaty to a world lying in wickedness. With this description of the judgment of the last day, the august gathering of the nations—not before the Man of Nazareth, but the Son of God in all his glory—not in Palestine, but sitting on the throne of glory—not with a few fishermen of Galilee, but with all the holy angels; with these solemn and awful words, he ended his public ministry. On leaving the temple his eye rested upon the treasury, and "he beheld how the people cast into it money." A certain poor widow passed him and threw in a farthing. Cheer up, lonely one, the Master's eye is upon thee. Thy gift is immortalized, and the thing thou hast done shall be told to the latest generation. Night coming on, he departed from the City of David to sleep as he was wont in Bethany.

The Sixth Day answers to our Wednesday. Clouds thicken about Jesus. The darkness is denser. He nears Calvary. He closed his miracles with the raising of Lazarus. He took leave of the City of David and of his father's when he made his home with Mary and Martha. He walked no more openly in Judea, for his time had not come to die. He met his combined enemies, and triumphed over them in the presence of the people. He laid bare the wickedness and hypocrisy of the rulers, and denounced the doom of the nation, and did so in sorrow and in tears. A sorer trial now awaited him. Tender ties of affection were to be severed. Yesterday he bade adieu to man as a teacher. Now he bids adieu to friends. Human friendship must end as the great work of redemption draws near. Farewell, Bethany! So beloved. Clustering interest hangs around thee, home of beloved ones! Footsore, weary, and oppressed Jesus never sought repose there in vain. Now Bethany, Mary, Martha, Lazarus, farewell! farewell! Human affection and loving associations must break, when the Captain of our Salvation girds himself for the awful conflict. Mother, brother, friend must not cling to those garments, soon to be dyed in the baptism of blood. He spoke the last words of affection as he left that loved family on the morning of this sixth day. The last human tie was sundered. He turned from that blessed home to enter it no more.

Not far from Mount Zion, where the tomb of David stood above the accursed valley of Hinnom, near the palace of Caiaphas, the defeated and chagrined conspirators then met in conclave. The day had been to them one of signal shame, and signal triumph to Jesus. They went out in the morning, confident of success, confident that one or all his foes would silence him. In confusion and shame he would retire from the contest, and the indignant multitude, denouncing him as an impostor, would demand that the Romans deliver him to death. The evening found the chief men of the nation discomfited. On all points their weapons had been turned against them. Not only had they not involved the prophet of Nazareth with the government, but they had embroiled themselves on the matter of the tribute with the people. The Sadducees had been confounded out of their own sacred books, and their ignorance exposed. The Pharisees had met with a signal rebuke, and their champion nearly converted. Hot was their rage, intense their determination, to put him to death. But "how to take him?" The affection of the people was not lessened by the conspiracy. It was dangerous to arrest him in the open day, or at the feast, or in the presence of the multitude. It would create an uproar. But Jesus must die. How shall he be taken? Into this perplexed and agitated conclave unexpected relief came. Up from the valley of Moloch's bloody rites, up the rugged sides of the steep hill on which the palace stood, stealing stealthily along like a thief and a robber, wrapped close in his cloak to escape recognition, a messenger was at the door of the palace. "Whom have we here? Uncover. Surely this is one of the disciples of Jesus. Why disturb this conference at this hour of the night?" Hear the hoarse answer from that voice agitated with guilt and fear and shame: "I was one of the twelve. I am one no longer. I know your wish. You demand the person of Jesus. You fear to take him openly whom the people adore. I know his secret retreat. I can guide you where you will find him alone. At midnight he has an appointment with his disciples in the garden of Solomon, at the foot of Olives. His friends are few, unarmed, and timid. The people who would rescue him are asleep. The great city sleeps. Give me money, and I will guide you to his presence. I will salute him as Master, and whom 'I kiss that is he, lay hold on him.' What will ye give me, and I will betray him unto you?" The delighted and relieved conspirators closed the bargain. Back, back the traitor took his way unto his Master—in season to enter his protest against the waste of precious ointment, which might have been sold and given to the poor—in season to witness the anguish of the disciples as the Lord said: "One of you shall betray me" —in season to take the sop from his hand, who authoritatively commanded Judas to do quickly the thing he was to do—in season to go from thence and earn the wages of infamy, to hasten from the betrayal, to despair, confession, suicide, and hell.

The Seventh Day corresponds to our Thursday. The hour grows darker and darker still. Zion, Moriah, and Calvary are at this hour each invested with new interest. To the Jew, the Feast of the Atonement engrosses his thoughts; the lamb of expiation will soon be offered for the sins of the nation. Yes! and near the same spot, at nearly the same hour, the Lamb slain from the foundation will be offered for the sins of the world. Joy reigns in the palace of Caiaphas on Zion. Men need seek no further to entrap or to lay hold of the Son of Mary, for one of his own disciples will betray him. The Prophet of Nazareth will soon be in that presence chamber, and his speedy death will follow. The palace is filled with the members of the Sanhedrim, and others, exchanging congratulations in view of the delivery of Jesus. On Moriah, priests and servants on the eve of the Passover are preparing in the Temple for the great sacrifice. On Mount Calvary, preparations are making for the sacrifice of the Lamb of God. Orders have gone forth for the crucifixion, and menials are digging for the three crosses that to-morrow are to be put up on Calvary. How significant that these three summits, connected with the most thrilling and momentous events in the history of the race, should each bear a part in the lifting up of the Son of God on the Cross on this eventful day.

On Mount Zion, near the foundations of David's palace, on the same night on which he was betrayed, in the darkest hour the Church ever knew, in an upper room, by appointment, the little band received at the hands of the Lord those mementoes of his love and memorials of his death and shame which shall abide till time shall be no longer. The prospects of the Church were never brilliant to human view. Its Founder had borne poverty, disgrace, and hatred, in which his disciples in a measure shared. A man of sorrows, a homeless, houseless wanderer, his eventful life was to close, and the manner of his death to be a legacy of perpetual shame and reproach to his friends. But of that reproach and shame the supper was to be an undying memorial. This our Lord knew when he consecrated the supper, saying: "Do this in remembrance of me." Men desire immortality. The best things and the worst are done to live in the coming generations. Mighty men have exhausted the resources of nations; sacrificed millions of lives; turned the world into a vast battle-field; filled it with captives, groanings, and agonies; become oppressors and scourgers of their race, to live forever. On that night in which he was betrayed, the Son of David immortalized his cause and reared his own monument. It has outlived the brass and marble of the mausoleum of kings. The rust of ages has not soiled it. The convulsions of kingdoms, revolutions, earthquakes, and the shock of battles, have not loosened it. It stands as its builder left it. Its deep foundation, cemented with his blood, is unmoved. Severely simple, reared by his own hand, built by his own might, it cost no tears, no sacrifice, no blood, but his own. Amid sorrow, treachery, and feebleness; in agony and ignominy; with the magnitude of sin, the worth of the soul, and the cost of a sinner's redemption inscribed on each particle of bread and blushing in every drop of wine, the Redeemer gave the Communion to the Church. Precious legacy! Glowing memorials of dying love! The redeemed sing, and will ever:—

> Yes, we'll record thy dying love,
>   Thou dearest, tenderest, best of friends;
> Thy matchless love, the noblest praise
>   Of long eternity transcends.
>
> 'Tis rapture more than earth can know
>   Thy passion through these veils to see;
> Thy table food celestial yields,
>   How blessed are they who sit with thee.

Dark and sorrowful was that hour on Mount Zion. "With desire have I desired to eat the passover with you before I suffer," said the Lord. "One of you shall betray me. One deny me. All flee. The shepherd shall be smitten, and the flock scattered." Fear and anguish paralyzed the little band. Trembling, they sang the paschal hymn and passed out into the Mount of Olives. At its base, near the gate of Benjamin, was a small enclosure, known as Gethsemane. It was quiet and shady, surrounded by an ancient wall, and supposed to be a part of Solomon's garden. It was the favorite resort of Jesus when he would be alone with God, or hold sweet converse with those whom he loved, and loved to the end. "Judas, also, which betrayed him, knew the place; for Jesus oft-times resorted hither with his disciples." It was the hour of midnight. Jesus had taken leave of the world. The ties of human affection had been severed, all save one, and that was to be broken on the cross, when he appointed a home for a poor widow, whose soul was pierced with the prophetic sword. He had a few words to say to his chosen friends, to whom his kingdom was committed, and who, after the panic and bitterness of the hour of darkness were passed, and the morning light should gild the mountain peaks of the world, would stand boldly forth, and preach to the nations Jesus and the resurrection. Through the mist, the darkness, and the blood of that hour, he saw the clear shining of that morning. Words of blessed comfort, support, and tenderness, were to be spoken to that fearful band, words that should bless and comfort the Church in all ages. Within the enclosure of Gethsemane were many olive-trees mighty with years, beneath which the kings of Judah sat, oft ate from the fruit of the climbing vine, and were sheltered from the dews of the night by the thick foliage of limb and vine. The Son of David took his seat beneath the trees that sheltered his fathers, and there he uttered those sweet words of consolation, that are such a precious legacy to the sorrowful, suffering soul who turns to Jesus for comfort: "Let not your heart be troubled." "In my Father's house are many mansions." "I will not leave you comfortless." "I will pray the Father, and he shall give you another comforter, that he may abide with you forever." "He shall teach you all things, and bring all things to your remembrance." "Peace I leave with you, my peace I give unto you." "Let not your heart be troubled, neither let it be afraid."

Doubly precious are those words when we recall that midnight hour—that garden of woe—the blackness of the hour of darkness in that enclosure of agony—the Redeemer alone with his disciples and the great events that had been crowded into so short a space. How strange the manner and words of the Saviour, as he handed the sop to Judas, at the supper! Was he understood aright? Did sorrow, desertion, and shame lie in their pathway? Why this meeting, in that dark hour, in that lonely place? Why such tenderness and sorrow mark the utterances of Jesus? These allay not their fears. As men hear the footsteps of the coming tempest, or read advancing troubles in the signs of the times, so the stricken disciples were in terror, that the presence of their Great Master could not remove. Under those olive-trees, which sheltered him from the dew of the night, he took affectionate leave of those he loved so well. The clinging vine, that adorned the branches of the tree over his head, indicated the intimate and tender relation between himself and the Church. "I am the vine. Ye are the branches: abide in me."

But his work was not yet done. With a tender adieu to his loved ones, he went out to meet the god of this world, and to hold his final conflict with Satan. Alone he must meet him. The deep sleep of sorrow fell on his disciples. No human eye could look on the agony of the Son of God in Gethsemane. The bitterness of that cup which he was to drink, when he tasted death for man, was the "wine cup of the wrath of God." How terrible that anguish, and how awful that curse borne, let the agonizing prayer, the Saviour's blood wetting the soil of Gethsemane, and the sustaining hand of the Angel of God, tell! No common agony wrung out the impassioned cry: "Save me, oh, save me, Father, from this hour." No mortal suffering or temporal woe wrung the life-blood from the Redeemer. He did not flinch under the lash. He did not shrink or supplicate when nails were driven through his hands and feet. He was silent on the cross, as a lamb led to the slaughter, till he felt his banishment from God, and uttered his death-cry. It was his soul's agony, as he wrestled with Satan. It was the curse borne for sinners that pierced the sky with importunate prayer. The sins of men felled him to the earth as he made himself an offering. But, this conflict over, how calm and serene his brow, how gentle his touch, how tender his tones, as he wakes his disciples out of sleep and says, "Rise, let us be going: behold he is at hand that doth betray me."

> " 'Tis midnight—and on Olive's brow
>   The star is dimmed that lately shone;
> 'Tis midnight—in the garden now
>   The suffering Saviour prays alone.
>
> " 'Tis midnight—and from all removed
>   Immanuel wrestles lone with fears;
> E'en the disciple that he loved
>   Heeds not his Master's grief and tears.
>
> " 'Tis midnight—and for others' guilt
>   The Man of Sorrows weeps in blood;
> Yet he who hath in anguish knelt
>   Is not forsaken by his God.
>
> " 'Tis midnight—and from ether plains
>   Is borne the song that angels know;
> Unheard by mortals are the strains
>   That sweetly soothe the Saviour's woe."

Judas was true to his bargain. He knew Gethsemane well. With a band of men and officers, he went thither with lanterns, and torches, and weapons, "to take the Saviour in his retreat." The token he gave the soldiers was this: "Whomsoever I shall kiss, that same is he; hold him fast, and lead him away." Jesus saw his enemies approach, and went forth to meet them. No cloud was on his brow. No trace of sorrow or agony furrowed his serene face. He was taken by the soldiers, and his disciples fled. Bound, and led to the palace of the High Priest, where the forms of law were to be observed in solemn mockery, he was arraigned for blasphemy, and was adjudged guilty. Till Pilate could pass on his case, the rabble were allowed their sport. They mocked him—smote him—spit on him—covered his eyes, and demanded of him who did the craven deed—bidding him prophecy.

The Eighth Day, the most momentous in the creation, a day seen from the foundation of the world. The people came together at an early hour. Jesus was with the guard. The Sanhedrim had convicted him of a capital crime. Yet the Jews could put no one to death. The consent of the Roman Government must be had, or the victim would escape death. A surging crowd surrounded Pilate's house. The rulers and the rabble demanded that Jesus should die. Pilate found no fault in Christ. He sent him to Herod, who put many questions to him, who made sport of him with his men of war, set him at naught, arrayed him in a gorgeous robe to deride his claims to royal honor, and then sent him back to Pilate. The terrible responsibility of putting an innocent man to death, or incurring the rage of maddened men, Pilate had tried to avoid. He sent Jesus to Herod, that the king might share the odium of the condemnation. Three times he appealed to the Jews to effect his release. The warning voice of his wife rang in his ears: "Have thou nothing to do with that just man."

The claims of the populace prevailed. Pilate gave command that it "should be done unto Jesus as the rulers desired," and then, calling for water, he washed his hands, to indicate that he was free from innocent blood, leaving with the Jews their awful malediction: "His blood be on us and our children." Reluctant or willing to sign the death-warrant of Jesus, the permission to put him to death was what the Jews wanted. He delivered Jesus to their will. The soldiers led him at once into the common hall. The band who arrested him were called in to behold the sport. He was stripped, and a royal robe put upon him. He was a king, crown him with thorns. He would rule, put a sceptre in his hands. "Bow the knee to his Majesty." "Hail King of the Jews!" Even Pilate was moved at the woe of the Son of God, and cried to the maligners: "Behold the man!" But they had no pity. To all appeals they gave but one answer: "Crucify him! his blood be on us and our children." Why is not that crowd sunk to hell? Where are those twelve legions of angels, we ask. But the Saviour's eye rebukes us—"Peace, be still." "For this hour came I into this world." The scarlet robe was removed when the brutal sport was done, and the company started for Calvary. Nothing was omitted to make his death shameful and ignominious in the last degree. He had been betrayed by one of his own disciples. He had been denied by another, under his own eye, and in the presence of the people. He had been adjudged guilty of blasphemy by the great council of his own nation. He had been the sport of rude and profane soldiers—mocked as a king by insulting homage while under guard, and derided as a prophet.

The death of the cross, itself, was excruciating as well as shameful. It was the last mark of detestation on the vilest of men. The nails driven into the hands and feet, the body thus supported, the head swinging to and fro in agony, the lacerated back exposed to the hot sun, made each movement an addition to the anguish, and the death of the cross awful. On his way to death, Jesus was compelled to bear his cross. Since the supper on Zion, it is not probable that he had taken any food. He was exhausted. His lips were parched with thirst. He was lacerated by the scourge. His wounds, bleeding and unwashed, made him faint on his way. He fell beneath the burden, and was bruised by its heavy weight. Still the procession moved on. On the back of a young stranger the cross was laid, and onward the unpitying company compelled the man of sorrows to walk. He was not alone. He was dear to the public heart. "A great company of people and women followed him." The women of Judea bewailed and lamented him. "Daughters of Jerusalem," said the compassionate Lamb of God, whose eye fell on those weeping women, "weep not for me; weep for yourselves and your children."

In the midst of two infamous men he was lifted to the accursed tree, to indicate that he was as vile as they. The same fiendish malice that mocked him in the hall of Herod and Pilate, pursued him to his death. He hung bleeding and in anguish, faint for want of food, and in deep woe. Beneath him sat the soldiers, gambling for his seamless robe, and watching him on the cross. The multitude reviled him. The rulers derided him. The priests passing by insulted him. The chief priests mocked him, saying: "Let him come down from the cross, and we will believe him." Even the thieves cast the same in his teeth. He was a spectacle to men, angels, and devils. "Who shall declare his generation!"

But on the cross, as elsewhere, the incarnate Lamb of God was mindful of others, not of himself. Bleeding hearts, loving, throbbing, came together to see that sight. His acquaintances and the women that followed him from Galilee beheld him. The home of Bethany was represented in that hour. The widow of Nain, leaning, perhaps, on the arm of her "only son," whom Jesus had given back to her in the hour of her great calamity. Mary, his mother, stood near; Joseph was no doubt dead, and she a houseless, and soon to be childless, widow. His last act was to provide a home for that forsaken and lonely one. It was high noon before the measure of his woe was complete. The victim on Calvary suffered in silence from the sixth to the ninth hour. The sun was darkened, and over all the earth the black veil of sorrow was flung. Not a bright thing was seen on the face of the globe. Heaven and earth sympathized with Calvary. The awful stillness was broken by the Son of God. The hour of abandonment came. Jesus could hold silence no longer. The anguish was too great to be borne. "My God! my God! why hast thou forsaken me?" In bitter woe he cried: "I thirst." That short sentence teaches the infinite suffering of that moment. That death-cry sounded through all the world: "It is finished. Father, into thy hands I commend my spirit." "He bowed his head and gave up the ghost." The earth quaked, and the dead came out of their graves. The great veil in the Temple was rent from the top to the bottom. The Roman commander confessed Christ and glorified God. In that hour, angels who attended him in Gethsemane heard the appalling death-cry.

Minutely must the sacred scriptures be fulfilled. The poor victim who had no home must "make his grave with the rich." Into the family tomb of his ancestors he could not be laid. The death of the cross had made him accursed, and from the family sepulcher he must be excluded. His mother, a poor, lone widow, could not find him a sepulcher. He had few friends among the rich. But he was not forsaken. Joseph of Arimathea was a noble and wealthy Jew. Led by an impulse he knew not of, he had hewed him a tomb out of the solid rock. It was still empty. In it no man had been laid. He was one of the council, "but was not consenting to the death of Jesus." He lifted up his voice against the outrage, but in vain. A secret friend of Jesus, he was so no longer. The death-cry, that extorted the confession from the heathen centurion, called Joseph forth, an open disciple of the Lamb of God. The Master had need of him. The sepulcher that he made was for his Lord, and by that the Word of God in the jot and tittle would be fulfilled. Boldly he went to Pilate, and begged the body of Jesus. Nicodemus, a brother councillor, and now an avowed disciple, joined him at the cross. Tenderly, and with deep affection, the body was lowered, and wrapped in linen clothes, "with myrrh and aloes, according to the manner of the Jews." As the sun lingered on dome and minaret, Jesus was borne to his burial "in a new sepulcher, wherein was man never yet laid."

Deep darkness settled on Calvary. The cause of the Prophet of Nazareth seemed lost. His few disciples had left him. All alone he slept in the new tomb. A stone was rolled up, and the seal of Imperial authority was put on the mouth of the cave. Soldiers paced their silent rounds to guard the dead, and broke the silence of the night with the cry: "All's well! all's well!" Not deserted is the great Prophet. Judas had gone to confession and suicide. Peter, alone and in shame, weeps over his cowardice and profanity. The disciples were scattered. Their dream was over. They separated to their own callings. But not alone in the tomb of Joseph, not without true friends, lies the body of our Lord.

> "Meek woman, with unblenching faith,
> Stood by him to the last."

These had not left him since he fell beneath the cross. And now, lest the body should be taken away, or the tomb be unmarked, they sit over against the sepulcher, and watch the spot where the son of God was laid. They knew nothing of his resurrection, but they loved him in the deep disgrace that was on his memory. In three days all fear that his disciples will steal him away would be gone; the guard would be withdrawn; the seal be broken. Then the friends of Jesus would have the solemn satisfaction of embalming the body, and laying it away till the general resurrection should call up all the dead. The god of this world had triumphed. Hell exulted as the Prince of Life was laid low. O grave! shout over thy victory. O death! be exultant. Thy sting is invincible. The Son of David, in the city of his fathers, sleeps the sleep of death. "This is the power of darkness!"

VIII.—CALVARY, AND THE HOLY PROPHETS.

> "He came to earth: from elder years,
>   A long and bright array
> Of prophet bards and patriarch seers
>   Proclaimed the glorious day;
> The light of heaven in every breast,
>   Its fire on every lip,
> In tuneful chorus on they press'd,
>   A goodly fellowship."

"How shall we know the word which the Lord hath not spoken. When a prophet speaketh in the name of the Lord, if the thing follow not nor come to pass, that is the thing which the Lord hath not spoken." Such a test God gave his people, to distinguish the true prophet from the false. The prophets of God were inspired. On record are many surprising predictions, which ran along the line of nations, foretelling the destruction of mighty empires, and the establishment of kingdoms yet unborn. Our Lord and his Apostles accepted the prophecies as from God, called their authors "holy men of God, who spake as they were moved by the Holy Ghost," whose teachings were "not cunningly devised fables," but oracles of the living God. The most famous of those predictions center around Calvary, and have their fulfillment at the cross. God revealed to Daniel, the beloved, the time of the Messiah's sacrifice—not his birth—but the time in which he should die. According to this prediction, Christ must be " cut off in threescore and ten weeks, not for himself, but for the sins" of men. So the angel Gabriel said as he "laid his finger on Daniel, at the time of the evening sacrifice." The birth of Jesus was glorious, but his death was that of a God. When the seed of the woman was promised, it was with a body wounded for sin. In the accepted offering of Abel, the Lamb slain from the foundation of the world was typified. In the spotless paschal lamb, laid on the altar, the Lamb of Calvary, without blemish and without spot, was seen by those holy men, who, walking by faith, saw the Messiah's day. The sprinkled blood-post in Egypt indicated that blood of sprinkling that saves the soul. " Of Jesus gave all the prophets witness." " The testimony of Jesus is the spirit of prophecy."

"Isaiah saw Christ's glory, and spake of him." How full, how rich, how minute, how glowing the record, culminating in Calvary! His graphic pen delineates the character of the Son of God—his doctrine, and the coming—the kingdom of God—the pathway the Messiah should tread, and the minute events of his life. But it is around Calvary that the prophet lingers with the fondest and most tender interest. Tender and truthful are those words spoken seven hundred years before the babe of Bethlehem was born. Graphically the Son of God stands out before us, as the pencil of the divine artist sketches the outline. We see him in his humiliation; his visage marred more than any man's; with no beauty of person to draw toward him the fickle crowd; seeking justice at the king's mouth, which is closed to him; preaching to a faithless generation; a root, dry and uncomely to the popular eye; rejected as a teacher from God, and despised; drenched with sorrow; familiar with grief; talking to men who, with averted faces, heard his report; stricken, smitten of God, and afflicted; wounded for the sins of men; bruised for the iniquity of the world; staggering under the weight of redemption; taken from prison and from judgment; bruised and put to grief; making, at last, his soul an offering for sin; making his grave with the rich and the wicked in his death; numbered with transgressors, to bear their sins and make intercession for them. So completely were all the predictions fulfilled, and so minutely, that men are compelled to accept the Redeemer, or deny the truth of the prophets, or affirm that the prophecies must have been written after the coming of the Son of God. But unto the "Jews were committed the oracles of God." Isaiah wrote many hundred years before the Saviour was born. The Jews held this prophecy in their hands at the time the Saviour came. It was a portion of their sacred writings, and was long before used in the temple service. From these Scriptures our Lord read, in the synagogue, when he became a public teacher. To them, constantly, he appealed, to prove that he was the Son of God. "The Scriptures in which you trust, they shall be your judges." As librarians, the Jews had it in their power to confound the Son of God, if he spake not according to the law and the testimony. Those sacred books held the promise of a coming king. In that coming the Jews believed. For it they had waited long. Some of their holy men had received a promise from God,

4*

that they should not die till they had seen the Lord's Christ. All that was marked about this coming Prince was minutely related by the prophets. The line from whence he should spring; the family to whom he should belong; the city of his birth; the time he should be born; and the attending events. When Jesus appeared, came he earlier or later than the prophets predicted, came he from another tribe or family than that set forth; with circumstances of birth unlike those in sacred record, all the Jews had to do was to appeal to the Holy Scriptures, and in the synagogue, each Sabbath, point out the discrepancy, and reject the Messiah as an impostor. The enemies of the Christian faith being judges, all things spoken of the Messiah in the prophets meet in the Son of God. He was of the kingly line of David. He was born of a virgin. He was a Nazarene. He came in the fullness of time. His birth-place was Bethlehem. Herod, alarmed at the birth of the young child, proclaimed by the wise men from the East to be born King of the Jews, "demanded of the Chief Priests and Scribes"—men competent to answer—"where Christ should be born." They were compelled to say—"In Bethlehem of Judea, for thus it is written by the Prophets."

How significant and beyond human foresight was that uttered by Jacob on his death-bed! He was an old man, and in his palace-home in Egypt he called his sons around his dying couch, that he might tell them "what should befall them in the latter days," and leave with them his dying blessing. He spake not only of what should befall his sons in their own person, but what should attend their descendants till the Messiah should come. He loved the tent home of his fathers more than the royal court of Pharaoh. He chose the sepulcher of Machpelah, where the ashes of Abraham and Sarah reposed, above any mausoleum the wealth of Egypt could build. So he took an oath of Joseph, his son: "I will lie with my fathers," said the old man; "carry me out of Egypt, and bury me in their burying-place." Around his couch his twelve sons gathered, to learn the future of their race. Of Judah he said: "The sceptre shall not depart from Judah, nor a lawgiver from between his feet, till Shiloh come." It has been conceded both by Jewish and Christian writers of note, that this is a prophecy of Christ the Saviour. It is one of the most remarkable. It demanded a national and kingly existence; the rise and fall of nations still in the future. It demanded ages of the world's history to complete its fulfillment. So it came to pass. The twelve families swelled into twelve tribes. God made them a nation, guided them by the pillar of cloud in the day, and the column of fire by the night. He fought their battles, and made them a great name among the people of the earth. The majesty of David's reign was their inheritance, and the glory of Solomon's kingdom their joy. Revolutions swept over the world. Nations arose and fell. Empires, so mighty that they seemed destined ever to abide, held the scepter, had their day, and vanished. New continents were discovered. Still the twelve tribes held on their unbroken way. Sin humbled them. They forsook God and he brought them low, till at last all passed away save Judah, and she, in the word Jew, gave her own name to all that was left of Israel. In due time, Shiloh, the salvation of God, came; when, where, and as, the prophets had said. To make the long-before-spoken prediction of the Shiloh true, it must appear that Judah remained, with her scepter grasped by her own king, and that her own lawgiver sat between her feet. That on the coming of Christ all was changed; the scepter broken, and Judah, no longer ruled by her own laws, ceased to be numbered among the nations of the earth. On the morning that the angels awoke a slumbering world with the song that will be sung "till the kingdoms of this world are become the kingdoms of our Lord and of his Christ," Judah was all that remained of the numerous and once powerful descendants of Jacob. Judah had a national existence. She had her lawgiver. Though a conquered people, she was ruled by her own kings, in subordination to Rome. The noble Temple, the pride of the Jew and the wonder of the age, crowned the summit of Moriah. The nation went, as of old, three times a year to worship before the Lord in Zion. Proud, haughty, defiant, with no symptom of decay in the national body; imperious as Babylon in her strength when she shouted, "I shall be a lady forever;" with scorn on her lip, with words of derision and an imperious spirit; Judah heard that in the lowly manger in Bethlehem one was born who claimed to be her king. Sudden and swift her doom came. Broken was the scepter. Departed the lawgiver. A few short years completed the fulfillment of this wonderful prediction of the patriarch Jacob. Within twelve months after Shiloh came, Herod, the king, died on his throne an appalling death. Step by step the impending ruin came. Revolt brought on Judah the heavy arm of the Roman power. Civil war lifted its gory front. The kingdom was rent, and Judah fell to rise no more. Without a scepter or seat of authority, with no temple and no home, she now dwells alone, an outcast among the nations. Alien in the land of her fathers, carrying about with her the evidence of a faith rejected, holding still fast her sacred books, which condemn her unbelief.

> "Fallen is thy throne, O Israel!
>   Silence is o'er thy plains;
> Thy dwellings all lie desolate,
>   Thy children weep in chains.
> Where are the dews that fed thee
>   On Elam's barren shore?
> That fire from Heaven which led thee
>   Now lights thy path no more.
>
> "Lord! thou didst love Jerusalem—
>   Once she was all thy own;
> Her love thy fairest heritage,
>   Her power thy glory's throne;
> Till evil came, and blighted
>   Thy long-loved olive-tree;
> And Salem's shrines were lighted
>   For other gods than thee.
>
> "Then sunk the star of Solyma,
>   Then passed her glory's ray,
> Like heath that in the wilderness
>   The wild wind whirls away;
> Silent and waste her bowers,
>   Where once the mighty trod,
> And sunk those guilty towers,
>   While Baal reigned as God."

Moses, and all the prophets, spoke of Christ, and of his death. In the opening sermon, with which our Lord began his ministry, he applied the lesson of the day, taken from Isaiah, to himself, saying: "This day is the Scripture fulfilled in your ears." To the Jews he said: "Had ye believed Moses, ye had believed me; for he wrote of me." Andrew, the first called of the apostles, with Philip, finding Nathaniel, urged him to join the new cause, saying: "We have found him of whom Moses, in the Law and the Prophets, did write—Jesus of Nazareth, the son of Joseph." The ministry of our Lord was devoted to explaining and enforcing the Law and the Prophets. After the resurrection from the dead, to the despairing pair on their way from Jerusalem to Emmaus, he "opened their understanding, that they might understand the Scriptures," and said, "All things must be fulfilled which were written in the Law of Moses, and in the Prophets, and in the Psalms, concerning me, for it was written that it behooved Christ to suffer, and to rise from the dead the third day; and that repentance and remission of sins should be preached in his name, among all nations, beginning at Jerusalem." He made his apostles witnesses of the prophecy, and of its fulfillment. The sermon at Pentecost, the dying address of Stephen, and the ministry of the apostles to the close, were little else than an appeal to the holy prophets, then in the hands of the Jews, to show that they were holy men, inspired by the Holy Ghost; a day-star from heaven; a light shining in a dark place, to guide the way-worn, weary, bewildered traveler along the pathway that led to Calvary. When the promise of Christ, on the Mount of Olives—given as he lifted up his hands to bless, and was parted from them and carried up into heaven—that they should "be endued with power from on high," came in the form of cloven tongues, like as of fire, filling the disciples with the Holy Ghost, giving them utterances with tongues of all nations, confounding and amazing the multitude; Peter, standing up with the eleven, lifted up his voice and said, this is that which was spoken by the prophet Joel. He affirmed that David foresaw the taking and crucifying of "Jesus of Nazareth by wicked hands, and spake of the resurrection of Christ, in that his soul was not left in hell, neither his flesh did see corruption." After healing the lame man in the Temple—which act caused " all the people to run together unto Peter and John in the porch, which is called Solomon's, greatly wondering"—Peter said that the God of Abraham had glorified his son, Jesus, of whom Moses truly said, unto the fathers, "A prophet shall the Lord your God raise up unto you of your brethren, like unto me! him shall ye hear in all things whatsoever he shall say unto you. And it shall come to pass, that every soul which will not hear that prophet shall be destroyed from among the people." And he adds, "Yea, all the prophets, from Samuel and those that follow after, as many as have spoken, have likewise foretold of these days."

The march of events, that attended the Saviour from Bethlehem to Calvary, are predicted and minutely stated. David, speaking by the Holy Ghost, sets forth the divinity of our Lord, and his expiatory sacrifice. He relates the proposal made by the Divine Son, in the council in heaven, to give himself an atonement for sin. He predicted the crime of Judas, the price of blood, and his suicide; the events that attended the death of Jesus on Calvary; the piercing of his feet and hands; and the gambling for his garment at the cross. He asserts that not a bone should be broken in that sacred body, and repeats the death-cry of the great victim. He spoke, also, of the resurrection from the dead; of the coming of the Holy Ghost; the calling of the Gentiles, and the universal spread of the Messiah's kingdom, from the rivers to the ends of the earth. We read, with wonder, the voice of God in the prophets, as the great events meet in their fulfillment. How unborn nations must arise and fall; how imperial decrees go forth and municipal laws be created. How God's word and Gospel must run along the line of national existence, while his enemies are swift to execute his word. The birth of John the Baptist was a miraculous event, and was in answer to prayer, though Elisabeth was well stricken in years. Yet, seven hundred years before that event, Isaiah predicted the birth of John, the forerunner of our Lord, and his words are quoted. He included in his prophecy the birth of Jesus from a virgin; the divine power and miracles of the Son of God; his preaching; the unbelief of the Jews; the calling of the Gentiles; the passion and death of our Lord; and the universal spread of his kingdom among men. His words are cited in all parts of the New Testament, and applied to the Gospel. Hosea knew that Christ must flee into Egypt. Micah predicted the birth-place of Christ. His words were read by the chief priests to Herod, when he "demanded where Christ should be born." Amos spoke of the cutting off of Israel, and the bringing in of the Gentiles. Nahum, as quoted by Paul in his letter to the Romans, proclaimed the scattering of messengers on the mountain, with good tidings of salvation, publishing peace. A passage in Jonah's life, when he was three days and three nights in the belly of hell, is made by our blessed Lord a type of his descent into the grave. Zephaniah utters God's call, in the Gospel, to the impenitent, to turn and live. Jeremiah is full of Christ. Paul quotes him in all the strength of his statements about the new and better covenant that God would make with his people in the latter times. Habakkuk proclaims the great truth of Justification of Faith. Daniel closes up the probation of the race, and sets forth in solemn words —made more solemn as cited by Jesus—that there shall be two resurrections—the one to life, the other to damnation. Haggai, Ezekiel, Obadiah, and Malachi, are cited in the New Testament, with their testimony for Jesus. Truly the holy men of God spake by the Holy Ghost, and by them God has taken care of his own honor and his own word. No link in the chain of evidence, from Eden till now, is wanting. No ancient work is so well attested as the Bible. No one can prove that Homer lived, or Plato wrote, with a thousandth part of the evidence that can be brought in favor of the truths of the prophets. No history is so confirmed as that of the Old Testament. Not only are all the prominent historic events approved and used in the New Testament, but their truth is confirmed in a marvelous manner. Buried cities are unearthed, and seas, and tombs, and national records, come daily to light, to vindicate the Word of God. Judah still abides, a wonder and a monument. She survives and worships as in the days of David. She worships the God of her fathers as he was worshiped in Zion. She holds the same Scriptures that were read by Jesus, at Nazareth, to which he appealed to prove his divinity, and from which the apostles proved that Jesus was the Christ. She still rejects the Son of God, and hopes for the Redeemer; keeps the Sabbath of her nation, and lifts up the cry to-day, "Come, Elijah, and bring redemption." Librarians of the Christian Church, she has for eighteen hundred years held in her own hands the proof that Jesus is divine. Christians can knock at the door of every synagogue of the Jews, in all lands and climes, and, from the Scriptures read by these people from Sabbath to Sabbath, prove that Shiloh has come, and that the seed of the woman has been born.

IX.—CALVARY AND THE HOLY GOSPELS.

"Through David's city I am led,
 Here all around are sleeping;
A light directs to yon poor shed,
 Where lonely watch is keeping.
I enter—ah! what glories shine!
Is this Immanuel's earthly shrine?
 Messiah's infant temple?"

PECULIAR was the condition of the world when God sent his Son to redeem it. It was a remarkable era, known as the "pacific age." One vast power ruled all the civilized world. It held war and peace in its hands. The great war temple of Janus, opened when war raged in any part of the world, was closed when the Prince of Peace was born. God held the passions of men in his hands. He subdued the lust of conquest while he ushered his blessed Son into the world.

"No war nor battle's sound was heard the world around,
 No hostile chiefs to furious combat ran;
But peaceful was the night in which the Prince of Light
 His reign of peace upon the earth began."

No such age was ever before known. A mighty prophet of God was expected. We have a fine illustration of this in the temple on the day of circumcision. Among the dwellers in Jerusalem was an aged man, Simeon by name. He was devout. His equal in the public estimation had not been seen since the time of Moses. He was held in great repute as a learned doctor of the law. He walked with God, and had this testimony, that he should not die till Christ came. According to the sacred books, the time for the coming of the Messiah was at hand; the time foretold ages before and long waited for. One desire burned in all hearts. One prayer was breathed from all lips: "Let the Messiah's day be in my day. Let him spring from my house." For his coming,

> "Kings and prophets waited
> And sought, but never found.
> Prophets and kings desired it long,
> But died without the sight."

When the parents of Jesus "brought in the Child, to do for him after the custom of the law," Simeon, guided by the Holy Ghost, came into the temple. He knew Mary and Joseph well. The Word of God and the events in Bethlehem were familiar to him. He was a type and the first fruit of his nation. In his withered arms he took the babe and blessed God, ready now to die, for his eye had seen the salvation of God.

At no time other than that which marks the Christian era could Christ have come into the world. With great care God has guarded the Gospel from the advent of his Son to now. History, sacred and profane, writers Christian and heathen, run the history back to the exact time when the prophets said the Messiah would appear. All concede that we have now a sect called Christians. They are counted by millions. They are found in all parts of the world. As Napoleon said of them at Helena: "Millions of men would die for Christ to-day." These people have sacred books which profess to hold the life, teachings, miracles, success, sufferings, and death of their exalted Head. This sect existed in the tenth century, for the Crusades were commenced, to rescue the Holy Sepulcher from the hands of infidels. In the year 300, Christians had a position and a name among the nations of the earth; for Constantine, the Emperor of Rome, became a Christian. In the year 200, Christianity ran through all the Roman empire, as Gibbon admits, and "spread into every city." In the year 176, Celsus wrote. He undertook to show from the Gospels themselves that Jesus ought not to be received as a divine teacher. He quotes from all the Gospels, and calls them by name. He calls Jesus "the man of Nazareth," says he "was followed by a dozen fishermen or sailors," and was "put to death by a Roman judge." These sacred books must have been in existence at that early time, or Celsus could not have cited them against the Church. In the year 107, Pliny, in doubt what should be done with the numerous Christians in Judea, all violating the law of Rome, wrote his celebrated letter to Trajan for instructions. The Christians were guilty in that they "worshiped a man whom the Jews had put to death." He states their number; speaks of their godly life; how they worshiped Christ as God, and sang hymns to his sacred name; exhorted one another to obey the law of the land, and to lead pure and holy lives. He could not find it in his heart to harm them. In the year 54, Nero lived. His persecutions are matters of universal notoriety. Sacred as well as profane history record his acts.

From Eden to John the prophecy came to men. From this point, where we live, the history of the Church starts and runs back. It pauses at the cradle of John, who came to prepare the way of the Lord. It touches the altar of incense, on the right side of which Gabriel stood when he announced to Zacharias the birth of a son. Joined to this is that long line of Christian fathers, who take us into the presence-chamber of Jesus and his friends. Polycarp looked on John, who leaned on Jesus' bosom. Ignatius walked with Paul, so Chrysostom affirms. Profane writers add their testimony. Men contemporary with the Apostles quote their words to approve them. Many quote to condemn, showing the existence of the Gospels. The multiplying the books of the New Testament; the reading of them in the public assemblies from the time of the Apostles; the jealous care with which the Church watched these sacred books; the vigilant eye of their enemies, which was continually on them, to note any alteration—all this amounts to a demonstration that the Gospels were written at the time, and by the men who claim to have penned them, and did so under the guidance of the Holy Ghost. Calvary vindicates the truth of the Gospels.

X.—CALVARY AND THE CHURCH OF GOD.

> "Fling to the heedless winds,
>   Or on the waters cast,
> Their ashes shall be watched,
>   And gathered at the last;
> And from that scattered dust,
>   Around us and abroad,
> Shall spring a plenteous seed
>   Of witnesses for God."

The Church of God was "purchased with his own blood." Its existence is due to Calvary. Without the blood of the cross no sinner could have been pardoned, and no one could have sung praises to him who had redeemed men to God. A glorious thing is the Church. It is the oldest thing in creation, and it will be the last. Built on the rock of ages, it stands on "the foundation of the prophets and the apostles, Jesus Christ himself being the chief corner-stone." The Church of both dispensations meet at the cross of Christ. She was ministered to by Abel as well as St. John. Melchisedek was her priest as well as St. Paul. Enoch was her preacher as well as St. Peter. The miracles that marked her later career, shed a halo of glory over her earlier triumphs. Abraham, and those holy men "who obtained the promise," and had respect unto the recompense of reward, were members of her communion. She has existed in all ages of the world. She measures her years by centuries. Dynasties are the waymarks of her history. She reared her altars amid the untamed frenzy of the middle ages. She preached the Gospel to the iron soldiery at Rome. She looked down on the glory of Nineveh and Babylon. From the windows of the ark she beheld the deluge. She knew how the young creation looked when it came fresh from the hand of God. To her pertains the blood of confessors and martyrs for six thousand years. Prophets who spake by the Holy Ghost, lived in her bosom. Apostles who looked on Christ, ministered at her altar. On her behalf the course of nature has been changed, rivers and seas been opened and closed, bread rained from heaven, the rock of flint turned into flowing waters, the sun arrested at midday, and corruption and death have yielded back their prey.

Calvary unites the Church of the Old Testament and the New. Both harmonize. They are one. Jesus was in the Church of the elder dispensation as well as in the later; as the sun is in the twilight as well as in the meridian splendor. Christ repealed nothing. The old dispensation faded into the full glory of the new as the earlier tint of morning merges into the clear, full light of day. All the types and shadows ended when the full glory came. To Abraham was the Gospel preached as well as to Paul. Of the "Rock of Christ" all drank who ran with patience and hope the race set before them. St. Paul likens the Church to a tree planted before the flood, its natural branches broken off, and the wild olive grafted in their place. It was the same tree under which heavenly visitants took shelter when they came to earth, and under it holy men reposed when they entertained angels unawares. Miracles attended it before Christ came. In the one, they came from men whom God appointed to subvert the order of nature. In the later, they came from the hand of our Lord alone, who said: "My Father works, and I work."

The Church has been the great power in the earth. She began the march of freedom and civilization around the globe. No freedom exists to-day but where her altars have stood. No philanthropy, no moral reform is worthy of the name which she does not originate and bless. Clothed with immortal vigor, she will abide among men till her work is complete; till this revolted world bows at the name of Jesus; till all the ends of the earth remember and turn to the Lord. Endless duration is her destiny. Endless conquest her crown. All who oppose her will be ground to powder. She has survived assault, apostasy, and treachery. Ignorance and corruption have struck at her, only to make her luster more apparent and glorious. Amid almost universal ignorance and crime, she has held all the learning and purity of the world. No weapon formed against her has prospered.

She has outlived her foes. She saw the old world sink beneath the flood. She was safe in Zoar when God rained down on Sodom fire and brimstone out of heaven. She survived the awful persecutions that for two hundred years raged after the ascension of her Lord; while Rome, then the proud mistress of the world and the author of her tribulations, has long since ceased to exist. Nations, kingdoms, dynasties, and councils have joined to destroy her. She abides, but they are not. New continents have been discovered; she has attended their earliest voyage. She has tracked commerce around the globe. Where gain and glory have tempted men to go, she has followed with the cross and the consolation of salvation. And, alone and solitary, she has taken her way "where heroes fear to tread." Science has enlarged her domain, but can not outrun the Church. New inventions and new discoveries mark the age, but the Church is nobler than them all. She sails with the new motive power; prints her Bibles with the latest improvements; sends messages of salvation along the iron pathway; and flashes truth along the wires with the velocity of light. All things change, but the Church. Like her incarnate head, she is the "same yesterday, to-day, and forever." The same Gospel which was read in the first Church at Jerusalem, when the Apostles stood at the altar, is read in our places of worship to-day. We chant the same psalms that awoke the echoes of Palestine in the time of David and Solomon. We worship in the forms that were hallowed by the example of her great head. Poetry, art, statuary, paintings, music, and refinement are her servants. To her shelter all are called. Wide open are her doors. Safe are all they who dwell in this city, beneath the canopy of God's covenant love. God is in the midst of her—all such will be borne across the river of death to join the Church above.

'One army of the living God,
    To his command we bow;
Part of the host have crossed the flood,
    And part are crossing now."

XI.—CALVARY AND THE SABBATH OF EDEN.

> Hail, holy day! "So calm, so bright,
> Bridal of earth and sky."

> "And now his conquering chariot-wheels
>   Ascend the lofty skies;
> Broken beneath his powerful cross
>   Death's iron scepter lies.
> This day be grateful homage paid,
>   And loud hosannas sung;
> Let gladness dwell in every heart,
>   And praise on every tongue."

We keep the first day of the week as holy time, and not the seventh. Men complain of this, and ask: "If we must keep one day holy unto the Lord, why not the day God made, on which he rested from all his labor, and which he hallowed as the Sabbath of the Lord our God. Why not keep the seventh rather than the first, and so Jew and Gentile worship God on the same day?" The answer is, that the day now called the seventh is not the day of original consecration; while the Christian Sabbath is the day of original appointment. The first day of the week as we compute time, will be seen to be the day that God called the seventh, which he blessed and sanctified. Calvary restores the old, and vindicates the Sabbath of the new dispensation.

The common term for the first day of the week in the early Church, was the "Lord's Day," and it was as well understood as the "Lord's Supper." The term was not used without a purpose. Many hundred years before the Redeemer came to earth, David spake of him, and, as Paul affirms, so spake by the Holy Ghost. Among other things David detailed was Christ's rejection as the "chief corner-stone" by the people to whom he was sent—his suffering as a man—his betrayal, crucifixion, and entombment, and his resurrection from the dead, as "it was not possible that the grave should hold him." The day on which Christ was to rise from the dead is called by David "the day the Lord made," in which by worship and song the Church should "rejoice and be glad." That day should be ever "marvelous in the eyes" of the saints, for it should mark at once the Sabbath of Eden and the triumphant resurrection of Christ from the grave. That "this day" refers to the day that Jesus arose from the dead is proved by the express statement of St. Peter, when he addressed the rulers of the people and Elders of Israel, saying: "Jesus of Nazareth, whom ye crucified, God raised from the dead. This is the stone which was set at naught of you builders, which is become the head of the corner." It was no human impulse that led to this utterance, for Peter, when he spoke those words, "was filled with the Holy Ghost." Our blessed Lord cites the same words of David, and applies them to his own death. It was the purpose of God that his own blessed day should be honored by the resurrection of his own holy Son, and by the worship of the Church on that day in all lands and climes. He who sent his Son to "shake heaven and earth, that things that could not be shaken should remain," intended to thus honor the "Sabbath on which God rested from his works." When the angel of light rolled back the stone and sat on it, it was the first act in the great drama of restoration, never again to be lost to the Church till time should end.

In one sense God never made and never owned but one day; as, in one sense, Jesus is the only Son of God. God always reserved an ownership in the things of life. The Lamb without blemish was his. The first-fruits of the fold and field were laid on his altar. A tenth of the treasure of the world he claimed. One of the tribes and a part of the temple were holy unto the Lord. An inclosure marked what was sacred when the people dwelt in tents. Man or beast that touched the sacred mountain died. So one day in seven God called his own. "It is mine." "I made it." "Touch it not." "Six days take your pleasure and do all work." "The Sabbath is holy to me. Will a man rob God?" By his own divine example he hallowed the Sabbath. He connected it with the noblest blessings that could fall on a people. The rain and dew should not be withheld if his people were true to the commandment. The fertile field and fruitful fold, peace and national prosperity, should be their inheritance.

Amid the unbelief, sin, and idolatry of his people—their ignorance of the law—their change in the computation of time—God kept his eye steadily on the holy Sabbath, and in the fullness of time he restored the ancient day to his Church, to be perpetuated in worship and marked by that precious ordinance that shows forth the Lord's death till he come. So the Church accepted it. The Lord's Day became the name of the Sabbath. So met the disciples. The descent of the Holy Spirit found them at worship on that day. John on Patmos, on the "Lord's Day, was in the Spirit," when he had glimpses of the home of the Redeemed, of which the Lord's Day is a type. Eden and the Millennium join hands at Calvary.

But, were the revelation of God silent on the Christian Sabbath, the change of day would not affect the keeping of the holy time by the Church. Suppose Jesus did not arise from the dead on the Sabbath day of Eden, it is for the rejecter of the Christian Sabbath to prove that the so-called seventh day of this century is the original Sabbath. Changes and revolutions affect computation as well as other things. The Jews "made void the law of God by tradition," and the day of worship was quite as likely to be affected as any thing else. In the long captivity of the Jews they lost their language, had hardly a tradition, and forgot almost wholly the Holy Scriptures, as the reader of Ezra and Nehemiah will learn; and they could easily have let slip the day on which their fathers worshiped God. More than this, the "Son of Man is Lord of the Sabbath." He could, if he would, change the day. Six working days and one of rest is what the law of God contemplated, and what the nature of man demands. He who made the original Sabbath could alter the time if he chose. We celebrate the birthday of the Father of his Country on the 22d of February. But Washington was born on the 11th day of February, and not on the 22d. It was agreed in all parts of the civilized world, to answer a great end, that eleven days should be added to the calendar. It was done. No one was harmed. No interest damaged. No man made older or younger by the change. The Lord of the Sabbath could have changed it from the seventh to the first, had it been needful; and so have called the Church together to mark the resurrection of its Exalted Head on that day. But it was not needful to alter the legislation of God on the Sabbath. Jesus was to "restore all things." To restore the original Sabbath was one object of his mission.

The Sabbath is not a "Mosaic institution." It was hallowed ages before Moses was born; before the tribes of Israel existed; before the father of the nation lived. Like a diadem, God placed it on the new creation when it came fresh from his hand, when the Divine Architect pronounced it "Good." It began its mission with labor, justice, and devotion; and will attend them to the end. It was kept in the wilderness before the law was given from Sinai. The miracle of the manna, on the sixth day, when it came in double quantity, and could be kept over the Sabbath, and on no other day, marked holy time, with which Israel was already familiar. "To-morrow is the rest of the holy Sabbath unto the Lord." "To-day is the Sabbath of the Lord; to-day ye shall not find manna in the field." And so in the wilderness, God put special honor on his day.

It was introduced into the law, not as a new institution, but one with which the people had been long familiar, of which they needed only to be put in remembrance. A new ordinance, ceremony or festival, garment or service, was introduced with explanations and orders how to use it. In most instances a pattern was given. But the terse and brief statute—"Remember the Sabbath day"—carries with it a previous knowledge of its purposes and duties, on the part of the people to whom it was given. We find the command in the center of a moral code, all now binding. To steal, to slander, to commit murder, to worship idols, are as sinful to-day as if the code of Moses, in all its parts, were binding. These sins against God and against man existed, and were forbidden, before the law came. So was it with the Sabbath. Like Jordan, through the Lake Tiberius, the Sabbath holds its unbroken way through all nationalities and all ages, from Eden to now.

No one understood Christ to loosen the binding force of the Sabbath. When accused of breaking it, he vindicated his conduct by his divinity as Lord of the Sabbath, and cited extreme cases, in the Old Testament, where men were excused for violations of the law, only by the stern necessities of the case. No word from his lips indicated that the Sabbath was to be closed by his coming. A finger can not be put on the repealing clause. He repealed no statute of God. He came to fulfill. He threw the whole force of his example into the Sabbath. He had a "custom" of going into the synagogue on that day to worship God, which he kept to the end. To the Samaritans he enlarged the sphere of service, but did not meddle with the day. The women who "beheld the sepulcher where the body of Jesus was laid," had too much regard for holy time to continue that office of affection. They went to their own homes, "and rested on the Sabbath, according to the commandment." Full forty years after the crucifixion, in that great judgment by which God would wipe out the Jews from among the nations, the Church had so much conscience on keeping the Sabbath, that, beyond a Sabbath-day's journey, they would not travel to escape ruin. Christ bade them pray that their "flight, in the evil hour, should not be on the Sabbath day" —a Sabbath-day's journey being only three miles, it was not far enough to carry them to a place of safety.

The "Lord's Day"—the holy Sabbath—the Sabbath of the Lord our God—or by what name soever known—is the same in spirit in both the elder and later dispensations. It had no local or municipal origin. Like the priesthood of Melchisedek, it has no beginning of days, nor end of life. It abideth forever. All that demanded its appointment, demands its perpetuity. The reasons that created it, require its preservation. It was made for man, and for all time. It was made before nations were known, and when but one man existed in the world. In the original appointment we are told, "God blessed the seventh day, and sanctified it; because that on it he had rested from all his works, which God created and made." That fact will ever remain. Before sin blighted this fair world, or sorrow's strong wave rolled over the human soul, the benevolence of God created the Sabbath, adapted it to man's moral and physical necessity, and the same benevolence has given it immortality while man's probation endures. No limit has been assigned to its observance, for it was made for the race. Some laws are limited. But the statute that called the Lord's Day into being is not one of them. We need the Sabbath as much as the Church in Eden or the home of promise—with all its aids to man's physical comforts, its sanitary power, its intellectual good, its ability to fit us for heaven, of which it is a type.

It is a practicable statute. Some laws become obsolete, or end, because it is not possible to keep them. The Sabbath is not one of those. It is not more difficult to keep it now than it was in Eden, or in the pathway of Israel from the Red Sea to the Jordan, or in Judea in the time of the Saviour. Its observance violates no statute of nations or government. It endangers no man's life. It runs counter to no physical law. It gives men ample time to do all the work that can be done with safety and profit. It creates no broils. It promotes no civil or domestic strife. Observed by nations, it lengthens their tranquillity, and enables subjects to lead quiet and peaceable lives. It harmonizes with the law of our being, and prolongs human existence. It raises the value of men and of property. It is God's gift to man. It is too humane—too beneficial—to owe its origin to man. The ruler, the tyrant, the oppressor would not shut up the workshop, end toil, lift up the yoke, and let the sons of labor rest, one day in seven. The Sabbath is God's day to the poor, and it was created by him who sent his Gospel to the poor. The rich can take their rest when they please. But who will come to the aid of the poor workman, if the Sabbath is not preserved. Life to him must be an endless round of toil. Those who call for the abolition of the Sabbath, who attempt to remove the sacredness of the day, or throw from society its binding power, are doing the work of the devil in Eden, carrying sorrow, woe, and death into the homes of men.

XII.—THE MOUNTAINS OF NEBO; OR, THE DEATH-SONG OF MOSES.

"Remember ye his parting gaze,
　His farewell song by Jordan's tide,
When, full of glory and of days,
　He saw the promised land—and died."

AT the age of one hundred and twenty years, at the command of God, Moses " went up from the plains of Moab unto the mountain of Nebo, to the top of Pisgah, that is over against Jericho. And God showed him all the land of promise from Gilead unto Dan, and all the land of Judah unto the utmost sea, and all the land of Canaan, which he had given unto the children of Israel for a possession." Moses had trespassed against God at the waters of Meribah. Not his long and devoted life nor his faithful service and suffering, could atone for the wrong-doing of that hour. He had longed to tread the soil of promise beneath his feet; to inhale the fragrance of the vale of Sharon; to lead the children of Israel across the Jordan as he had led them across the Red Sea; and to "eat with them the old corn of the land." But importunate entreaty, earnest prayer, and sacrifice were in vain. The decree went forth: " Thou shalt see the land before thee, but thou shalt not go thither into the land which I give unto the children of Israel." There seemed no reason why Moses should die. "His eye was not dimmed, nor his natural force abated." He was as able, as Joshua, to have led the people into the land of promise, and to have established them among the nations of the earth. But his work was done. The pen of the lawgiver must give place to the sword of the conqueror. God said to him: " Get thee up unto the Mount of Nebo, and die in the mount whither thou goest up, and be gathered unto thy people, as Aaron, thy brother, died in Mount Hor, and was gathered to his people." Moses received the decree with no sullen spirit. He uttered no complaint against the severity of the sentence. He did not cry out as did Cain: " My punishment is greater than I can bear." He bowed his head in heroic submission. In the presence of all the people he vindicated the righteous judgment of God, saying: " All his ways are perfect; just and right is he." His heroic death-song, which makes the closing portions of Deuteronomy, is the sublimest of human compositions. No reproach escaped his lips. He took with cheerfulness and unblenching faith the bitter cup commended to his lips.

His life had been an eventful one. Born in captivity; hid three months in defiance of the king's decree; cast upon the waters and watched by his sister; rescued by a royal lady, whose heart God touched, he cradled his infant head on the beating bosom of his own mother. As he grew in years, he defended his oppressed brethren; fled the land; and in Midian led his flock as a shepherd on the sacred sides of Horeb. Out of the burning bush God instructed him to go down to Egypt and redeem his people. He crossed the Red Sea triumphantly; and, with Miriam and the thousands of

Israel, sang that anthem of the free, which in heaven is to be joined with "the song of the Lamb." He gave the nation the law he received at Sinai, amid the awful manifestations of divine power. He led them to the borders of the land of promise. "There arose not a prophet in all Israel like unto Moses, whom the Lord knew face to face." August was his burial. He was alone with God when he received the law. He was alone with God when he threw himself between his guilty nation and the wrath of Jehovah. He was alone with God when he ascended the top of Pisgah to see the land he could not enter. "So Moses, the servant of the Lord, died there in the land of Moab." Deep among the rocks, "in a valley of Moab, over against Bethpeor," his grave was dug by the Almighty hands. His tomb was hidden from the eyes of all living, for "no man knoweth of his sepulcher unto this day."

> "God amid rocks buried him
> In his lonely grave on Nebo, where he died.
> The rocks clave asunder 'neath his corse,
> The mountain o'er it closed,
> And Moses, buried by the hand of God,
> Lay in his secret grave."

XIII.—JERICHO; OR, THE SCARLET LINE IN THE WINDOW.

"Room in the Saviour's bleeding heart—
There love and pity meet;
Nor will he bid the soul depart
That trembles at his feet."

"In the days of Ahab, king of Israel, Hiel, the Bethelite, did build Jericho. He laid the foundation thereof in Abiram, his firstborn, and set up the gates thereof in his youngest son, Segub, according to the Word of the Lord." The ancient city of Jericho has great renown. It has been the theater of marked events in the march of God's people. It is situated about twenty miles east from Jerusalem. It was a walled town, and was the key to that part of Palestine.

It was a rude collection of huts when Deborah judged Israel under the palm-trees. Israel was pitched near Jericho when Balak sent for Balaam to "curse Israel and defy Jacob." And near this city the spoil of the Midianites, with the captives, were brought into the camp. The discomfited and depressed messengers of David, who suffered at the hand of Hanam, were commanded to "tarry in the city till their beards were grown."

Jericho was identified with many of the marvelous works of the Son of God. He called and saved

Zaccheus on his first visit to this ancient city; and when Bartimeus called for mercy from the Son of God, it was the last visit of Jesus to Jericho.

Moses completed the work committed to his hands. He died in the fullness of strength at the great age of one hundred and twenty years. The sword of the conqueror must succeed the pen of the lawgiver, to allow Israel to take her place among the nations of of the earth.

Joshua, a valiant and heroic captain, was chosen to lead the people into the promised land. The conquest and subjection were sure. God had said it; God would secure it, if again he rode the cloudy pillar, and made the stars and the rivers fight the battles of his people.

Jericho was a walled city and a fortress. Its strength or weakness must be known. Valiant men were sent forth to spy out the condition of the king and his hosts. It was quite easy for the spies to enter the city, but not so easy to be hid. The encampment of an immense host near the city was well known. Such a people, with Jehovah for a leader, were no common foe to meet in battle, and terror had fallen on the city.

The people of Jericho knew the history of the Israelites—"How the Lord dried up the waters of the Red Sea"—knew "what he did to the king of the Amorites, and Og, whom he utterly destroyed." No wonder the "inhabitants of the land were faint" with fear because of the presence of such an army, or that the coming into the city of two strange men, supposed to be scouts from that invincible host, should spread terror and general alarm, or that "men went at once and told the king."

The spies found a friend in the city, whose house was built on the walls. It was a woman, named Rahab. She was probably a hostess or an innkeeper, for so the term applied here may mean. She was perhaps a Jewess or a proselyte. Certainly she was well acquainted with the dealings of God with his people, from the passage of the Red Sea to that very hour. She knew the errand of the men whom she entertained; knew the doom of the people; knew that God would deliver the city into their hands.

She received the spies in peace; hid them from their pursuers; made a covenant with them on the roof of her house; which covenant included the salvation of herself and family, in that terrible hour when Jericho should be given up to carnage.

She trusted in the covenant, and had unflinching faith in the honor of the men whom she entertained.

Yet she distrusted herself. She would have some visible token of the compact, to which, from time to time, she could turn—on which she could look, and revive her waning faith, as the dark and terrible day drew near.

She demanded of the messengers a symbol. She let them down from the wall by a line, during the darkness of the night. That line was a common house-cord. It happened to be scarlet. The men said unto her: "Thou shalt bind this line of scarlet thread in the window which thou didst let us down by, and it shall be a true token."

The scarlet cord was nothing by itself; but as a true token—a symbol—it held the salvation of Rahab, and all in her house. Once placed in the window, and all the conditions kept, her salvation was sure. Kept elsewhere, or destroyed, and her ruin, with all her house, was certain.

The history of Rahab is cited both by St. Paul and St. James. The one, to show that Rahab was saved by faith; the other, to show that she was saved by works. Such seeming contradictions are common in Divine revelation. In one place we are commanded to "answer a fool according to his folly," and the reason is assigned. In the next verse we are forbidden to "answer a fool according to his folly," and the reason is given. If a man, dealing with a fool, does not know when to speak and when not to, he does not know enough to answer a fool at all; and the passage does not concern him. We are told that, "If the iron be blunt, and he do not whet the edge, then must he put to more strength; but wisdom is proper to direct." If a man has a day's work to do with an ax, it would be profitable to take time and grind the tool to an edge. But if the limb of a fellow was under a fallen tree, it would be better to strike harder, "put to more strength," rather than let his friend die while he went to grind the ax. If a man did not know enough to decide whether to "whet the edge" of the blunt iron, or "put to more strength," he would not know enough to handle edge tools at all, and the directions need not concern him.

To a class of people who prided themselves on good

works, without the foundation of faith, it was needful to show that faith underlaid all that Rahab did. To a people that relied on a sound creed, regardless of a holy life, it was needful to say that Rahab's faith was seen in her acts; and that, had she not kept the conditions of the covenant, and done the work commanded, she would have perished with those that believed not. Two farmers might dispute about which was the most valuable part of a tree, the root or the branches: one contending that the root could bear no fruit without the branches and the foliage; the other as earnestly contending that the limbs would be parched and withered without the root. It would be as easy to settle the dispute by showing how each were dependent, and how worthless were the root and the branches unless mutually sustained. St. James says: "As the body without the Spirit is dead, so faith without works is dead also." Faith needs her symbols. She has them. Her ordinances are simple. Faith is spirit and life, and not form. But the water of life can not be reached unless we have a pitcher to draw with; and the oil of life must be put into a vessel, or it can not give light to all in the house. The sash that holds the glass that lets in the light of day, should not be heavier than is needful to hold firm the glass, lest the thickness of the frame keep out the light of day.

Men want some tangible thing in religion to help their weakness, as they cry out, "Lord, I believe; help thou my unbelief." Rahab believed, and was saved by faith. But, after the covenant was sealed, and its execution sure, she exclaimed: "Give me a true token that you will deliver our lives from death."

To answer this yearning of the soul, God gave to each tribe of Jacob a standard, around which each could rally. All nations have symbols in the flag that embodies the national power. It is the only thing that can be insulted or honored. It is a frail thing, indeed, that national banner; but it is the strongest thing in the nation. It commands all the swords, which in its defence fly at once from the scabbard. It commands every man in the realm, who, to avenge its sullied honor, leaves home and kindred to fill a patriot's grave. It commands all the treasure of the land. An infant's hand could rend the flag, but nations must not trample on it. No government could live, none ought to live, who can not or will not defend its colors.

When the Russian fleet were in the waters of New York Bay, the daily lowering of the national ensign was a most attractive sight. The crew stood on deck; the officers, bareheaded, stood on the quarter-deck; the band played the national air of Russia; and, amid the booming of cannon, the Russian banner came to the deck. The presence of Alexander, the Emperor, on board the flag-ship, would not have been a more real embodiment of the sovereignty of Russia than was that frail piece of bunting, saluted with such honor, for it was a true symbol of loyalty and Russian nationality. I once saw a review of one of the corps of the Army of the Potomac; members of the Cabinet, Senators, Governors, and other dignitaries were present; but one man held the eyes of all present—he was the commander-in-chief, who held the review. He rode to the front of the line, and sat alone, less moved than the noble animal he rode. Column after column went by, and his keen eye glanced at each soldier as he passed. At length the band filed out and stood in front of the commander-in-chief, and soon the color company came by, bearing the national banner. The commander raised his hand reverently to his head, removed his cap, and sat bareheaded as the sovereignty of the nation passed by, symbolized in the American flag—saluted by the band, amid the huzzas and the waving of handkerchiefs by the assembled thousands; the sight thrilled the heart of the people, who saw the reverence paid to the embodiment of national honor and power.

When Nelson was buried, the flag that floated at at the mast-head of his vessel when he fell fatally wounded, was placed on his coffin and lowered into his grave. The brave men who had followed him through seas of blood removed the old flag from the coffin, tore it into ribbons, and placed the pieces near their heart, to be buried with them when they died. It was a memento of a brave man whom they loved.

The same spirit is seen in the household into which death has come; the broken top or whip, the mutilated doll and worn shoe, are more precious than jewels. It was said that the famous Earl of Ripton had a chest kept near his bed, that bore on it these letters: "To be saved first in case of fire." During his absence his residence was consumed by fire. On his return, his first inquiry was for the favorite chest. When told it was safe, he said, calmly, "It is well—it is enough." His servants supposed the chest contained jewels that were heirlooms in the family. It held nothing but the play-toys of a beloved child, whom in deep sorrow he had borne to the grave.

God has given his Church symbols of his undying love. They are the bread and the wine that symbolize the scarlet blood of the Son of God, indicating that we are not our own, but are bought with the precious blood of the peculiar Son of God. With these symbols of the cross—not our churches, not our prayer-books, not worn as ornaments on the brow of beauty, but on the heart—we may await the coming doom of the world, as Rahab waited the hour of destruction to Jericho; while the scarlet line was in the window she was safe; and with the atoning blood of Christ on our souls, as the blood of the Paschal Lamb was on the Hebrew door-posts in Egypt, we may welcome the angel of destruction as our deliverer.

Blessed confidence of faith! Not stoicism, not indifference, but confidence in Jesus. "I know in whom I believe." And when we die, a seraph's song will be heard above the roar of the river of death. And as the scarlet line of Rahab, so shall the crimson blood of the Lamb be to thee when God shall take away the soul.

XIV.—VALE OF SODOM, AND ITS LESSONS.

> "Beneath whose sullen lake
> Sleep the guilty cities of the plain;
> Unlike other lakes,
> It sends no tribute to the ocean."

THE historic portions of the Old Testament, by quotation and approval, are made a part of the New. Both stand or fall together. Buried cities come forth to defend the histories of the Word of God. Nineveh and Babylon, Egypt and Shushan, verify the great events of sacred story. The Vale of Sodom is full of God. Once it was the hotbed of vegetation. It was watered by the Jordan, which then held its onward way to the Red Sea. It "was as the Garden of the Lord—like Egypt coming from Zoar."

Abraham and Lot came up from Egypt. Both were rich in cattle and flocks, and gold and silver. They encamped not far from that spot where, in after-times, God appeared to Jacob in the night-watches, and made the desert a house of God and the gate of heaven. Grass and water would fail in that dry and thirsty land. Contentions would arise between the herdsmen of Lot and the herdsmen of Abraham. The patriarch saw the end, and knew that himself and kinsman would soon be involved in perpetual quarrels with their servants. It was better to separate at once. The land was all their own. They could roam as they pleased. With the generosity of a noble mind, that was not afraid to make advances or concessions for the sake of peace, Abraham gave Lot his choice to "go to the right hand or the left." The Valley of the Jordan was a tempting spot for one to whom water and grass were the greatest boon, and whose wealth was mainly in the field and fold. The only drawback was the character of the people. Lot was a godly man, and the "men of Sodom were wicked and sinners before the Lord exceedingly." Lot did not like either their character or their company. But he went to Sodom from business considerations, "and he must take the world as he found it." Like many a one since, he thought personal preferences must give way to the great ogre, Success. A good place to increase his wealth was to him of more importance than a good place to bring up his family. Many so conducting have been compelled, as was Lot, to flee at the last, losing all the property for which they bartered the chief good of life, leaving in the ruin wife and children, often, for for whom the gain was intended. But the well-watered vale, "watered everywhere as the Garden of the Lord," was too attractive, and Lot became a resident of one of the great cities of the plain. Mamre's pleasant acres became the tent-home of Abraham, not far from the city of Hebron, where the tomb of the patriarch still is kept.

In the cool of the day, Abraham sat at the door of his tent. To three men passing on their way he extends the hospitalities of his board, and was rewarded by entertaining angels unawares. In return for the refreshment offered, and the bowl of water to lave their dusty feet, the visitants gave the host the great promise of a son, to be born of the incredulous Sarah. They dash the cup of joy with bitterness as they announced the doom of Sodom. Twenty miles from the spot, not far from the same hour, Lot entertained two men, whom he attempted to hide from the men of Sodom, who sought to destroy them. They came not only to warn him of coming danger, but to deliver. The time was short: "Up and away!" was the imperious order. "Escape for your life. Look not behind. Stay not in all the plains. Flee to the mountains." Affection and trade are the two great hinderances to personal salvation, as set forth by the Redeemer in the parable of the supper: "I have married a wife. I have bought a yoke of oxen." So Lot found in his family. His daughters were allied to the men of Sodom, and were unwilling to flee. His wife had her heart in the city and in the homes of her children. The warning and entreaties were to the "sons-in-law as one that mocked." Even Lot lingered in the city till the angel laid hands on him and his and drew them away from the doomed place.

On the same day that Lot went out, Sodom was destroyed. "God rained on all the cities fire and brimstone from the Lord out of heaven." "He overthrew those cities, and all the inhabitants of those cities, and all that grew upon the ground." The smoke of the country went up as the smoke of a furnace. Abraham stood at the door of his tent, twenty miles away, and saw the destruction, as those accursed towns sank beneath the hot, surging tide.

For five thousand years the lake and the surroundings have been an "admonition and a beacon to all who should hereafter live ungodly."

The Dead Sea, which covers the site occupied by the cities of the plain, is one of the most remarkable things in the Holy Land. To all who look upon it, it tells its own fearful story. The sluggish waters lie in a deep caldron about ten miles southeast of Jerusalem, and are plainly seen from the summit of Olivet, near the Mount of Ascension. The Sea lies fifteen hundred feet below the level of the Great Sea. On all sides it is surrounded with naked hills. No green things grow on its banks; all is desolation for miles around. The trees seem petrified. No living thing swims on its bosom. A high embankment, thrown up when God overthrew the guilty cities, holds the lake in its bed. It has no outlet. It receives from the Jordan six million tons of water daily. It sends no tribute to the ocean, as if its own sullen bed were the only fit receptacle for its own accursed waters. In color, taste, and character, the waters of the Sea are unlike any other. They are bitter, and "as brimstone to the taste." They buoy up the swimmer with great power.

The Dead Sea, and its surroundings, tell to all beholders the story of Sodom's guilt and Sodom's doom. The wild Arab looks with awe on the mysterious water, hears the strange sounds that still come forth from its bosom of sterility and death, and flees from its presence. The pious are awe-struck as they tread, after a lapse of centuries, the soil so evidently accursed of God, and which to-day tells the story of

Admah, Zeboam, and their sisters in guilt, quite as graphically as it is told in the Word of God.

It was a common tradition among the Jews, that the "pillar of salt" was still standing, and to that common faith our Lord referred when he said, "Remember Lot's wife." Josephus alluded to it, Clement of Rome, Irenæus, and others of the fathers. But all investigations were dangerous. The Turk could not or would not afford protection, and the wild man of the desert was, to all explorers, like a "bear robbed of her whelps." But years have wrought great changes, and it remained for the Government of the United States to vindicate the sacred history about the pillar of salt, and confirm the opinion of eminent Jewish Rabbis, that it stood to this day.

In 1847, under the authority of the United States Government, an officer fitted out an expedition, with boats, tools, and all needed authority. Amid universal solitude—amid withered boughs, without birds, flowers, or grass—where no boat had fretted the waters since the day God destroyed Sodom, the little craft was launched. Tradition pointed to one spot, on which the foot of man for centuries had not pressed. Here hidden things were brought to light, and the Word of God found a marvelous corroboration. A marvelous mission! Our national banner was the first to be wet with the spray of the Dead Sea; the first to float over Sodom; the first to salute Lot's wife, and hang over the pillar of salt; to drag out from their mysterious retreat the hidden evidences of four thousand years to the truth of God's

Word. The search and the pillar are thus described in the official report made to Government:—

"Soon after, to our astonishment, we saw, on the eastern side of Usdum, one-third the distance from its northern extreme, a lofty round pillar, standing apparently detached from the general mass, at the head of a deep, narrow, and abrupt chasm. We immediately pulled in for the shore, and Dr. Anderson and I went up and examined it. The beach was a soft, shiny mud, incrusted with salt, and a short distance from the water, covered with saline fragments and flakes of bitumen. We found the pillar to be of solid salt, capped with carbonate of lime, cylindrical in front and pyramidal behind. The upper, or rounded part, is about forty feet high, resting on a kind of oval pedestal from forty to sixty feet above the level of the Sea. It slightly decreases in size upward, crumbles at the top, and is one entire mass of crystallization. A prop or buttress connects it with the mountain behind, and the whole is covered with debris of a light stone-color. Its peculiar shape is, doubtless, attributable to the action of winter rains. The Arabs had told us, in vague terms, that there was to be found a pillar somewhere upon the shores of the Sea; but their statements, in all other respects, proved so unsatisfactory, that we could place no reliance upon them."

The lessons this history teaches us lie on the surface. The admonition runs through the Bible. We live in a world doomed to destruction. Plain and timely warnings are given. Messengers who have sounded the cry, "Up and out of this place," have laid their hands on us, as the angels did on Lot, to urge our escape. We have the conditions of deliverance, and may, if we will, escape the coming doom. We must be more than awakened. Lot's wife had this. We must do more than start on the way of salvation. We must run on, and keep the conditions to the end. Worldly ties are powerful. Human affections are strong. The unbelief and jeers of the ungodly are mighty. By them many a strong runner has halted in the race, and been overtaken and slain. With an eye on the point of safety—deaf to all cries that can impede, retard, or turn his step—the panting fugitive can not rest till he reaches Calvary, and lies down at the foot of the cross.

XV.—TOMB OF RACHEL; OR, THE DEATH OF CHILDREN.

> "There is no flock, however watched and tended,
>   But one dead lamb is there;
> There is no fireside, howsoe'er defended,
>   But has one vacant chair.
>
> "The air is full of farewells to the dying,
>   And mournings for the dead;
> The heart of Rachel, for her children crying,
>   Will not be comforted."

In the sweet vale of Ephratah, near the cradle of our divine Lord, Rachel, the beloved wife of Jacob, was laid in the tomb. As he journeyed with his family from Bethel to Bethlehem, sudden labor came upon Rachel. She gave birth to Benjamin, and died in agony and sorrow. Jacob loved her with a deep and tender love, that twenty-one years of wedded life had not cooled. To all her descendants her sepulcher has been sacred. Over her rural tomb the munificence of strangers has placed a noble mausoleum, which to this hour is held in reverence by all her descendants.

Faith and affection have clustered much poetic beauty around this tomb. Rachel is regarded as the matron of Jewish maids and mothers. Hebrew poets represent her as holding a living and intimate oversight of all that concerned the happiness of children. When the King of Babylon conquered Jerusalem, the sons and daughters of Judea were gathered near her sepulcher, and, as long lines of captives assigned to bondage and the sword passed by her tomb, filling the air with loud cries and wailings, the faithful mother of Israel is represented as rising from her grave. A loud lamentation, weeping, and much mourning were heard in the field of Ephratah. Rachel refused to be comforted amid the sorrow and exile of her children.

The Babe of Bethlehem invests the tomb of Rachel with new beauty. He was born not far from the grave of the mother of Benjamin. His birth created general alarm among the rulers who dwelt in Jerusalem. The attendance of angels at his manger cradle, the worship of wise men, the star in the east, proclaimed the advent of some mighty personage. The chief priests added to the consternation by declaring that God, by his prophets, had said that the King of the Jews should be born in Bethlehem of Judea. It was resolved to end the reign of the young monarch by taking his life, and Herod sent out the bloody decree that "all the children that were in Bethlehem and the coasts thereof, from two years old and under, should be put to death." The execution of this bloody law followed the command. The infant children of Bethlehem were the first martyrs for Jesus's sake. The wail of the mother and the shriek of the child rent the air of Ephratah; they disturbed the repose of the dead. The memory of Rachel was sweet to the daughters of Zion. In the hour of their great calamity they looked on her tomb, and invoked her aid. Wailing and loud lamentation went out among the hills and plains of the City of David. Rachel could not rest in her grave. Again she came forth, as of old, from her tomb at her children's cry for help. She joined in the general lamentation. She again seemed to hear the cry of Benjamin, for whom she gave up her life in anguish. Her race was to be cut off by the cruel decree of Herod, and she would not be comforted. Eastern mourners bewail their dead at the door of the sepulcher; and Rachel is represented as weeping and lamenting her dead at the entrance of her own tomb.

A few strokes from the celestial pencil throw light on one of the darkest events of life—the death of children. Why live at all, if to die so soon? Why the peril and woe of birth, the brief gladness, the fleeting sunshine of a moment? To what purpose has it lived? Apart from the sad experiences of life, no one could believe that infancy was a time to die. The death of a child is one of the great mysteries of God. The great congregation of the dead is composed of the young. But such have not lived in vain. That child, that reposed a moment on your bosom, whose smile, like the rod of Moses, smote the rock of your soul, and bid new waters gush forth, whose feeble wail thrilled your life-blood, that child has fulfilled its mission. It has touched and tinged all your life. Its voice sings through all your chambers. Its tiny step is heard in all places. Its smile lingers in house and home; and, when you look in the vacant cradle, or awake suddenly at night and miss the babe from your arm, and cry out: "Why this waste, this brief gladness, to end in gloom and sorrow," the Gospel answers: "The Lord hath need of him." "She has gone up to the throne of love." "Its angel doth always behold the face of my Father in heaven;" and with the Saviour, redeemed by his blood, its infant voice shall join the elder spirits in praising redeeming love.

Childhood is a blessed time to die. The memories that attend its life are sweet, fragrant, and enduring. Its existence has been an abiding beauty. Many may come, many children be added to the household. But the absent child is a reality. With Jacob, we say still: "One is not." Its death will aid us in our preparation for a better world. "It is well with the child. It is well with thee." "Can I bring the child back again?" said the stricken monarch. The death of a child makes heaven more real and more dear to us. Many stricken parents have turned away from the death-bed of a dear one to feel how real heaven was, when the heart's utterance came forth with the words: "We will meet again, my child." We want to know more of that world to which our loved ones have gone. We want to walk with them those golden streets trodden by the celestial feet of dear children who on earth were bone of our bone and flesh of our flesh. We want to see them in that world "where the wicked cease from troubling, and where there is no more death." A sweet little boy, who had learned much of Jesus, lay on his death-bed. Two little brothers had been taken away, and he had often talked of them in the home of their Heavenly Father, and seemed to feel that he should not be long away from that bright, blue world. Just as his spirit took its flight, he stretched out his little hands, bade good-bye to his mother, and added: "I'll give father's love and mother's to Charlie and Willie." To those bereaved hearts heaven had a real existence, and seemed the more so with three happy children around the throne. What though the brightest seem to die, and the most endeared and lovely fade soonest? They shall be gems in the Saviour's crown.

> "That sun went down in beauty,
>   Yet it shineth sweetly now
> In the bright and dazzling coronet
>   That decks the Saviour's brow.
> But oh! that cup of bitterness!
>   Let not my heart rebel!
> He gave—he took—and he'll restore,
>   He doeth all things well."

One of the sweetest instances of resignation in the Bible is found in connection with a case of peculiar bereavement. A humble but pious woman dwelt in Israel. She was poor, but the wayfaring man was ever welcome to what her poor board afforded. The prophet of God often was refreshed beneath her roof, and a plain chamber was fitted up for his reception. The man of God had influence with the king, and offered her promotion. "I dwell among my own people," was the modest but decided reply. Long and ardently had she prayed for a son, and this coveted boon was sent to her from God. The son grew to become a rugged lad. He had mastered the diseases of childhood. He was full of promise, that child of many prayers. One day he went out into the field unto his father. He left home with the glow of health, with a mother's permission and a mother's kiss. Such a child wins the deepest love. There was no thought of harm in that good-bye. Suddenly he was stricken down. He cried only: "My head! my head!" He was carried to his mother. "On her knees he sat till noon, when he died." To the prophet on Carmel, to whom she looked for consolation, she said, in answer to his query: "It is well with the child." An heroic answer, given by a bereaved mother on the death of an only son, long wished for, coming as the gift of the Lord, suddenly removed, his sun going down while it was yet day, accepted as the gift of God, and given back too soon. "It is well with the child."

> "She is not dead—the child of our affection—
> But gone unto that school
> Where she no longer needs our poor protection,
> And Christ himself doth rule."

A mother's love is the highest form of love. To it God likens his own, which differs from human love in this, that while the mother may forget her child, and cease to have compassion on the son she has borne, God's love is an everlasting love. A mother's love for a first-born and only son is regarded as the most sacred of all human things. An affection such as this avails with God. And what is a mother's affection? Go to the bedside of a sick child. What form, uncomplaining, wears away the dreary hours and refuses to be relieved? What eyes refuse to sleep? What hand mixes the healing cup? What heart feels all the agony, and would bear all the pain? "It is well with the child." Refuse not to be comforted.

A voice comes from the tomb of Rachel to the cradle in Bethlehem and the tomb of Calvary. Thank God for the great boon sent to create such change in you. Bless God for all the pleasant memories, fragrant and eternal, about that little one gone up to the house on high. Repine not that the brightest die first, and that God calls the loveliest. For, remember,

> "In that great cloister's stillness and seclusion,
>   By guardian angels led,
> Safe from temptation, safe from sin's pollution,
>   She lives whom we call dead.
>
> "Day after day we think what she is doing
>   In those bright realms of air;
> Year after year, her tender steps pursuing,
>   Behold her grown more fair.
>
> "Thus do we walk with her, and keep unbroken
>   The bond which nature gives;
> Thinking that our remembrance, though unspoken,
>   May reach her where she lives."

Burdened and strickened one, cast all your care on him who asks, in tender tones, "Woman, why weepest thou?" Think of your babe among the angels, radiant and lovely. Gather up the broken whip, the mutilated doll, and the worn shoe; roam through the vacant chambers; but remember, amid all your sorrows, "It is well with the child." Take words of infinite consolation, and say:

> "Thou art gone to the grave! but we will not deplore thee,
>   Though sorrows and darkness encompass the tomb;
> The Saviour hath passed through its portals before thee,
>   And the lamp of his love is thy guide through the gloom.

"Thou art gone to the grave! we no longer behold thee,
   Nor tread the rough paths of the world by thy side;
But the wide arms of mercy are spread to enfold thee,
   And sinners may hope, for the Sinless hath died.

"Thou art gone to the grave! and, its mansion forsaking,
   What though thy weak spirit in fear lingered long;
The sunshine of Paradise beamed on thy waking,
   And the sound which thou heardst was the seraphim's song.

"Thou art gone to the grave! but we will not deplore thee,
   For God was thy ransom, thy guardian, and guide;
He gave thee, he took thee, and he will restore thee,
   And death has no sting, for the Saviour hath died."

XVI.—THE FIELD OF BOAZ; OR, CONSECRATED AFFECTION.

> "People of the living God,
>   I have sought the world around,
> Paths of sin and sorrow trod,
>   Peace and comfort nowhere found.
>
> "Now to you my spirit turns—
>   Turns, a fugitive unblessed;
> Brethren, where your altar burns,
>   Oh! receive me into rest."

NEAR Bethlehem is the field of Boaz. He was a mighty man of wealth, and was held in great honor among his people. In the time of harvest he came from his home in Bethlehem to look on his reapers in the field. He met them with the ancient salutation, "The Lord be with you." To which the men replied, "The Lord bless you." Gleaning among the reapers was a maiden of foreign manners and foreign birth, unknown to Boaz. "Whose damsel is this?" he said. And the servant that was set over the reapers answered and said, "It is the Moabitish damsel that came back with Naomi out of the country of Moab: and she said, I pray you, let me glean and gather after the reapers among the sheaves: so she came, and hath continued even from the morning until now that she tarried a little in the house." This damsel was Ruth, a daughter of Moab. Her life had been an eventful one. Its fragrance preceded her on her way to Bethlehem, the new home she had chosen among a strange people.

Into the land of Moab came a family from Bethlehem for bread. Famine, that scourge of the land, drove them from the fields they loved. Two daughters of Moab, Ruth and Orpah, formed the tenderest of ties with the Hebrew children, and one of them married Mahlon, and the other Chilion, the sons of Naomi. These formed her family, in which the true God was worshiped. Affliction came on that house. The father and two sons died. Rich in the love of her husband and in the affection of her sons, with a weary step Naomi came back to her people. "All the city was moved at her approach, and came out to meet her" on that bitter day. Touched by the great public sympathy, and stricken to earth by her great woe, she cried out, "Call me not Naomi, call me Mara; for the Almighty hath dealt very bitterly with me."

On the burial of her husband and sons, Naomi's heart yearned for her home and kindred in Bethlehem. The three stricken widows met under one tent. Moab had now no charms for Naomi. She had not heart to take from kindred and altar the young women that loved her for the sake of the dead. Ever dear, and now doubly dear in their mutual bereavement, Naomi told Ruth and Orpah her resolution to seek her own people, and urged them to return to their homes. "Go, return each to her mother's house; the Lord deal kindly with you, as ye have dealt with the dead, and with me. The Lord grant you that ye may find rest, each of you in the house of her husband. Then she kissed them; and they lifted up their voices and wept." Orpah went back with reluctance, and in tears. But Ruth refused all entreaty. Her resolution was firm. Her position taken. With unalterable affection and impassioned eloquence, she cried out: " Entreat me not to leave thee, or to return from following after thee. For whither thou goest, I will go; and where thou lodgest, I will lodge; thy people shall be my people, and thy God my God; where thou diest will I die, and there will I be buried." Beautiful exhibition of affection and unblenching faith, sanctioned by religious trial! A young girl leaves house and kindred, the religion of her youth, and the sepulchers of her people, going out on a long journey to a strange land and a new religion. It was not simply love for the dead. Orpah had this, and went back. It was not simply a love for the living. The humble piety of Naomi won on Ruth. It had won her to the altar of the Hebrews. "Thy God shall be my God." In her heart the true faith was ardent, constant, and a living principle. By it all sacrifice was easy. Cheerfully she could tread the rugged path, hold up the weary step of Naomi, and glean and toil for her on the way. Along the trodden way matron and maiden trod, footsore and weary, amid many a tender glance from the passer-by, through many a hospitable town, with many a "God bless you" from hearts touched by sympathy. At length the gates of Bethlehem were seen. Their coming and their story ran on before them. The great men of the city bid them welcome. As Ruth went out for food on their arrival, for they were poor as well as hungry, "her hap was to light on part of the field belonging to Boaz." A right royal welcome the maiden received from the lord of the land. "Hearest thou not, my daughter? Go not to glean in another field, neither go from hence, but abide here fast by my maidens; let thine eyes be on the field that they do reap, and go thou after them. Have I not charged the young men that they shall not touch thee? And when thou art athirst, go unto the vessels, and drink of that which the young men have drawn." Well might Ruth fall on "her face, and bow herself to the ground," and say: "Why have I found grace in thine eyes, that thou shouldst take knowledge of me, seeing I am a stranger." Well did Boaz answer her: "It hath fully been showed me all that thou hast done unto thy mother-in-law since the death of thy husband; and how thou hast left thy father and thy mother, and the land of thy nativity, and art come unto a people which thou knewest not heretofore. The Lord recompense thy work, and a full reward be given thee of the Lord God of Israel, under whose wings thou art come to trust."

In the humble walks of life, in the quiet home in Moab, trusting, true, confiding, sustaining, comforting, and guiding the weak and afflicted, gleaning in the hot sun for food for her mother-in-law, and doing all in the fear of God, asking no reward, save that found in love of the mother of her husband, whose memory cheered her on—how wide her fame, how fragrant! In that weary journey, she was doing work that should tell till time shall be no longer. Deeply she laid the corner-stone of her grandson's fame, when, as king and priest, in Jerusalem, he should reign on that throne on which her greater Son should sit forever. Orpah's affection was human. It clustered around the dead; it held fast to the living. It could be loosened, but with sorrow, with tears; it could leave Naomi alone to her hard journey, and go back to seek new, or revive old affections. Not so the love of Ruth. She had been won to the better faith. She accepted the God and the people of Naomi. And that love that waters can not quench, that can cut off the right hand, and leave father and mother for God, was hers. Human affection is strong, but it is brittle. Many love you for your talents, your position, or your hold on popular favor. Take these away, and the fickle multitude seek others, or go back to their idols of old. But religious consecration come out in dark and tearful scenes, and is the tenderest and truest in the time of disaster.

Friendship, true as human friendship can be, is seen in tears and desertion. Friendship sanctified by grace shines in Ruth, lives and labors for loved ones, takes part in the peril and dust of long journeys, sheds tears with adieus, but puts its face as a flint toward the new destination, saying: "Whither thou goest, I will go; where thou diest, I will die, and there will I be buried. Naught but death shall part thee and me." What lessons come from that field of Boaz! How rich the reward for filial affection! How humble piety blends with the daily duties and adorns the homely virtues of domestic life! How firm a stay, and how divine the refuge of that humble piety that guarded the maiden of Moab, and made her friends and patrons on all her lonely way, and, while shielding the head of the mother of her husband, was rearing a home for herself, and sending down to all time, her name with Mary, Elisabeth, and other holy women who are immortalized in sacred history in connection with the humanity of the blessed Son of God!

XVII.—JOSEPH, A TYPE OF CHRIST.

> "But who shall see the glorious day
> When, throned on Zion's brow,
> The Lord shall rend that veil away
> Which binds the nations now?
> The fount of life shall then be quaffed
> In peace by all who come,
> And every wind that blows shall waft
> Some long-lost exile home."

The old patriarch was about to die. He had attained the full ripe age of "one hundred and forty-seven years." When he stood before Pharaoh, he said: "The days of the years of my pilgrimage are a hundred and thirty years; few and evil have the days of the years of my life been, and I have not attained to the days of the years of the life of my fathers in the days of their pilgrimage." His life had been checkered, but his end was peace. He died in a royal abode. He loved the tent-home of his fathers more than the palace of kings. He wished his dust to repose in the sepulcher of Machpelah, where the bodies of Abraham and Isaac, Jacob and Rebecca were laid. He gave his dying blessing to all his sons. To Joseph he gave a double blessing, as a type of the coming Messiah, and elevated the lion-hearted Judah as the one from whom the Shiloh should come. As the type of Christ, Joseph stands out prominently:

I. IN THE NAME HE BORE IN EGYPT, which was

above every name. Besides Pharaoh, it was the greatest name in all the land. It was omnipotent to open and close prisons. At it all Egypt was to bow. It was supreme. Men were to honor it as they honored Pharaoh. All dishonor to Joseph was dishonor to Pharaoh. So ran the royal command. So all Egypt knew and obeyed. It is thus with God's highly exalted Son. To him a name has been given that is above every name. At it men and angels are to bow, and all who insult it, insult God, who gave him that name. "Wonderful," "Councillor," "the Mighty God," "King of kings," "Creator," "Redeemer," "Judge," the "Prince of Peace," are among the names by which the Lord of life and glory is named among men.

II. BREAD COULD BE HAD ONLY IN THE NAME OF JOSEPH. By it the granaries in Egypt were full. Bread, and to spare, in that land was garnered. But it could not be sold nor distributed unless the name of Joseph was invoked. No appeals to Pharaoh could avail, for it had pleased him to commit the distribution of the precious food in the time of famine to Joseph. Men who would appeal to Pharaoh, could only approach him in the name of the great ruler and savior of the land, to whom all rule had been committed. Hungry, suffering, starving men, who came from the surrounding country to get bread, lest their wives and little ones should die, found the doors barred, and all appeals in vain, till they sought relief in the name of Joseph. "There is none other name under heaven given among men, whereby we must be saved, but the name of Jesus Christ of Nazareth."

Jesus presides over the treasury of grace. He garnered up those stores of mercy, that in the house of his Father "there should be bread enough, and to spare." For this purpose he was bruised and put to shame, and his soul made an offering for sin, that he might "give repentance unto men and remission of sin." "No man can come unto the Father but by the Son." "All who come unto God through him" will be accepted. All who reject the Son must die in their sins.

III. He blessed those who did him the greatest wrong. Joseph was the most affectionate of the sons of Jacob. He neither did nor thought his brethren wrong. It was not his fault that his father loved him too well. It was not his fault that there was given to him the coat of many colors, a badge of his sire's partiality. He was not responsible for the interpretation his brethren put on his dreams of the sheaves in the field, or the obedience of the sun, moon, and stars to the single star that shone in its magnitude. Yet envy and hate, without cause, fired their bosoms, and they resolved to kill him. When the opportunity came for the maddened brothers to put their bloody resolves into execution, Joseph was on a visit of kindness to them. He sought them, laden with tokens of a father's affection. He roamed from field to field to find them. "Behold! the dreamer cometh," they cry; "let us kill him, and we shall see what will become of his dreams." On an errand of mercy Jesus came from heaven, when he was seized by wicked hands, crucified, and slain. His mission was full of peace and good-will to men. "He came to his own, and his own received him not." He went from place to place, filling the cities and homes with blessings. He was holy, harmless, and undefiled. "He did not cry, nor strive, nor lift up nor cause his voice to be heard in the streets." Yet men cried: "Away with him! It is not fit that such a fellow should live." No man can read the trial of the Son of God, see the rabble in Pilate's hall, look on the insults to the person of the Saviour, the mock array, the scourge, the dreadful march through the narrow street of Jerusalem, while he was crushed to the earth by the heavy cross laid on him, amid the jeers, insults, and blasphemies of priests and people, and not cry out: "Is there a God in heaven? Why don't he open the earth, as he did when, for a less aggravated sin, he sank Korah and Dathan down to hell?" Not so felt the merciful High-Priest of our profession. "Father! forgive them," he cried, as he gave up the ghost. Men had no cause to hate the Lamb of God. He was not their enemy. He was not in rebellion. His miracles, and they were many, were wrought for others' good, and not his own. Yet not one of those cruel men were excluded from the august benefits of his death. "Begin at Jerusalem," was his omnipotent command, when he sent men out to preach the salvation of God.

IV. Joseph's path to the throne was one of the deepest ignominy. To his brethren he said, when he revealed himself to them as "Joseph," "God sent me before you to preserve you a posterity in the earth, and save your lives by a great deliverance." A dark pathway God called him to tread. Few could suppose that it would lead to a throne. Envy, hate, a jail, a prison, temptation, opportunity, importunity, disgrace, and a dungeon were all paths of the great programme that led to the steps of a throne and to unlimited power. Ages before Jesus came, his royal position was proclaimed, and he was crowned King of Zion. Before he could take the scepter, he must weep tears of infancy in the manger, toil beneath the hot sun of Palestine, be homeless and without a refuge for his head, endure the insult and ignominy of men, be accursed, and be adjudged guilty of the highest crime known to the laws of his land, be sold as a slave for thirty pieces of silver, be buffeted by Satan, abandoned, betrayed by his own brethren, and suffer at last the most ignominious of deaths. But that infamous pathway led him to the throne on which he is to ever reign King of kings and Lord of lords.

V. JOSEPH'S GLORIOUS REVELATIONS. Joseph's brethren saw him often, and knew him not. He was in no haste to reveal himself. He waited till the fullness of time had come. He seemed harsh and unfeeling, when his soul melted with tenderness, and he had to withdraw himself and weep. He treated them at times as a band of spies. He harshly bade them bring Benjamin, as if he would rob the old man at home of his last tie, and leave him childless in those he loved. He did not hesitate to plunge Jacob into the profoundest grief by what seemed a cruel demand. He put on Benjamin, the loved of his father, the semblance of a thief, and brought back the family in terror at the charge that the governor's cup had been stolen, and that Benjamin the beloved had committed the foul wrong, for in his sack the cup was found. All this was done to answer a great end in Joseph's heart—that the revelation of himself should be complete and glorious.

Before the full revelation could be made, or the curtain lifted on the glorious scene beyond, Simeon must come out of prison, Benjamin be brought into Egypt, and then Joseph, throwing off all disguise, could cry out, amid tears and sobs: "I am Joseph. Does my father still live?" "Now, therefore, be not grieved nor angry with yourselves that ye sold me hither, for God did send me before you to preserve life, and he hath made me a father unto Pharaoh, and Lord of all his house, and I am ruler throughout all Egypt."

So our blessed Joseph disciplines his Church. He leads them along dark and strange paths. To them often he seems a hard and stern ruler. He indeed is called "an austere man, reaping where he does not sow, and gathering where he hath not strewed." But he is his "own interpreter, and he will make it plain" in due time.

> "In the furnace God may prove thee,
>   Thence to bring thee forth more bright,
> But can never cease to love thee,
>   Thou art precious in his sight.
> God is with thee.
>   God thine everlasting light."

All the ends of the world shall remember and turn unto the Son, all kings shall serve him, all nations call him blessed. From sea to sea and from the rivers unto the ends of the earth shall his kingdom extend. And when the set time shall come, all flesh shall see the salvation of God, and one song shall employ all nations, and all cry: "Worthy is the Lamb, for he was slain for us." "A fruitful bough by a well" shall our Joseph be. Not simply beautiful for its verdure and grateful for its shade in a hot and sultry clime, but bearing fruit that is sweet to the taste. Not dependent for its green leaf and luscious fruit on the rain and dew of heaven, but a bough whose root strikes deep into an unfailing fountain, which drought can not consume, nor the withholding of the early or latter rain exhaust. "A fruitful bough by a well, whose leaf shall not wither."

VI. The archers shot at him—mean, treacherous, stealthy foes, where least expected, whose poisoned arrows of envy and calumny sped noiselessly through the air, and, while the hand that drew the bow was hid, the winged missile hit its mark, and did its deadly work. Archers who were both sly and cruel aimed at a noble mark. But God made his hands strong. Not the malice and envy of his brothers, not the casting into the pit, nor the sale into Egypt, not the rage and falsehood of Potiphar's wife, nor all combined, could keep Joseph from his destined throne. All opposition and attempts to work his ruin aided Joseph, and hastened him along the pathway that led to exaltation.

So "Herod, Pontius Pilate, the Jews, and the Gentiles" conspired against the Holy Child Jesus, against the Man of Nazareth, against the incarnate Son of God—conspired to do the exact thing that the hand of God and his "counsel determined before to be done." Man can fulfill, but can not destroy. He can hasten, but he can not retard the chariot of salvation.

VII. His branches run over a wall. As a fruit-bearing bough he was to shelter and feed the royal family and the people of Egypt. But to Egypt the blessing was not to be confined. Like a luxurious vine, whose wide-spread branches broke the inclosure, and ran over the walls, so that the poor, the stranger, and the needy could sit under the shade and eat from the hanging limbs, Joseph was to be a blessing to other lands. The good news of plenty in Egypt, in the time of general famine, spread far and wide. Men flocked to the garden of Nile from all lands to purchase bread, and every nation which sought food was fed by the bounty of Joseph.

So Jesus is a fruitful bough with branches running over the wall. His Gospel belongs to all the world. Men can not confine it. Men can not bind it. No walls of party construction or sectarian jealousy can be run up so high as to confine this blessed vine. There is nothing national about it, nothing sectarian.

> "While grace is offered to the prince,
> The poor may take their share;
> No mortal has a just pretence
> To perish in despair."

It is free to the Jew and the Greek, to the bond and the free. Its call is to the world, to the weary and the lost. Planted in Bethlehem, it has run over all the seas and rivers of the earth. It has spanned the oceans, and broke over the barriers made by kingdoms and hierarchies to confine it. It will grow and spread till all nations shall enjoy its shade, shall eat, and live. It comes to all the folds where the sheep of the Good Shepherd dwell, like the sunlight of heaven, which no man can confine to his own little plot of ground. It comes, like the rain and dew, to all nations. It climbs over the wall, up the gnarled tree, gracing the knotty oak, along the watercourses, over brooks and streams, ever green, ever peaceful, on whose branches no hungry soul ever looked to find " nothing but leaves."

XVIII.—A FESTIVAL FOR ALL THE FAMILY; OR, THE HOME OF JESSE.

> "Oh! why should tears bedim the eye,
>   Or doubts obscure the mind?
> Away let grief and trouble fly,
>   As clouds before the wind.
> The fiercest tempests die away,
>   The roughest storms subside;
> So be our hearts serenely gay,
>   Whatever ills betide."

NEVER large, but honored above all the cities of Judea, a jewel on the crown of a lofty hill, sits the fragrant city of Bethlehem. It has been the home of the noblest of men. It will be held in all reverence, in all ages, as the spot where he was born among the straw who to-day, as Napoleon said on St. Helena, " has millions that would die for him." When princes are born, all that wealth and authority can do are put in requisition, with care and skill, to relieve the anguish of the mother, and give her comfort in the hour of her great trial. But when the Son of the King of kings came into the world, the royal peasant maiden came the long distance from Nazareth on foot, unattended save by Joseph. No mother's couch or mother's care awaited her in that dark hour. No bed made ready for the royal child. The inn was full, and Mary took her weary way to the stable, and, with the stalled oxen, laid down to become the mother of the Prince of Peace.

Bethlehem is about six miles south of Jerusalem. It stands on the sharp brow of a hill. Its main features are the same as when Jacob set up the pillar over Rachel's grave, and David came in from the sheepfold to carry the loaves to his brethren in the army. Its fertile fields still invite the flock to green pastures. Its valleys are filled with grain as in the day when the maiden of Moab gleaned beside the reapers.

Jesse dwelt in Bethlehem, and he was called "Jesse the Bethlehemite." The women of Bethlehem said to Naomi: "His name shall be famous in Israel." He was a noble old man, and trained his children in the fear of God. In dark and troublous times, when few were faithful, the rural home of Jesse stood fast in the faith. Within its bosom was found one worthy to take the mantle that was torn from the shoulders of the apostate Saul. When Samuel mourned for Saul, because God had rejected him, God said to the weeping prophet: "How long wilt thou mourn for Saul, seeing I have rejected him. Fill thy horn with oil, and I will send thee to Jesse the Bethlehemite, for I have provided me a king among his sons."

To the humble home of Jesse, in Bethlehem, the prophet Samuel came by the command of God. The Elders of the town trembled at his approach, and demanded of him: "Comest thou peaceably?" He replied: "Peaceably. I am come to sacrifice unto the Lord." Jesse and his elder sons were called to the sacrifice. One of these Samuel supposed was to be the Lord's anointed. A lad, the eighth son, too small and too inconsiderable to be a witness of the visit and partake of the religious service, was in the field. Of all the sons presented, the Lord had chosen none of them. "And Samuel said unto Jesse, Are here all thy children? And he said, There remaineth yet the youngest one; behold he keepeth the sheep. And Samuel said unto Jesse, Send and fetch him, for we will not sit down till he come hither. And he sent and brought him." "He was ruddy, and withal of a beautiful countenance, and goodly to look to. And Samuel took the horn of oil, and anointed him in the midst of his brethren."

Man in his home, with its relations and duties, fill up the Bible. It creates home, regulates it, binds men up with it. Send the Gospel anywhere, and it gathers the solitary into families. Send it among savage cannibals, or among the pirates in the islands of the Pacific, and homes will rise and social life will be created. Men who assail the Bible, in any land or age, strike at its domestic power, and hurl their masses against its social life. Till this is broken, nothing is done. The domestic power of the Gospel stands as an immense rock in the center of a railway. The incoming train must hold up, or be dashed to pieces. Polygamy and caste, in heathen lands, fall before the cross, and attest its onward march.

The Bible is full of allusions to home. The most vivid metaphors are taken from domestic customs. The holy men of God, by whom the Word of the Lord came, and to whom were committed the oracles of God, were men found in their homes, in the center of domestic affections and duties. "Noah, Job, and

Daniel," Abraham, Zacharias, and Joseph, are specimens. Women, to be holy and please God, were not shut up from the joys and sympathies of life, and were not gathered in houses filled with foolish virgins. Amid domestic associations, they reared their households in the love of God. Sarah, Rebecca, Rachel, Elisabeth, Mary, all so teach us.

Our Lord came not from a race of Bedouins, with no home or family ties. He came from the only nation of families—and that created by the Bible—that then existed on the earth. Amid a refined and civilized people, with whom art and industry flourished, who had schools and altars, social life and general public worship, his childhood was passed. His people had work and pastimes, festivals and amusements, all under the approval and guardianship of home. Our Lord gleaned his choicest and oft-repeated emblems from the sacred theater of home. He bound himself up with social life. He lived with men, ate, worked, and walked with them. When he left his home at Nazareth to go out on his great mission, he found a genial home in Bethany, which he kept till the night in which he was betrayed. To the common people he sent his Gospel, from them chose his Apostles, among them gained his first trophies. He spake to the people, in their own tongue, of the man who had two sons whom he sent to work in the vineyard, and of the marriage feast. He spake to men as he sat at meat. The merchant seeking pearls, the king making war, the merchant going into the city to get gain, the house on the sand, the woman and the leaven hid in the meal, had great power, because drawn from the daily customs of the homes of the people whom he addressed.

God made these homes cheerful by festivals and pastimes. They had their gala-days, in which age and youth, priest and congregation, king and subject joined. The merry-makings with the harp and pipe and cymbal bound the nation together. In the far-off land of captivity, by Babel's streams, these pleasant and fragrant memories came up, and the sacred song of home could not be sung in a strange land. Nations and families will and must have amusements. The social tie and social nature demand it. The only safe form is that which carries with it the sanction and the oversight of home. So amusement comes to us in the Word of God. Job was the holy man of the East—upright and perfect—so much so that the keen eye of Satan could find no flaw in him. His sons and daughters were many. He founded pastimes for them, to make them happy in their homes. Each day, after its duties were done, these eight children met at one of the houses agreed upon, and held a social festival, with eating, drinking, and music. And, lest they should at any time carry their pleasures too high, Job " made a sacrifice for them early the next morning." This home was made delightful, and religion hallowed and restrained the mirth.

Moses' home was dear to him. In his palace-chamber, the reputed son of Pharaoh's daughter, and heir to the realm, he loved the race of slaves from whom he came. He had power and learning. The throne of Egypt flashed before his eyes. But all paled before the joys of the home of poverty among his people, for whom he bartered all the good he had. He lifted up his hands to defend the oppressed, and fled into exile to await the call of God.

David had a happy home. He lived amid the glowing recollections of the past. On the hillside where he tended his sheep, the poetry and traditions of his fathers told him that Cain wandered in his wildness, and Abel kept his flocks. Abraham, the great father of his race, had pitched his tent not far from the home of Jesse, and from its door he could look on the spot where the mother of Israel died in agony. A great future was opened to him. Called when a lad, he was anointed as the future king of Israel. He could hardly miss success. He was bold, brave, courteous, and handsome. With the son of the king he was a favorite, and the king's daughter looked kindly on him. He was called into the royal family, and was among the honored of the land. But none of these could wipe out his love for the home at Bethlehem. And when the time drew near for the annual family gathering, he could not remain away from home. In the words of Holy Writ, "He earnestly asked leave to run to Bethlehem, for there was a yearly sacrifice, a feast there for all the family." In later times, amid the smoke, dust, and peril of battle, David yearned for the old well-curb, and cried out: "Oh! that one would give me to drink of the water of the well of Bethlehem, which is by the gate."

The welcome of the prodigal was a home welcome. The amusements that expressed the joy of that hour were common in the houses of pious Jews. It was a merry-making under the restraints of religion. It was such as all the neighbors and friends of that home could join. Impure pleasure is solitary, and hides itself from the public gaze. It revels in dark chambers, amid the long drapery of the tents of sin. It goes not in company—calls not parents and kindred to look on. But rational pastimes are demanded, and social kinsfolk and neighbors partake. If we would have the full blessing of domestic life, we must make it the center of recreation as well as of restraint.

The austerity of the Puritans abides with us still. We have not their excuse. In other things we have shaken off their yoke. The good of coming generations demands that we revise our amusements. In the time of our fathers, the recreations were earthly, sensual, and devilish. The light literature, the pastimes, and customs were bad. They came three thousand miles away to do as they pleased. So far away that those who did not like their customs need not follow them, and those who did not like their singing need not hear the tune. They intended to found a community of saints, without ungodly alloy. They put an end to all folly. In their domain there was to be no song, no dancing, no statuary, no paintings. Their churches were without ornament. Their sermons bare as iron pikes. Sunday was a sad day, in which it was almost a sin to smile. All was overdone; and men, like boys overstrained, swung to the opposite extreme. From the austerity of home, and the bald and hard training that had been called religion, their descendants made reprisal by abandoning the altars and faith of their fathers, and seeking in secret or abroad those pastimes denied them at home.

We have no national or domestic recreations that call priest and people together, and blend the national banner with social life. None that religion can sanctify or bless. In our homes and churches we have cut loose from the Puritan rule. We have brought back the unsightly Gothic, we recall the decorations, revise the paintings, and make some of our temples as gaudy as a circus, and as gay as a North River steamboat. But the iron rule holds in amusement. We need pastimes for our young and our homes. Superstition and business will clamor—but the want is felt. It will be met in the church or out of it, with its sanction and consent, or in defiance of both. We have the Fourth of July, we bow in the New Year, we welcome Christmas. Each are worth more than they cost. But we need more. Home has great power. Its influence should be wider. Many a wealthy man, living in pomp and style, sighs for the humble home of his youth, as David sighed for the waters of Bethlehem. The old well, the brooks, the school-house abide. He has made his mark, and reached the goal. He dwells in marble halls, sleeps under a crimson canopy that queens might envy, eats from gold and silver, and a coach comes at his call. His servants wear his livery. His wife and daughters revel in real sable and point lace. The wildest dreams of his youth are realized. Yet his happiest moments are when he dreams himself back to his boyhood home, and revels in the green fields of his early years. Then his comfort was flowing as the sea—he ate when he was hungry, drank when he was dry, went to bed when he was sleepy, dressed for his own comfort, lived to please himself, no slave to fashion—not led by a sordid set, not tyrannized over by fools who ate his dinners, drank his wines, and laughed at him when all was done—and when he had that "peace of mind dearer than all."

Nations are made strong and great by rational amusements. The pathway of the Jewish people from slavery to nationality was lined with festivals by the command of God. England owes much to her festivals. Her houses are the hidings of her power. To a Briton no clime is so fair, no grass so green, no throne so mild, no sovereign so loved. While the national pastimes hold, Britannia will need no bulwarks, no towers along the steep. No period is so hateful to an Englishman as the so-called Reign of the Saints. Under it no peasant could dance on the green, no child be crowned queen around the Maypole. Time-honored pastimes were voted a sin before God. The nation became sullen. Life was gloomy. Crimes swelled and raged as a flood. Had the Puritans let the pastimes alone, they could have reigned to this day, and the descendants of Oliver sat on the throne.

We want homes. Our men live in the marts of trade. Some hardly know their own children. Home, with its clinging affection, homes such as Joseph and David knew are rare among us. The demon of business possesses all bosoms. Farmers' sons look on life as an endless round of toil, and flee from the old homestead at an early day. Wife, child, home, religion, are all subordinate. The wife sits alone all the day, while the husband "seeks goodly pearls." Sons grow up without the eye of a father, and the daughter misses the firm, strong hand that should "be the guide of her youth." Buried beneath ledgers and piles of stocks, the husband and father allows to lie neglected and unheeded the noblest treasure mortals can receive—a woman's pure love: so strong that she would follow the man of her choice in poverty and disgrace to the ends of the earth. But, trampled down in the search for gold, jostled off the path in the chase for the phantom gain, clothed in purple and covered with diamonds, she would give them all for the early and quiet home, with the early and the true love. "This kind goeth out only by prayer."

XIX.—THE VALE OF ELAH; OR, HOME PREPARATION FOR LIFE'S DUTIES.

> "I would not have the restless will
>   That hurries to and fro,
> Seeking for some great thing to do,
>   Or secret thing to know;
> I would be dealt with as a child,
>   And guided where to go."

> "What shall I do to gain eternal life?
>   Discharge aright
> The simple dues with which each day is rife?
>   Yea, with thy might.
> Ere perfect scheme of action thou devise
>   Will life be shed;
> While he who ever acts as conscience cries
>   Shall live, though dead."

About three miles from Bethlehem lies the Vale of Elah, celebrated for the encounter between David and Goliath. It is on the Jaffa road, and will always be a point of great interest from the lessons that conflict teaches. The foes of Israel gave the people no peace. She had no standing army. To the patriotism of the tribes and families the government looked for aid to conquer the foe and expel the invader from the land. Jesse was an old man, but a true patriot. The real fire burned in his bosom, and he gave all he had to give to his country, three able-bodied sons, and kept at home only the lad David, who could, in the common estimation, be of no possible service to the army.

Jesse longed to know how the battle was going. He called David from the flocks, and sent him out to the Vale of Elah. Not empty-handed did he send him. Beside a present to his sons, he sent a gift to the commandant of the thousand among which were his own children. He was thus thoughtful, that the captain, remembered by the old man at home, might be careful of the lads under his care, and be kind to them. David came to the trench, and saw a sight that stirred his young blood. The host was going forth to fight, and shouted for the battle. Israel and the Philistines had put the battle in array, army against army. David left his carriage, ran into the camp, and saluted his brethren. As he talked with them, there came out a champion, the Philistine of Gath, Goliath by name, out of the army of the Philistines. He was a man of gigantic stature, being over nine feet high, and of great strength. His helmet of brass, his coat of mail, his greaves of brass, his target of brass, his staff, and his spear's head of iron would have crushed any other man to the earth. He stalked up and down before the people, in sight and hearing of all, as the champion of the Philistines. He dared any man, from Saul downward, to a personal combat with him, proposing to save the effusion of blood, and by the fighting of two men to decide the fortunes of the day. He stood and cried unto the armies of Israel: "Why are ye come out to set your battle in array? Am not I a Philistine, and ye servants to Saul? Choose you a man for you, and let him come down to me. If he be able to fight with me, and to kill me, then will we be your servants;

but if I prevail against him, and kill him, then shall ye be our servants, and serve us." This challenge he repeated, day by day, morning and evening, for forty days. Saul and all Israel heard these boasting words with dismay and fear. They withered beneath his taunting, and looked upward for help when Goliath defied the armies of Israel, and said: "Give me a man, that we may fight together." David, a ruddy lad, in the simple garb of a shepherd's boy, bareheaded and barefooted, heard the taunt of this champion, and his spirit was stirred within him. "Not a man in all Israel able to cope with this Philistine? Not one man able to take away the reproach from Judah? Not one to trust in God and kill this boaster, who defies God and his hosts?" While all the warriors, pale with fear, fled from Goliath, David stood his ground and offered himself to vanquish the boaster. The arrival in the camp of the young stripling spread through the ranks, and carried interest everywhere. The proposal of the heroic lad was made known to Saul. And to the monarch he said: "Thy servant will go and fight with this Philistine." "Thou art but a youth," said the king, "and he a man of war from his youth." Not in his own strength did David propose this combat. God, who had so signally and oft delivered his people, put the purpose into his heart, and to his name David ascribed all the glory. While keeping his father's sheep, he had delivered his flock out of the mouth of a lion and a bear. And said David: "The Lord that delivered me out of the paw of the lion, and out of the paw of the bear, will deliver me out of the hand of this uncircumcised Philistine. As the lion and the bear shall he be, seeing he hath defied the name of the living God."

Behold the champion of Israel! A lad fresh from the sheepfold, with no weapon but a sling, and a shepherd's bag containing a few stones—but bold, daring, athletic. His courage had been proved. The story of the lion and the bear was known in all Israel. He held the courage and faith of the olden times, when armies fled at the uplifted hands of a man of God. He went forward as if the pillar of cloud and fire guided him, and horsemen and chariots of fire filled the mountain. No wonder Goliath received him with derision. No wonder he disdained his youth, his ruddy and fair countenance. When he looked on his own array and weapons of war, his strength and his military power, he felt insulted at being confronted by a half-clad lad, green from the sheepfold, with no apparent weapon but a shepherd's crook. He cried out, in indignation: "Am I a dog, that you come to drive me away with staves?" And he cursed David by his gods, and boasted that the beasts of the field and the birds of the air should feast on his unprotected body. To all this bravado David returned a reply far beyond his years, and worthy of the ablest captains of the world. "I come to thee," he said, "in the name of the Lord of hosts, the God of the armies of Israel, whom thou hast defied. This day will the Lord deliver thee into mine hand. I will smite thee, and take thy head from thee. I will give the carcasses of the hosts of the Philistines this day unto the fowls of the air and unto the beasts of the earth, that all the earth may know that there is a God in Israel—that all this assembly may know that the Lord saveth not with sword and spear, for the battle is the Lord's, and he will give you into our hands."

David had great occasion thus to magnify God. In his home-training in Bethlehem, in the rugged necessities of his daily life, trained to toil amid danger, he had prepared himself on this broad theater to be the champion of Israel, and in after times its king. Courage, industry, the frost by night, and the smiting sun by day, had trained him. Beasts of prey, and men more savage, prowled around his flock. Bravery and a stout heart made him equal to any occasion. He needed weapons of defense. These were necessarily limited to the staff, the bow, and the sling. On the hillside, tending his flocks, his harp, which afterward made him an inmate of the royal palace, filled his leisure hours and guided his devotions. Leading his flock into green pastures, or in dark ravines, like the Valley and Shadow of Death, his sling became in his hands a mighty weapon. The Benjamites were left-handed men, and all famous with the sling. We read in one of the great battles that of "this people there were seven hundred chosen men left-handed; every one could sling stones at a hair-breadth and not miss." With this famed weapon David was intimately familiar. It was the attendant of his pastimes. He had played with it thousands of times. He knew the form, size, and smoothness of the stone that was to whiz from the sling on its mission of death. On his way to meet the giant, as he took from the brook five smooth stones, and put them in his shepherd's bag, he was only repeating the custom of his shepherd's life. Fighting Goliath with his own weapons, he would have been felled to the earth ere he had reached him. Protected as Saul would have protected him, with armor and helmet and coat of mail, and his sword girded on his armor, he would have been crushed beneath the heavy blows that would have made his carcass fit food for the beasts of the field.

But God inspired the young champion. At a glance, as Goliath passed before him, he saw his advantage. All the armor worn by the warrior would afford him no protection against the unerring aim of the shepherd boy. So far as David was concerned, Goliath might as well have been clothed in a shepherd's garb too. The bare spot was the only one that would have served David. He had confidence in his unerring aim. He knew how near he could approach his adversary with safety. He knew how to add to the power and deadliness of the blow by his own speed. He hailed with shouting the advance of the Philistine. "David hasted and ran to meet him." "He put his hand in his bag and took thence a stone, and slung it." Whizzing through the air, and lost to sight, with unerring exactness it was planted in the center of the mark, and sank into the forehead of the Philistine. Israel and Judah shouted as the giant fell. The shepherd boy had won. To God belonged the victory—showing how preparation for life's great duties are learned in the lowly and common pursuits of life.

God finds men when he wants them. But he finds

men—men who have made the most of their position, have used their gifts, talents, and opportunities well, and thought only to do the will of God in the position in which he placed them. Men want riches, talents, and position that they may serve Christ. He asks no poor man to do a rich man's work—no unlearned man to do the work of a scholar—no one in humble life to bear the cross of the titled. We serve God best when we serve him with all our heart in the position which he has given to us. So was it with David. He did not go out in the spirit of bravado to attack a lion and a bear. But when one attacked him or his flock he showed his courage. He did not present himself as a candidate for the throne, but was called in from the sheepfold when Samuel desired to anoint him. On this wise speaks the word of God: "He chose David also his servant, and took him from the sheepfold. He brought him to feed Jacob, his people, and Israel, his inheritance. So he fed them according to the integrity of his heart, and guided them by the skillfulness of his hands."

Joseph prepared himself for ability to rule in Egypt by fidelity in the lowly position of a slave. Daniel rose from a captive's couch and chain, to which he had been consigned in youth, by principle, by doing all things well, by seeing that the king's business suffered no harm. And the trials and vicissitudes of his lowly walk, faithfully improved, made him the ablest prime minister that Babylon ever knew. Had Saul of Tarsus been less devout and earnest as a Pharisee, less a student at the feet of Gamaliel, less learned in the law; had he been indolent, thriftless, and an undevout Pharisee, his conversion would not have ranked him as the great Apostle to the Gentiles. Had Luther been less enthusiastic and sincere, less earnest and conscientious as a monk, had he wasted what talents and light he had, he would not have been the great champion of the Reformation. Like David, he formed his own weapon, and became expert in its use before he became the great commander of the armies of the Lord of hosts against the hosts of darkness.

So all the battles of life are to be fought. The simple weapons God has provided are the powerful ones. The world can beat us with their own weapons. In their generation the "children of this world are wiser than the children of light." The philosophy and wisdom of men will overmatch us if we go to them with armor, coat of mail, and helmet of their own stuff and workmanship. David could not cope with Goliath in Saul's armor, but with his sling he could do what all the army beside could not do. As well incase the shepherd lad in the armor of Saul, who was head and shoulders above all Israel, and had him fight Goliath; as well put a small boy in the great boots of his father in time of danger, and bid him haste for the doctor in a matter of life and death, as to place in the pulpit the philosophy of men to break the ranks of the enemy. The cross that the heathen conqueror saw in the sky, with the motto, "By this conquer," that led him and his nation to Calvary, is the only truth before which infidelity bows. It can plant altars on every hilltop, and make every vale vocal with the praise of God.

Error has always some vulnerable part—some vital point not covered by the strong and costly armor she wears. Achilles has his vulnerable heel. The concessions of men, their admissions, their idle and contradictory boasts, the fruits all systems of irreligion bring forth, the acknowledged value of religion to nations and men, its power on the head, intellect, and life, enable the champion of truth, who will use the sling and the smooth stones taken from the brook that flows from the throne of God, to fell the giant of error, and cut off his head with his own sword.

XX.—THE ARK OF GOD ON A NEW CART.

> "Should all the forms that men devise
> Assault my faith with treacherous art,
> I'd call them vanity and lies,
> And bind the Gospel to my heart."

DAVID was king in Zion. The ark of God was in a distant part of the kingdom. It was the symbol of the Divine presence. It held the tables of the law, Aaron's rod, and the manna. It held the affections of the people. It was needed by David to make his throne stable. It could do more for one, whom many still regarded as a usurper, than armed men. Its presence in Zion would produce loyalty in the capital and the land, and stamp out the remaining seeds of rebellion. It would be to the king what the pillars of cloud and fire were to his ancestors. Long absent, conquered, and dishonored, the people panted to see it the center of sacred worship in the tabernacle.

Special messengers were appointed to carry the ark from Kirjath Jearim to Zion. It was a solemn trust, and the messengers felt their responsibility. They resolved to do honor to the symbol of the Divine presence. They made a new cart and set the ark thereon, and, with oxen, they started for the sacred city. The paths in Palestine were not made for carts. They were rough, uneven, and dangerous. The ark jostled, "for the oxen shook it." One of the messengers, named Uzzah, put out his hand to steady the ark; he touched it, and fell dead beside the cart. Consternation seized the people. General alarm prevailed. Even the king was afraid to remove the ark to his own house, and "carried it aside to the house of Obed-Edom, where it abode for three months."

Uzzah's crime was this: he disobeyed positive law. In his great zeal to honor the ark, he forgot to ask the direction of God. He did not inquire whether God had said any thing on its removal. The ark was his. The removal was a religious work. If moved at all, it must be in the manner God prescribed. But Uzzah forgot to consult the law. He put sacrifice before obedience. He took a grand and expensive course to magnify his office. God had asked no such sacrifice or service. His command was plain on the removal of the ark, and it was imperative. No common man must touch it. It must be borne on the shoulders of the priests, and those beside, that touched it, should die. Passing by this law, the messengers chose an imposing way, more worthy of God, they thought. But to Uzzah it proved the way of death. His intentions and motives were good. But right things can not be done in a wrong way. He knew the law well, and should have obeyed it. If he had been ignorant, he could have gained knowledge at the hands of men learned in the law.

The business of life is conducted on this rule. Men who run railway trains must obey positive law. It is the only rule of safety. A large part of the collisions come from good intentions, which lead to violation of rule. One thing that makes military law so efficient is, that it is imperative. In time of war, men must obey or be shot. Good intentions don't save men when they violate natural law. A man who walks off a precipice, thinking he is in the plain, safe road, meets with all the consequences that he would meet were his precipitation intentional. The natural law is, that a man must know where he is treading. A mother, who arises at night and seizes a bottle of poison, supposing it to be medicine, kills, as really, her only child, to whom she gives the dose, as if she intended its death. The natural law is, people must keep their poisons and medicines separate. A man went out with his brother to hunt a bear that was doing mischief to their fold. They separated to make the search better. One of them saw what he thought was a bear among the limbs of a tree. He fired, and brought, not the bear, but his brother's mangled corpse to his feet. The law is, that men must know what they are shooting at, whether it be a bear or a man, and good intentions can not save the victim.

It was so in the case of Uzzah. God had appointed men to move the ark. He had forbidden all others to touch it. The law was imperative, and the penalty well known. But the ark shook, and if Uzzah had not steadied it, it would have fallen and broken, perhaps, the tables of stone. But had Uzzah obeyed God, the ark would have needed no steadying, nor would the precious contents been exposed to damage. His disobedience created the peril that called forth his sacrilegious touch, for which he died. On the shoulders of the priests it could have been borne safely, and no hands been laid on it but those whom God commanded to touch it.

Had it been otherwise, it was Uzzah's duty to obey, and leave the results with God. God had made ample provision for the removal of this ark. A new cart, with oxen attached, was not among them. Uzzah's care was self-created; his labor was for self-glorification. In defiance of God's command, he put the ark on a new cart. He drove over a rough road. He put his hand out to steady the ark. God struck him down. He lay a corpse beside his own new invention.

Men complain of religion, that it is severe and bigoted, in that it will not accept of good intent and sincerity, instead of true faith and certain acts done. We are often told that it matters not what men believe, if they are only sincere; that one way to God is as good as another way, if men only believe it. It was not so with Uzzah. You can not persuade a farmer that cockles are as good as wheat, if he is only sincere. The man who shot his brother and thought him a bear, was sincere; but it made some difference with the mangled brother whether he or the bear was shot. The mother who gave her babe poison, and thought it was medicine, was sincere; but sincerity did not save the life of the child. You could not persuade a pilot off Cape Hatteras, in a gale, with a thousand souls aboard his bark, that a chart of the Bay of Fundy was as good to sail by in those stormy waters, if he was only sincere, as any other. In all these cases, we know the value of being right as well as honest.

This history disposes of the objection made to the justice of that rule which rejects the sacrifices of the wicked, and makes the prayers of the insincere an abomination. Right things must not only be done in the right way, but with the right spirit and right intent. Outwardly Cain's sacrifice was as good, as costly, and as appropriate as Abel's. "Abel was a keeper of sheep. He brought unto the Lord of the firstlings of his flock and the fat thereof." "Cain was a tiller of the ground, and he brought of the fruit of the ground." "The Lord had respect unto Abel and to his offering. But unto Cain and his offering he had not respect." Cain's heart was not right in the sight of God. "His works were evil, and his brother's were righteous," said the disciple whom Jesus loved. A kiss is a token of affection, of true devotion, of sincere love. But what was the worth of the kiss of Joab, or of Judas? As valuable as the dagger of the one, and the foul bargain of the other. Prayer is the soul's sincere desire. But of what avail are those long, hypocritical prayers, denounced by the Son of God, from which those who offered them turned away to devour widows' houses and bind heavy burdens on men?

Neither in religion nor in daily life can men do right things, save in the right way, and with the right spirit. A man can not hold his own unless he does so lawfully. The absence of the legal number of witnesses, or some informality, may defeat the intent of one who makes his will, and frustrate the lifelong purpose of his heart. Personal safety and freedom can be enjoyed only by following the rule prescribed by law. Nor is a man allowed to redress his own wrongs in his own way. He must take such redress as the law gives, or have none. An absent clause, want of a seal, or some apparently immaterial form, has changed vast estates. Men exist whose duty is to teach in all these matters. And the maxim of law is, "Ignorance of law is no excuse to any man." Before men act in the affairs of this life— buy, sell, or meddle with the affairs of their neighbors—they must consult the statutes, and know what they may and may not do. A New York gentleman died some time since, and left an estate of a million of dollars, to be disposed of by will. But some informality in the will caused it to be set aside by the courts, and the disposal of this vast property was changed entirely.

Religion comes to us in the Word of God. "Search the Scriptures" is the command.

> "This is the judge that ends the strife
> When wit and reason fail,
> My guide to everlasting life
> Through all this gloomy vale."

The Word of God shows us the way of salvation. It teaches us what we must do to be saved, on whom believe, and what life we must lead. It is idle to object to such strictness, for we must do God's work in his way, and ask that way at his hands. If we would enjoy the fruits of the earth, we must not only labor, but labor and sow in good soil, and in due season. The work of May can not be done in January, because we feel like it at that time. The "time to sow" is the only one to cast the seed into the furrow.

To bless and save men, God has set certain instrumentalities in the world. All reforms, all human elevation, all attempts to raise up degraded humanity, without those, are in vain. The Church, the Bible, the Sabbath, the living ministry, are God's chosen instruments: all beside these are carts for the ark of God. Men malign the Church of God, and count the ministry a vain thing and foolishness. But God has chosen this instrumentality to save men. He chose it out of all the world, and has perpetuated it for eighteen centuries. What have men gained who have broken away from those? Where are their monuments? No permanent reforms, no institutions of humanity, no schools or hospitals, have they founded who are enemies to these. The path of human reform, aside from the Bible, is studded with dead Uzzahs, who lay beside the new cart on which they have attempted to carry the ark of God. What religion can not do, can not be done by man. All departures, all royal roads and new schemes, that have not in them the cross of Christ, will lead where Uzzah's work led him—to death.

We live in an age of experiment. Men who are not swift to do the will of God are swift to do what God does not demand. Uzzah took no thought to ask the Lord how he would have him act, but was quite ready for the expense and labor of a new cart. Men have "better things" than the Gospel—more "costly, efficient schemes" for human elevation than the Bible. As of old, "they promise us liberty while they are the servants of corruption." Against the social life of the Bible they place Fourierism; against the work of the spirit they place spirit-rapping and table-tipping; against regeneration and a solid piety they place "promises of life to the wicked, though they turn not from their wicked ways and live." But such bear not the sign-manual of the King. It is the work of Uzzah, putting the ark of God on a new cart. We want the old paths, and for these we must "stand in the way and inquire for the old ways, and walk therein."

XXI.—THE MOUNT OF OFFENSE; OR, PERILS OF AGE.

"Where is the strength that spurned decay,
The step that rolled so light and gay,
 The heart's blithe tone?
The strength is gone, the step is slow,
And joy grows weariness and woe.
 When age comes on.

"Our birth is but a starting-place,
Life is the running of the race,
 And death the goal.
There all those glittering toys are brought;
That path alone, of all unsought,
 Is found of all."

THE Mount of Olives has three summits. On one of these—the most southerly—Solomon committed his great offense, from which the eminence takes its name. Of this matter the Sacred History makes the brief but graphic record: "King Solomon loved many strange women of the nations concerning which the Lord had said, Ye shall not go in unto them. It came to pass, when Solomon was old, that his wives turned away his head after other gods; and his heart was not perfect with the Lord his God, as was the heart of David his father. He builded altars, and sacrificed to the abominations of the Moabites, the goddess of the Zidonians, and the abominations of the Ammonites." A part of the Mount of Olives was included in the royal gardens, and this fact may explain why Solomon chose the spot opposite the temple on Moriah as the place of his apostasy and idol worship.

There is a marked and sad contrast between the youth and age of Solomon. At the early age of twenty-six years he ascended the throne of David. It was a splendid throne, and he a splendid monarch. It was a time of profound peace. His kingdom was fortified. He was on good terms with all the kings of the earth. He was appointed king by his father. His appointment was hailed with acclamation by the whole nation. Riches multiplied in the city as dust in Jerusalem. He was a young man, rich and handsome. He had a noble position. No element of a brilliant career was wanting. He had power, position, wealth, and taste. He had all the appliances of success. He possessed a painter's eye and a poet's fancy. God gave him wisdom exceeding that of all men. His decision filled the people with awe, and the rulers who came from afar to hear his wisdom counted even his servants happy who attended on his steps. He was allowed to build the temple to the Lord on Moriah. He dedicated it as king and priest. God accepted the gift, and filled the house with his presence. He knew that unaided he could not rule so great a people. He supplicated aid from on high. God came down to him. He gave him wisdom and a large heart, and made him a model ruler and a finished monarch. When he was old, he forsook the God of his fathers, and bowed down to idols. He deserted the altar of Jehovah, and soiled his fair fame. He formed alliances with the heathen women, which

God had forbidden, and such as would have ruined Isaac.

Who that saw Solomon at the altar of the Sidonians on Olivet, in full sight of the Sacred Temple, could believe that in his youth he had laid the foundation of that gorgeous edifice, and at its completion uttered the sublime prayer of dedication. He was now an apostate priest, a disloyal king, the champion of error, undoing the work of a lifetime —he who had been so blessed, and saw such visions! No one who saw the bridal pageant when the king led the woman of Egypt to the altar, could have predicted such an end. But "his wives turned away his head after idols." On the summit of Olivet he built heathen altars. He bowed down and worshiped the work of his own hands. He sent on the curse to his children's children. No doubt he repented, and the book of Ecclesiastes was the work of his repentant old age.

Youth is not the only season of peril. Increasing years demand increasing vigilance. It is no time to lay down the watch, call off the guard, and invite temptation. Age has dangers peculiar to itself. When Solomon was young, strong in God, and guarded by his fear, no heathen woman could have led him astray. But when he was old he was an easy victim. The sin that kept Moses from the land of promise was the sin of ripened years. The crime of Eli, that could not be purged "with sacrifice nor offerings," was committed when the priest "was very old." David, when he quailed before Nathan the prophet, in the matter of Uriah, seems not the same person who, as a ruddy youth, defied and defeated the uncircumcised Philistine.

The best things men do have been done in comparative youth. The worst, in age. Men usually publish their best works and establish their fame before they reach mature life, or not at all. Those who apostatize from the truth, and attempt to destroy the faith they once preached, usually wait till they become old. Arnold was a young man when he was wounded in the cause of American liberty. But when he became old he bartered the honor of his country for gold. Paine, Voltaire, Bolingbroke wrote their vile works against the religion of the Son of God after they had passed the meridian of life. The passions of men, their presumptuous but secret sins gather strength from age. They get dominion over men.

Each season has its own peculiar peril. That of youth attends the start. Age is dangerous as it nears the close. The noble ship, that has braved the tempest and the gale, comes in from its voyage around the globe, and goes down within sight of land. The soldier, home from many a bloody battle, who walked unharmed as the red-hot missiles of death rained around him, saw thousands of his comrades die on the battle-field, from which he passed out unhurt, dies within sound of the church-bells of his own loved home. The traveler comes back from the abode of the plague, and amid the healthy breezes of his native hills lieth down, and riseth not till the heavens are no more. He who for gain or glory sleeps where the pestilence with its silent tread walks forth on its mission of death, gives up the ghost in sight of the smoke that curls from his own hamlet. So age often stumbles when near the end of its race. When memory holds not the things of yesterday, when the strong man bows himself, and strand after strand of the silver cord is snapped, and the passions seem to have died out, temptations come with terrific power, sweeping away the reputation of years, and hurling the old man into a dishonored grave. Men master the perils of youth, overcome the temptations of manhood, then welcome the enemy, and, when their heads are bleached with years, fall from their steadfastness, and are blotted out from among the good. The Mount of Offense is full of warning to age.

XXII.—THE PLAIN OF ZAANAIM; OR, BUTTER IN A LORDLY DISH.

> "Sin has a thousand treacherous arts
> To practice on the mind;
> With flattering lips she tempts our hearts,
> But leaves a sting behind.
> With names of virtue she deceives
> The aged and the young;
> And, while the heedless wretch believes,
> She makes his fetters strong."

An ignominious peace is worse than a righteous war. A servile submission to wrong is a greater evil than garments rolled in blood. In the time of Deborah the government of Israel was weak. Among forty thousand men, there was not one soldier, nor one shield or spear. Armed men and robbers overran the land. Marauders and highwaymen made life insecure. No home was safe. Women were shot as they went to the well for water. Business ceased. No furrow was turned—no seed sown—no trade prosecuted. Men were effeminate, and God raised up a woman to save the land. Deborah arose, and she called Barak to be captain. But little patriotism was there in the land. Some willingly responded to defend the nation. The "governors of Israel offered themselves willingly among the people." Reuben was divided and chose to abide among the "sheepfolds, to hear the bleating of the flocks."

Gilead was safe beyond Jordan. Dan remained in ships. Meros refused to come "to the help of the Lord against the mighty." But a noble company were ready to "jeopardize their lives unto the death." The cowardly, the timid, the selfish were sent away. Yet there remained to Deborah the noble army of forty thousand, who would turn their backs on no foe.

God helps those who help themselves. Unexpected aid came. The stars in their courses fought against Sisera. The river Kishon swept away the foe. The great captain, with his war-chariot, horsemen, and mighty men of war, were routed and broken, and Sisera fled alone, in dismay and disgrace. Beyond the camp of Israel was pitched the tent-home of Heber, the Kenite. He was a Gentile, and a friend to Sisera's master, the king of Hazor. "There was peace between the house of Jabin, the king of Hazor, and the house of Heber." The discomfited captain "lighted down off his chariot, and fled away on his feet;" "he fled away on his feet to the tent of Jael, the wife of Heber the Kenite." The reception was all he had expected. He was well known to Jael. She saw him approaching, with the shame of defeat on his brow, who had left her tent so short a time before in the pride of a haughty conqueror. His splendid army had been cut to pieces, "and there was not a man left." All his chariots were captured, and his "horses' hoofs broken by the means of the prancing of their mighty ones." An oriental welcome awaited him. Jael went out to meet him. She bade him enter and "fear not." "She covered him with her mantle." "He asked for water, and she gave him milk. She brought forth butter in a lordly dish."

He was weary, and soon was fast asleep. He confided in his covenant with Heber, and felt safe. That covenant of peace between Heber and Jabin did not include Heber's wife. When the devil makes a covenant with the husband, it does not always include the wife! Probably Jael was an Israelite at heart. She may have been a distant relative of Moses' wife, for she was a Kenite. Moses' name and memory were dear to this people. Jael was a believer in the true God. She saw, in Sisera, an enemy and a scourge to a people whom she loved. She saw the fair land desolated by the hoof of his horses. She saw the terror of the people, and the devastation of an armed mob. She knew her power, and used it. She beguiled Sisera into her tent. She used lawful strategy to end a bloody struggle, and give peace to the land. When the armed warrior was heavy with sleep, Jael "put her hand to the nail, and her right hand to the hammer; and with the hammer she smote Sisera, she smote off his head, when she had pierced and stricken through his temples." And for this aid the inspiration of God pronounces her "blessed among women."

Not unlike the fascinations and temptations of life were the seductive arts of Jael to entrap and disarm the discomfited captain. She seemed a friend when all was lost. She gave him a warm and genial welcome amid disgrace. Not the offer of a tent, and a cup of water, at the earnest and almost dying call of a forlorn and disgraced man, but a coming out of the seclusion of her tent to call in the fugitive, lest he should go by; a right royal welcome, giving more than he asked, and in his disgrace recognizing the royal state of his master the king; bringing milk when he asked for water; bringing butter, and that too in a lordly dish; not calling him to the ordinary couch, but spreading her own mantle, to make him a bed of honor; and by all these flatteries, attentions, and seeming honors, lulling all suspicions, to make the destruction of her victim easy and sure.

Irreligion is well represented by this conduct of Jael. Counsels that lead to destruction drop from lips "sweet as honey-comb," and from mouths "smoother than oil." Lying in wait, with flattering of the tongue, with enticing words and "engaging eyelids," promises of "beds decked with coverings of tapestry, with carved work, and with fine linen," "couches perfumed with myrrh, aloes, and cinnamon," promises of good with fair speech—so the messenger of evil leads astray and downward, "young men void of understanding," causing them "to yield," till the seductive form is followed, and the victim "goeth as an ox goeth to the slaughter, as a bird hasteth to the snare, and knoweth not that it is for his life."

A walk among the temptations of city life, a glance at those avenues which lead to death, and whose steps take hold on hell, teach what fascinating allurements are held out to the expected victim. Butter in a lordly dish; open conservatories, fragrant with rare and splendid flowers; paintings, gildings, statuary, and art; music to entice and lull; the syren song to tempt; the sparkling cup, red with the ruby wine, "when it giveth its color in the cup, when it moveth itself aright," are all beautiful to see. The canopied couch invites to luxurious repose. Danger is banished—fear removed. Pleasures promise to rule the hour, and give a solace of love. Beautiful to the eye and the sense are those chambers of sin, where men, young and old, gather to squander their birthright, fortune, repute, and life, in gaming. But all these seductions are the cup and platter of the Kenite, with butter in a lordly dish. How fine and gay, how elegant the entertainment. No dull saints sit at that board. No gloom of religion gives the soul a shudder in those tents of sin. The pathway trodden is broad and flowery. The door stands wide open, and men and women cross the path of those who "would go on their way," and "cause them to turn in, and," with the "flattering of the lips, force them to yield." Pleasure attends, promises of good seduce, gay associates plead. "No gloom," "no long faces," "no long prayers," "a merry life, if a short one," are mottoes that adorn the walls of pleasure's voluptuous abode.

How like the fascinations that lured Sisera on to his doom! A weary, faint, and discomfited man; a tent-home with door wide open; milk instead of water; butter in a lordly dish; a warm welcome; generous and elegant hospitality; an elegant hostess comes forth to welcome the comer, more than anxious to impart the luxuries of her home; an open-handed provision for the wants of the invited; a compassion for the misfortune that sent him out to seek the needed shelter. Where can one be safe if not here? Where may the weary form spread itself, and take the needed rest, and sleep in security, if not in the house of Heber, where hospitalities are dispensed by Heber's wife? Alas for Sisera! Could he, ere he fell into that sound and final sleep, have gazed behind that curtain, seen the hammer and tent-pin to which the hand was to be put, and the right hand to be placed, how he would have aroused himself, and escaped the impending evil. Few who enter the tents of sin see the end, or look on the nail and hammer, or think of peril nigh. Men see the wine cup, and are charmed with its color. It is fascinating and harmless to the view. But at "the last it biteth like a serpent and stingeth like an adder."

The plains of Zaanaim are studded with Kenite tents. Long lines of Siseras enter for rest and happiness. We see them go in; but when come they forth? Look into this seeming pleasant abode; pull aside the tent-cloth, and look on that ghastly form, and know that the "dead are there." At home, the mothers of our modern Siseras wait their return, looking out of their window, crying through the lattice: "Oh! my son, my daughter, come home." Alas! they will never come. And when you ask for your child, the modern Jael will answer: "Come, and I will show the form whom you seek." And she will show you your child, "dead, with the nail in his temples." In vain in bitter anguish will you cry with King David: "Oh, my son! my son! would God I had died for thee."

XXIII.—THE PLAIN OF ONO; OR, RELIGIOUS STRATEGY.

> "Hark! the onset! will ye fold your
> Faith-clad arms in lazy lock?
> Up! oh, up! thou drowsy soldier;
> Worlds are charging to the shock.
> Worlds are charging—heaven beholding—
> Thou hast but an hour to fight;
> Now, the blazoned cross unfolding,
> On! right onward! for the right."

AMONG the children of Israel born in Babylon during the captivity was the prophet Nehemiah. He was of the tribe of Judah, and of the royal family. He obtained promotion in Babylon, dwelt in the palace Shushan, and held the confidential position of cup-bearer to the king. He loved the land of his fathers with a deep and abiding love. Certain men of Judah, who were left of the captivity in Jerusalem, visited the prophet in his royal home. They could say little of the city of David, and that little filled the heart of Nehemiah with sorrow and affliction. His brethren told him that the remnant left of the captivity were in great affliction and great reproach. The wall of Jerusalem was broken down, the gates were burned, the city in ruins, the holy temple a waste, the altars of sacrifice scattered, and the fires gone out.

A captive in Babylon, a slave to the king, living amid idolatry and impiety, his upright walk and noble integrity bore him above all others, and the king confided in him as the chief of his household. Like Daniel in Babylon, there was an excellent spirit in the prophet. Like him, he was preferred above the presidents and princes concerning the kingdom, and he took care that "none should find occasion nor fault; for as much as he was faithful, neither was there any error found in him." He made the best of his position for himself and his brethren. He was as humble in his princely apparel, with the gold chain about his neck, and in his sumptuous home in Shushan, as was Elijah with his rough garment around him in his cave on Carmel. His fervent piety and unblenching integrity raised him to his high position. He maintained a cheerful spirit, and, during his long service as cup-bearer to the king, his countenance had at no time been sad in the royal presence. But the sad news of the desolation and reproach of the city of his fathers filled him with the deepest sorrow. He shed bitter tears over the dishonored dust of his beloved Zion. He entered the king's presence with a sad countenance, and, as he took up the wine to give it to the king, the monarch marked the change in his appearance. He tenderly asked: "Why is thy countenance sad? It is nothing else but sorrow of heart." Many days he had kept from the king's presence. He had wept and mourned, fasted and prayed before the God of heaven. He was fitted for his interview with the king. The God of heaven put words into his mouth as he touchingly replied: "Let the king live forever. Why should not my countenance be sad, when the city, the place of my fathers' sepulchers, lieth waste, and the gates thereof are consumed with fire?" The prophet sought wisdom of God, and then preferred his request to the king. He obtained permission to visit the city of his fathers' sepulchers, and build it. He obtained letters to the governors beyond the river, letters to the keeper of the king's forest, and all the authority that was needed to build up the wall of Jerusalem, and take away the reproach. The "king sent with him captains of the army and horsemen." So he came to Jerusalem, no man knowing what God had put in his heart to do. He arose in the night with a few confidential men, compassed Jerusalem, and learned the extent of the desolation that was to be repaired. He then called together the rulers, the priests, the nobles, and those that were to do the work, and "told them of the hand of God that was good upon him, also the king's words that he had spoken." And the people said: "Let us rise up and build." This work was a religious work. It began in tears and mourning, fasting and prayer. It was commenced with a perfect understanding of the extent of the work. All had a part in it—the rulers and the peasants, the noble and the humble, the aged and the strong, women and children. All classes were assigned to that portion of the toil suited to their ability, capacity, and taste. Selfish ones, found in all communities, who will only join in public works where their own interests are promoted, were allowed to "build the wall over against their own house." A few weeks repaired the desolation of many years, "for the people had a mind to work." The sacred places were dedicated with solemnity and magnificence. The prophet reformed the corruptions that had crept into public affairs. He curbed the inhumanity of the great, and obliged the hard-hearted to release from slavery the unfortunate. Heavy mortgages were removed from the lands of the poor, and alienated estates restored. Marriages with idolatrous women were dissolved, the observance of the Sabbath enforced, honor and justice maintained, and public worship re-established. The book of the law of Moses was brought forth with all honor, and read in the presence of the people by the Levites, who "read in the book of the law of God distinctly, and gave the sense, and caused the people to understand the reading." So God revived his work in Zion, and poured out his spirit upon his tabernacle.

This great work was performed in the face of the most violent and persistent opposition. While Zion was in affliction and reproach, the walls broken down and the gates burned with fire, and the people in the deepest disgrace and distress, these enemies of God were quiet and contented. When they heard that there was come a man to seek the welfare of Judah, and to take away her reproach, it grieved them exceedingly. Sanballat the Horonite, Tobiah the Ammonite, and Geshem the Arabian embodied and led the opposition to the work of restoration. They affected to despise the effort, and laughed to scorn those who attempted to rebuild the city, contemptuously asking: "What do these feeble Jews? Will they make an end in a day? Will they revive the stones out of the heaps of the rubbish which are burned?" One suggested that a fox going up on the wall would break down even their stone wall. The ridicule failed of its effect. Their reproach was turned on their own head, and the wall went speedily up. The authority of the prophet to rebuild the city was next denied. Sanballat said: "What is this thing which ye do? Will ye rebel against the king?" He attempted to intimidate the people against joining in the work by asserting that Nehemiah was about to make himself a king. He showed an open letter, "wherein was written, It is reported among the heathen, and Gashmu saith it, that thou and the Jews think to rebel; for which cause thou buildest the wall, that thou mayest be their king." He affirmed that prophets preached at Jerusalem, saying: "There is a king in Judah," and he threatened to report these words to the king. This also failed of its effect. The conspirators, very "wroth that the walls were made up, and the breaches begun to be stopped," came together to fight against the builders, and to hinder the work. They intended to take the builders unawares, and slay them. But God brought these councils to naught. The prophet was a soldier as well as a civil ruler, and under his direction "every one had his sword girded by his side, and so builded. One half labored, and half of them held the spears, from the rising of the morning till the stars appeared." Knowing that God would fight for them, their hands were not weakened nor their work stayed. The wall was finished in fifty and two days. "All their enemies heard thereof, and all the heathen that were about saw it with their own eyes, and perceived that the work was wrought of God." As neither ridicule, denial of the prophet's authority to build, nor attempts to cut off by treachery the people, or the sword availed any thing, strategy was employed. Sanballat and Geshem all at once pretended to be favorable to the work and its success. They differed on some small points, and a conference was proposed. They said: "Come, let us meet together in some one of the villages in the plain of Ono." Ono was a city of Benjamin, and was located not far from Joppa. The plain of Ono was near the city. The way to it from Jerusalem was long and dangerous. It was filled with the enemies of Judah, who were ready to put to the sword the prophet and his friends. By craft and strategy, under the pretense of finishing the dispute by an amicable conference, his enemies endeavored to draw the prophet into an ambuscade in the fields, where he would be speedily dispatched, the abandoned walls of the city be again thrown down, the Jews, without a leader, speedily dispersed, and the desolation of Israel made complete and final. But all these schemes were defeated by the prophet, who declined the conference, saying: "They thought to do me mischief." "I am doing a great work," he said to his enemies, "so that I can not come down." Nothing stayed the work. The prophet spent no time in replying to the ridicule nor in repelling the injurious report of his rebellion against the king, nor in idle conference with treacherous foes. But, while his enemies gathered in force for battle, the wall went steadily up, and the desolation of seventy years was repaired in fifty-two days.

This history stands as a type of the reviving grace of God to a desolate Zion, and the manner in which those desolations are repaired when the people of God arise under the stirring appeals of his servants, saying: "Let us build up the wall, that we be no more a reproach." Nehemiah, as a wise master-builder, acting under the immediate direction of God, is a model to all those who seek to revive God's work in the world, and take away the reproach of the Church among men. The word of the Lord informs us that when God's servants "take pleasure in the scattered stones, and favor the dust of Zion," surveying the desolation with tears, and resolving to amend them, God will have mercy upon Zion, for the "set time to favor her has come." Sanballat, Tobiah, and Geshem are types of the opposition to the truth, embracing those who are nominal Christians and those who blaspheme. When the Church is cold and dead, and few come to her solemn feasts; when her members are cold and worldly; the rain of the land is powder and dust, and the soil seems iron or brass, there are no assaults on the kingdom of darkness, the enemies of truth look complacently on he desolation, and are still. But let the Church bestir herself; let fasting, prayer, and tears bear witness to her sorrow ; let her send out her prophets to compass the desolation and to wipe out the reproach; let it be known that men are seeking the welfare of Zion, and the enemies of truth will bestir themselves to hinder the work. The elements of opposition are the same in all ages. The gathering of God's people together, the confession of their sins before God, their tears and prayers and fastings, their impassioned entreaty to God to revive his work and save souls, is met with derision and ridicule, and the Church "is laughed to scorn and despised." If the work progresses, its divine authority will be denied. The work will be said to result from fear, from excitement, originating in the passions of men, and that those who guide in the work are seeking self-aggrandizement. If the work goes on, if the Church becomes active and fruitful, if bad men are reformed, and the impious become devout, then combined opposition will arise. Not only will sects combine, as did the Horonite, the Ammonite, and the Arabian, but a man's foes will often be those of his own house. If this is not successful, the same men who cast ridicule on the opening work, who denied its divine authority, and fought those engaged in it, will adopt the strategy of Sanballat, and, professing friendship for the work, will ask a union, a discussion, or a conference between the friends of Zion and her foes, hoping to withdraw the laborers from their work, scatter those that build, and, by craft, on some pleasant plain of Ono, make the friends of Zion a confusion and a snare.

Such fourfold opposition attended the ministry of our divine Lord. His enemies ridiculed his claim, his doctrine, and his friends. They denied his authority as a teacher, and accused him of blasphemy. His combined enemies conspired to destroy him; and his subtle foes, under the guise of friendship, endeavored to ensnare and entangle him in his talk. So has it ever been in the Church in all ages. So will it ever be when the people of God attempt to repair the desolations of Zion, and, strengthening each other's hands, cry out: "Let us rise up and build."

It is futile to spend time to argue with the enemies of divine truth, to answer their jibes, to vindicate the divinity of Christ, to waste time in idle controversies about the settled truths of religion or ordinances, or the duties she enjoins, or to expect good from the mask of friendship at times proposed, or the conferences offered on the plains of Ono. The arguments for and against the Gospel have been exhausted. A man who will not read the evidences of Christianity, is one of the class who "will not come to the light lest he be reproved," one for whose salvation the Church has no responsibility, of whom we may say as Paul said: "If any man be ignorant, let him be ignorant." If one has made himself familiar with the evidences of Christianity, and is still an unbeliever, such a one "would not be persuaded though one rose from the dead." His difficulty is in the heart, not in the head. He wants faith, not proof.

It has pleased the Sovereign Head of the Church to have set times to favor Zion, to repair her desolations, to bring his people to mourn over the waste, the reproach, and the degradation of the city of our God. He has often rained down righteousness upon the people, and in a few short blessed hours repaired the desolation of many years. We live in the reign of the Holy Spirit, whose office work it is to revive the work of God, and bring sinners to the cross. Let Christians with the spirit of Nehemiah prepare their own souls, by weeping, fasting, and prayer, for the great work they propose to do, and then, in the fear of God, resolve to take away the reproach from Zion, not by might, nor by power, but by the spirit of the Lord of Hosts. Then he who walketh in the midst of the golden candlesticks will be in the presence of his people ; then Zion shall arise and shine, her light being come ; her walls shall arise in strong, fair, and beautiful proportions, and the "headstone thereof shall be brought forth with shouting, crying, Grace, grace, unto it."

XXIV.—THE PULPIT OF WOOD; OR, THE POWER OF THE BIBLE.

> "Pillar of fire, through watches dark!
>   Or radiant cloud by day!
> When waves would whelm our tossing bark,
>   Our anchor and our stay!
>
> "Lamp of our feet! whereby we trace
>   Our path, when wont to stray;
> Stream from the fount of heavenly grace!
>   Brook by the traveler's way!"

In sorrow and captivity the conquered people of Judah sat down, by Babel's streams, to mourn over their sad desolation. The remnant not carried into captivity, who lived in the Holy Land, amid the ruins of its former greatness, were in a condition of greater degradation. Among the captives was Nehemiah, born in bondage. God gave him favor with the king. He dwelt in the palace Shushan, and held the confidential position of royal cup-bearer. Certain brethren, men of Judah, that had visited those left of the captivity, made Nehemiah acquainted with the affliction and reproach that attended the Jews who were in Jerusalem. They were down-trodden, and in great poverty. Jerusalem, the holy city, was a waste and a reproach; the walls were broken down, and the gates burned with fire. Nehemiah's heart sank within him. He wept and mourned certain days, and fasted and prayed before the God of heaven.

His prayers were heard. God inclined the heart of the king to be gracious. He was permitted to visit Jerusalem, repair her waste places, and set up the order of worship for the Lord's house.

The work done, the great festival of dedication was to be performed. For seventy years the people had been away from the house of the Lord; the language of the nation was lost, and the people had forgotten the word of the Lord. Now the "people gathered themselves together as one man, unto the street that was before the water-gate." A pulpit of wood was erected, capable of holding thirteen persons, among whom was Ezra, the scribe. With great fervor Ezra brought the law before the congregation; and from the law of God the Levites "read therein, before the water-gate, from the morning until midday. The ears of all the people were attentive unto the book of the law. They read in the book of the law of God distinctly, and gave the sense, and caused them to understand the reading."

Mighty results followed that public reading of the law. The great heart of the people was stirred. A revival of religion followed. So deep was the sorrow of the Jews for having forsaken and forgotten God, that the holy men of the nation were obliged to command the people that they should hold their peace, nor more utter their loud wailings, neither be more grieved or sorrowing, for the joy of the Lord was their strength.

God has always put honor on his own word, and magnified it beyond even his name. And the rivers of water are not more marked by their verdure, than is the track of the Bible distinguished by great results.

The great value of the Bible is its power over the soul, its intellectual might, and its ability to make men wise unto salvation. We can not over-estimate the value of the Bible on the future life. We may undervalue its influence on the life that now is.

It has great intellectual power. Its historical parts are among the oldest books in the world, written, some of them, six hundred years before Homer, the oldest Greek poet, lived. As a book of history it is peculiar. Without it, two thousand years of the world's history is lost—and that the most interesting. It tells how creation was made, how worlds were swung in their orbit, how man was made and fell, how the convulsions that changed the physical earth, carrying seas over mountain tops, were produced. It runs parallel with human history, minute where it need not be, till human history can go no further; and when it pauses, as reason pauses at the cross, then the Bible takes up the wondrous story, and holds on its solitary way, till it stands at the beginning of the creation of God, when this fair world was called into being, amid the anthems of the morning stars and the shoutings of the sons of God.

It is said in cavil that the Bible was written in a barbarous age; that its authors were rude, unlettered men; that they knew nothing of chemistry, geology, or electricity; that it is suited to an illiterate age; that a refined people can and do outgrow it. But who taught those ignorant men? By whom came the wisdom found in the Word of God? That wisdom that can be found to-day in no book but the Bible, and in no schools not learned in the Word of God? No problem of human life or destiny is passed by in the Bible. Under the black tents of Idumea, the great question of moral evil was discussed by Job and his friends as it has never been discussed since. All ages have panted for those truths found in the Bible. The wise men knew them not. Far-seeing sires prayed for such revelations. How came they revealed to barbarians, to peasants on the bleak sides of mountains? How came shepherds to be the mouth of God to men, so that ignorance confounds the wise, and babes teach the nobles of the earth? The cavil that the Bible was written in a barbarous age, rises to the dignity of an argument in its favor.

The Bible keeps in advance of the intellectual. Galileo was put to death for his theory of the solar system. But, ages before he lived, it was taught in the Bible that God "stretched out the north over the empty place, and hangeth the earth upon nothing." Socrates drank hemlock because he asserted that God was one, and not many. Yet in the wilderness of Sinai, to the thousands of Israel, the great truth was proclaimed: "Know, O Israel! that the Lord thy God, is one Lord." Men can not outrun the Bible, for it has in it the vitality of God. It leads the foremost nations of the world. Bury it, put thrones on it, it will come up in God's own time, as the Lord of light and glory came forth, breaking Pilate's seal.

Men with the Bible in their hand must think. It wakes up men and nations on whom its truth falls. It has started the marvelous inventions of our age.

It originated the common school and the college to educate the common mind. A traveler in Europe, ignorant of his locality, can tell at once whether he is in a Papal or Protestant country by glancing at the men and women, the cattle and crops, the fences and barns. Look at Italy, a Christian land without the Bible. With a clime that poets never tire of praising, with a population the vilest that dwells in civilized lands, who abstain from food at the command of the Church, and cut the throat of strangers for a dollar, whom no man can trust, with whom life and property are never safe. The Pope sits on his throne, with his three keys at his girdle, indicating that he bears rule in heaven, earth, and hell. His dear children kneel at his feet for a blessing. Yet, while they do so, if it were not for the foreign bayonets that guard the Pontiff to his prayers, they would tear the scarlet robe from his body, and trample it under their feet, and would oblige him again to flee from the city in the guise of a lackey on a coach-box.

Look at Luther, a monk, a beggar, with a mind as mighty as when he thundered at the gates of Leo, but torpid as a gorged beast in its cave. He was submissive under the despotic rule of the cloister. He made a fair monk. He swept the chapel, begged flax, eggs, and money for his convent, ran of errands, and any old monk that chose could flog him. Roaming through the convent one day, he found a part of a Bible. It started his life-blood. He became a new man. It ruined him as a friar. It made him worthless as a beggar. No monk could now lay hands on him. He dared the Pontiff, burned the bulls of the

Pope in the flames, defied the devil with his inkstand, and married a nun. It has so far proved, and will ever prove, equal to any age. Build your lines, and truth will be flashed over the wires. Lay your cable, and London and New York will talk of the great salvation. Cover the earth with the network of railroads, and the Church will send over them the swift messengers of peace. Build your fast presses, and they will multiply those leaves which are for the healing of the nations. Extend your domain of merchandise, and the Bible will track commerce around the globe.

How profuse the munificence of God, to give so much beauty in his statute book, which could have been as blank as a criminal code, and delivered its message: "Turn, turn, why will ye die!" God has committed his word to a golden censer. He has made it the fount of pure language. He has filled it with poetic beauty of narrative, poem, fable, story, proverb, and song. You find apples of gold in baskets of silver, the sword of the spirit in a diamond scabbard. In it are the heroic, the pathetic, and the sublime. Of this fount men drink, and live forever. It leads all true reform. It is the origin and perpetuity of civil and religious freedom. It is the arsenal of God, where hangs the whole armor we need to fight the fight of faith. Before it Dagon falls. By it temples rise and songs swell. It will crown every hilltop with glory, complete the conquest of the world, till one song shall employ all nations, and all cry: "Worthy is the Lamb, for he was slain for us."

XXV.—PALACE SHUSHAN; OR, BUSINESS INTEGRITY.

"Thy word, a wondrous guiding star,
On pilgrims' heart doth rise,
Leads to the Lord, who dwells afar,
And makes the simple wise.
Let not its light,
E'er sink in night,
But still in every spirit shine,
That none may miss thy light divine."

In the book of Esther an account is given of the palace Shushan. Its magnificence and splendor far exceeds any city known to the ancients, and indicated a degree of civilization and refinement that has led men to doubt its existence. It was the home of monarchs, and tradition asserts that it held the tomb of Daniel. Among other splendid peculiarities of Shushan were beds of gold and silver, on a pavement of "red and blue and white and black marble." Some time ago, an attempt was made to re-run the line between Turkey and Persia. Engineers from both of those Governments were appointed. To see that exact justice was done to both nations, an application was made to the English Government for an able engineer to attend the company. In their track lay buried cities. They unearthed the remains of national greatness, and, in solitude, where owls and cormorants have long reigned, they found the corner-stones and columns of palaces that echoed with the revelry of great kings, who believed that they would abide forever.

But, afar from all civilization—where no gain, or glory, or the zeal of the hunter had called man— these engineers came upon the remains of a former refinement beyond any thing found—vessels of gold and silver of elegant workmanship and of curious device, glass vases that would adorn any palace in the world to-day, and other numerous indications of a refined and rich people. But, unharmed, and as perfect as in the days of Mordecai, they came upon the variegated marble pavements of the Book of Esther, of red, white, blue, and black marble. Not far from this palace was a tomb, evidently built for some great man. On its façade was sculptured a cage, in which were lions, and a man in a reclining position, with a face at once fearless and serene. It was the tomb of Daniel, telling his remarkable story, in those wilds where the foot of man for ages has not trodden, as graphically as it is told in the Book of Daniel the prophet; adding another link to the great chain that tells us that all " Scripture is given by the inspiration of God."

Among the captives of Judah who sat down by the rivers of Babylon, who refused to sing their sacred songs in a strange land, who hanged their harps upon the willows and wept when they remembered Zion, was Daniel, the beloved of the Lord. He was but a youth when carried into captivity. But he loved the city of his fathers with an intense and holy love. He was of the royal line of David—manly, heroic, and pious. He entered on his life in a heathen court, while yet a lad, with his character formed and principles fixed. He dwelt in Shushan palace. The duty assigned him brought him in immediate contact with those who denied the God he worshiped and derided his religion. Blasphemy, idolatry, licentiousness, and debauchery ruled those with whom he must dwell and serve. The whole atmosphere of the court was impious, and bad examples and unholy conduct met his eye and offended his ear during all his life in the palace of the king. A young man, handsome, intelligent, and attractive, he was not only exposed to the temptations that surrounded him, but he was exposed to the deeper peril of a king's smile. Selected to grace the palace, the blandishments of the court and royal temptations assailed him on every side. He was from home, and far from the altar and sepulcher of his fathers. He was exposed to peculiar perils in his own person. He had great beauty, and was without blemish, well favored, and attractive. He was skilled in wisdom, in cunning words, and in knowledge. Political preferment, with its dazzling banners, flaunted before him. He ate at the royal banquet, and princes were appointed to see that the king's meat and the royal liquors were placed on his table. Daniel saw the drift of all this. It was to be a trial of three years, and he knew where it would lead. "He purposed in his heart that he would not defile himself with the king's meat, nor with the wine which the king drank." His resolution was early taken, his stand was firm, prayerful, and loyal to God. In an absolute court, in the midst of courtiers and priests who sought to destroy him, he walked the humble path of duty, amid terrible temptations. He clung to the simple fare of his Hebrew home; he had his closet and seasons for daily devotion, amid the revelries of the king's palace. He not only abstained from intemperance and idolatry; he not only maintained his devotions; but he resolved to honor God in his daily life. Industry and integrity marked all his movements. He was diligent in his business, and able to stand before kings. He had an "excellent spirit," which may mean kindness, good-nature, or courtesy. All that he did, he did well; and when envy, hatred, and jealousy put spies on his track, they were obliged to confess that "they could find none occasion nor fault; he was faithful, neither was there any error or fault found in him." He arose gradually and surely, till the purple robe, the golden chain, and the favor of the king proclaimed that the Hebrew captive was prime minister of the realm. High in authority in a heathen court, he was the humble worshiper of the God of his fathers. He was never ashamed of his nationality nor of his religion. He made the condition of his captive brethren pleasant, and gave them a share in his success. He obeyed the law of the land when it did not conflict with his religion. He refused no post of honor tendered to him. He wore the insignia of his rank, power, and wealth. He was as meek when ornamented with gold as when he wore sackcloth. He was as devout in purple as in chains. He was the same open-hearted, reverent servant of God in the palace as in the den of lions. He knew that industry was a blessing and indolence a sin, and he rose from the position of a serf no less by his intense industry than by his integrity. He acted on the truth that runs through the Bible, that God made men for business; that it is the duty and charm of life; that he put man into the garden to dress it as well as to enjoy it; that his blessed Son bound himself up with the toil of life, and earned the bread that sustained his humanity beneath the hot sun of Palestine; nor was there an indolent bone in the apostolic body, unless it was in Judas.

So life teaches. Nations that rule the world are celebrated for business. England is called a nation of shopkeepers—the sun does not set on her domain. Johnson objected to Scotland that the men and horses ate the same food; but he was asked where he could find better men or better horses. The native products of the soil of New England are said to be ice and rocks; but the alchemy of labor has turned the ice into gold, and the rocks into bread. The glory of a nation is not in her palaces, statuary, paintings, and jewels, but in her thousand workshops, in intelligent mechanism, in enterprise, in the hardy arm of industry, in the marts of trade, in the domain of commerce. These give abiding prosperity, civil tranquillity, that make her walls strength, and her gates praise. Brains and toil rear the massive edifice of national greatness, and stand as columns in the portico. Repose and piety God has not joined together. To live in a cave, and found the order of Nazarenes, and to make charity a trade, was not the purpose of the Son of God. No swarms of lazy mortals separated themselves from labor at his bidding. No houses full of foolish virgins, ignorant of the joys and hopes of life, were gathered at his command. The history of Joseph, Daniel, Paul, and Christ prove that industry and piety God hath joined together; let not man put asunder. A religion that will not bear the rough of life is not worth the having.

Religious principle underlaid Daniel's success, and was the corner-stone of his greatness. It was the basis of that courtesy, integrity, and industry that made him so great. It gave him courage for every duty. By it he battled his foes and wielded the great power of the realm. He was not offensive in his piety, nor did he fail in his duty anywhere. The king was absolute, but he rebuked him for his sins. He was not present at Belshazzar's impious feast, though it was given to his lords, and Daniel was the prime minister. His religion grouped and harmonized his traits of character and gave him success. He made friends of all classes by his excellent spirit, and won all hearts. He was exact in all his duties, and obliged the princes to give accounts, that the king should have no damage. He provoked no opposition. He made no unnecessary foes. He made no secret of his devotion. The princes who sought his ruin knew that they would find him in his chamber at the hour of prayer, kneeling before his God. He moved along the pathway of duty with majestic firmness. He was faithful to his king, but no royal decree could drive him from the altar of his God.

It is the theory of the world that business success and high religious integrity can not go together. Men affirm that fortunes are not made on Bible rules.

They do in associations what they would not do as individuals. They are "as honest as the times will allow," and consider "all is fair in trade." No one defends the morality of these maxims. But they are urged as the basis of success. But do all succeed who adopt them? Is not success the exception, and failure the general rule? It is estimated, on a careful and wise calculation, that in our large cities ninety-nine out of every hundred fail, and that property seldom descends to the third generation. The merchants in this country who have been permanently successful for fifty years can be counted on ten fingers; and, without exception, the houses represented by those men have been celebrated for business integrity and reliability, in which the purchaser obtained the very article that he bought. The United States Observatory purchases most of its instruments and lenses from celebrated houses in England, France, and Germany. These instruments are immediately mounted without examination or trial. The repute of the house is a guaranty for the article. That repute is capital. One bad instrument would spoil the market. The stamp of Rogers on a piece of cutlery, the name of Day & Martin on a bottle of blacking, passes them around the world. The uniform excellence of these articles creates the renown and fortune of their makers. Axes from the celebrated Douglas factory, in boxes packed by the maker, are found in the woods of Missouri and in the forests of California, untried till used by the hardy pioneer; but each article is known to be good, for that house could not afford to send out an imperfect article: the excellence of its work is its fortune. We have many men among us who commenced life poor; who left home with no fortune but good principles and the blessing of a mother; who added, to integrity and industry, piety. Such men rose steadily and surely to a fortune. Some of them have been succeeded in business by brothers or children, who took the code of the world for their guide instead of the code of God. In a few years they have scattered all that had been gathered; soiled a fair name; fell suddenly from affluence to want; fled from familiar faces to hide their shame abroad, or sought to drown it in the poison-bowl, or filled a grave by taking life by their own hands. All history proves that where there is no principle there is no permanent success.

Our own nation illustrates the truth that the principles that led Daniel from the position of a slave to the highest honors of the land are applicable to us. We speak of the men of the "old school." Such founded this nation. They had character, principle, and piety. They came from the plow, the anvil, the lapstone, and the printing-case, as well as from the store and college. They worked their way up as Daniel worked his. They were a match for the statesmen of the Old World. They met and conquered veteran soldiers on the battle-field. They created a flag, and defended it with their own cannon. They sent out the declaration of freedom, that rang over hill and dale, whose sound carried hope into dungeons, and made tyrants in their palaces turn pale. Tried by all tests, ours is the strongest nation to-day on the face of the earth. Neither domestic treason nor foreign assaults can destroy our Government. The waves of rebellion, mad and mountain high, can not overwhelm it. It stands as the Eddystone light-house—hid for a moment by the angry billows which roll over it, it comes forth, lifts its tall peak to the sky, and, throwing its steady and certain beams over the waters, guides the tempest-tossed mariner on his perilous way, into the haven of civil and political repose.

XXVI.—THE BLACK TENTS OF IDUMEA; OR, DEATH NOT THE GREAT ENEMY.

> "There are mansions exempted from sin and from woe,
> But they stand in a region by mortals untrod;
> There are rivers of joy, but they roll not below,
> There is rest, but it dwells in the presence of God."

UNDER the black tents of Idumea sat four men in silence and sorrow. Upon one of the wealthiest men of the East, one whom God had seemed to hedge about with every temporal good; whom he blessed in all the works of his hands, increasing all his substance in the land; who was happy in his children and in his position of honor among all the people; who was "perfect and upright, a man who feared God and eschewed evil," upon him a sudden and terrible calamity came. Messenger swiftly followed messenger with evil tidings, till all seemed lost, and strong temptation beset him to "curse God and die."

Each from his own place, came three friends to mourn with and comfort the man of the East, when "they heard that all this evil was come upon him." So changed was his appearance that his friends knew him not when they saw him afar off. "They lifted up their voices and wept, as they drew near; they rent every one his mantle, and sprinkled dust upon their heads toward heaven." In silence the company "sat upon the ground for seven days and seven nights, and none spake a word" to the sufferer.

The drama was opened by Job, who, in the bitterness of his soul, cursed the day wherein he was born, and all the events that prevented his birth from being untimely. From this point an interesting discussion goes on, embracing all the problems of God's moral government among men, his providence, the sufferings of the good, and the triumph of evil men on earth. One more able has never been recorded. No discussion of this knotty theme has been as exhaustive. At one time Job lifted his head in serene confidence, and said: "Shall we receive good at the hand of God, and not evil? The Lord gave, and the Lord hath taken away. Blessed be the name of the Lord." At another time he cried out, in the bitterness of his soul, asking for death and the repose of the grave, "where the wicked cease from troubling and the weary are at rest."

In some of his utterances, Job cried out: "I would not live alway." But these words came not from a pious spirit, made glad in God—submissive under the mysterious and awful chastisement of his hands—a heart weaned from lust and crucified to the world. His frame of mind was desperate. He was in despair. Tired with the battle, disgusted with his lot, he loathed life, and would none of it.

Job was one of the noblest of men. He had not the clear light that now shines on the providence of God and on the darkness of the grave. The Babe in Bethlehem had not been born, and the Man of Calvary had not been laid in the tomb, to throw the glow of an immortal life within the black charnel-house of the dead. He had a dim and misty hope of a better life. "There is hope of a tree," he said. Cut it down, and it "will sprout again." "Though the stock die in the ground, yet the tender branches thereof will not cease. Through the scent of water it will bud and bring forth boughs like a plant." But "man dieth; shall he live again? He giveth up the ghost, and where is he? He lieth down, and riseth not till the heavens are no more." Shall he then "be raised out of sleep?" To him shall the great "change come?" So amid the sorrows, woes, and reverses of life he panted and yearned for that better world which, as the subject of hope, God has so mercifully allowed to survive the fall.

We can not commend the gloom and despair with which Job looked on life. But his history shows the "end of the Lord—that he is very pitiful and of tender mercy." It stands in marked contrast with the great boon of eternal life, which our Lord has "brought to light through the Gospel." We may thank his holy name that the veil has been lifted from the eternal world, and that we have hope of immortality, "since the Sinless'has died." We are not left to grope our way up from barbarism, without faith, filled with fear of the grave, and despair at death; with gloom, depression, and desperation; with loathing of life; fearing, yet longing to lie down in the grave, so dark, so repulsive; yielding our bodies as a banquet for worms; knowing nothing of the great realm beyond the tomb; that this is not our portion.

In the faith of Christ, and in the heroic confidence of Christian trust, we may take up the refrain, and say:

> "Who, who would live alway, away from his God;
> Away from yon heaven, that blissful abode,
> Where the rivers of pleasure flow o'er the bright plains,
> And the noontide of glory eternally reigns?"

Death has two aspects. It is loss when a man leaves all his treasures below. It is gain when his treasures are in heaven. A willingness to die is not always a proof that one is prepared to die. The Bible teaches that the wicked often have no woes here, "are not in trouble as other men," and often have no "bands in their death." Bad men often seek death. They do so to hide their despair, or escape ignominious punishment. They do so to silence the worm that gnaws at the heart. They do so to avoid exposure. They fly from the ills that they have to those they know not of. In passion and in madness men and women often exclaim: "I wish I was dead;" "I hope I may die this minute."

But in no such spirit does a Christian say: "I would not live alway." With much to live for; with honor and a noble name; with a home filled with all good, and made radiant with children and friends; with wealth, taste, elegance, and refinement; with fragrant and balmy odors around; with youth, affection, and love; bound to the living by the tenderest ties, the Christian, with the hope of heaven in the soul, cries out: "'I would not live alway;' I have a nobler good in heaven, a better mansion; there friends do not die, flowers do not wither, and joys do not fade.

> "'No cloud those regions know,
> Forever bright and fair;
> For sin. the cause of mortal woe,
> Can never enter there.'"

Men in the elder dispensation groped in the dark. The Christian walks in the clear sunshine of endless day. To the one, the tomb was a gloomy haven, in which the tempest-tossed and wearied could hide his head; to the other, the sepulcher is warm with the presence and bright with the light of him who is the "resurrection and the life."

To one who dies in the Lord, Death is a conquered foe, and no longer a great and dreaded enemy; for

"The Saviour hath passed through his portals before us,
And the lamp of his love is our guide through the gloom."

In the war death wages, there is no discharge and no substitute. The river of death must be forded, and through the dark valley all must walk. But, as in some Eastern cities, conquered warriors and kings gird themselves to serve and wait on the children of the conqueror, so Death, robbed of his terror and disarmed of his sting, stands at the portals of eternity to hand the saved over the dark flood to their home on high. They tread the path their Redeemer trod, and follow in the way made radiant with light from his Father's throne, flung back upon it by him who has gone before to prepare a place for the redeemed. Well may such sing:

"I would not live alway! no, welcome the tomb;
Since Jesus has lain there, I dread not its gloom;
There sweet be my rest till he bid me arise,
To hail him in triumph descending the skies."

The Christian tires of this world. Imperfection and sin are stamped on all things below. He bears about with him daily a body of death. The whole creation groans with travail, woe, and sorrow. Famine's gaunt form stalks abroad. Pestilence, with silent footfall, moves on its terrible mission. The whole pathway is strewn with broken resolutions and vows unpaid—and the evil he would not, that he does. He says:

> "I would not live alway! thus fettered by sin!
> Temptation without and corruption within!
> E'en the rapture of pardon is mingled with fears,
> And the cup of thanksgiving with penitent tears."

The child of God knows too well that no relief can be found in this life. It is a war that ends only with the tomb. The experience of God's holy ones, for six thousand years, bears testimony to this solemn truth. All things tend to decay. Light and sound, tastes and power wax old and pass away. "The sun, the light, the moon and stars are darkened." "The keepers of the house tremble." The almond-tree blossoms. "The grinders cease." "The windows are darkened." "The grasshopper is a burden." The golden bowl breaks, the silver cord snaps, and solitary old men move about the streets as mourners, because companions and lovers have gone to their long home. So is it on earth. So all find it.

No man can be satisfied with this life. Gain it all, hold it to the end, and it is dust and ashes to the touch, as are the apples of Sodom. Much joy has the worldly man in his generation. He can gratify the eye. He can pull down and build greater. He can sow and gather a noble harvest. He can say to his soul: "Thou hast much goods laid up for many years. Eat, drink, and be merry." But on the walls of his banqueting chamber an armless hand draws blazing characters, that pale his cheek and make his knees smite together in terror. He toils for heirs—he knows not who. He may enjoy the pleasures of sin, but they last only "for a season." Nor can he keep from his soul that searching question: "What shall it profit a man if he gain the whole world and lose his own soul?" He repeats in the solitude of his chamber: "Naked came I out of my mother's womb, and naked shall I return thither. I brought nothing into this world, it is certain that I can carry nothing out." Beyond this life he has no inheritance and no hope.

Not one good thing on earth that a worldly man can enjoy is denied to a Christian. His Father made them all. He is an heir with God and a joint heir with Christ. He can woo, win, and enjoy this life; besides, he is heir to a glorious inheritance in heaven, where moth doth not destroy, rust doth not corrode, and time's tooth not gnaw. Death is his servant, to hand him across the narrow stream that divides the heavenly land from ours. And in that fair world into which Death introduces him, the Christian will have immortal bloom, eternal vigor, and endless youth.

Who then would live alway? Who, when the Master pleases, would not welcome death? Would the children of a king live always in exile, while the palace gates stand wide open, and a robe, a ring, and a sumptuous table await the comer? Shall the son always tread the dusty way, or halt at noon at the well-curb for rest? Shall the wayworn pilgrim always tread the perilous road—roads full of pitfalls, where lions prowl, and men more savage seek their prey? Beyond the rolling river is the mansion of God. Into it sin, pain, hate can not come. "There is rest for you," O Christian! there is rest for you.

"Over the river they beckon to me,
 Loved ones who've crossed to the other side;
The gleam of their snowy robes I see,
 But their voices are lost in the dashing tide.
We saw not the angels who met them there,
 The gates of the city we could not see—
Over the river, over the river,
 My friends beloved stand waiting for me.

"Over the river, the boatman pale,
 Carrying another, the household pet;
Her brown curls waved in the gentle gale—
 Darling blossom! I see her yet.
She crossed on her bosom her dimpled hands,
 And fearlessly entered the phantom bark;
We felt it glide from its silvery sands,
 And all our sunshine grew strangely dark.
We know she is safe on the other side,
 Where all the ransomed and angels be—
Over the river, the mystic river,
 My childhood's idol is waiting for me.

"For none return from those quiet shores,
 Who cross with the boatman cold and pale;
We hear the dip of the golden oars,
 And catch a gleam of the snowy sail;
And lo! they have passed from our yearning hearts,
 They cross the stream and are gone for aye—
We may not sunder the veil apart,
 That hides from our vision the gates of day.

We only know that their barks no more
  May sail with us o'er life's stormy sea;
Yet somewhere, I know, on the unseen shore,
  They watch, and beckon, and wait for me.

"And I sit and think, when the sunset's gold
  Is flushing river and hill and shore,
I shall one day stand by the water cold,
  And list for the sound of the boatman's oar;
I shall watch for the gleam of the flapping sail,
  I shall hear the boat as it gains the strand,
I shall pass from sight, with the boatman pale,
  To the better shore of the spirit land.
I shall know the loved who have gone before,
  And joyfully sweet shall the meeting be,
When over the river, the peaceful river,
  The Angel of Death shall carry me."

XXVII.—FIVE SMOOTH STONES FROM THE BROOK; OR, FUTURE LIFE AND RETRIBUTION CERTAIN.

> "Friend after friend departs:
> Who has not lost a friend?
> There is no union here of hearts
> That finds not here an end.
> Were this frail world our only rest,
> Living or dying, none were blest."

GOD chose "David, his servant, and took him from the sheepfold, to feed Jacob, his people, and Israel, his inheritance. So he fed them, according to the integrity of his heart; and guided them by the skillfulness of his hands." It was no caprice, or the movements of mere human affection, that led Jesse, in that hour of national peril, to call the ruddy lad from the care of the sheep to run to the camp and look how his brethren fared, carry them a present, and take their pledge. God was in all that arrangement. Goliath had defied the God of Israel as well as his armies; and God purposed to overthrow this impious and uncircumcised boaster, and to do so by such humble weapons as to prove that the victory belonged to God. He chose a shepherd lad—sent him to the fight in the rude garb of his calling— guided him to the brook from which he took the five smooth stones—aimed the blow—and gave the stripling strength to sling. David met the giant in the name of the Lord of hosts, whom the man of war had defied.

The armed giant of unbelief, in complete panoply, arrays himself against the great central truths of the word of God, which affirm a future life and a future retribution. If there be no future life, Christ lived and died in vain, men are yet in their sins, and preachers are false witnesses before God. If there be no future retribution, and death puts a full and final period to all woe and all punishment, then, indeed, did the Lord die in vain. He died to save man from the penalty of the law and the curse of transgression. Not here, for his children not only are not free from pain and woe and death, which is the common inheritance of the race, but often a full cup of bitterness is wrung out to them because they are disciples. Apostles and martyrs, who suffered and died for Jesus's sake, that they might obtain a better resurrection, were not only, as Paul says, "of all men most miserable," if in this life only they had hope, but of all men the most foolish. They met the bitter conflicts of life to win a crown, and that crown was certain without the conflict. The champions of error, from the preaching of John the Baptist till now, have in some form forged their weapons against the certainty of a future life and the certainty of a future punishment. These truths have felled the Goliath of error to the earth, and removed his head with his own sword. We will put them in this form:—1. Future life is reasonable. 2. Future life is certain. 3. Future retribution is reasonable. 4. Future retribution is certain. 5. The peculiar features of the final trial.

1.—FUTURE LIFE IS REASONABLE.

> "So Jesus slept; God's dying Son
> Passed through the grave and blessed the bed:
> Rest here, blest saints, till from his throne
> The morning break, and pierce the shade."

MAN has a threefold nature. But God has made provision only for the full and complete development of the body. The intellect can do something, the soul less. God has made nothing in vain; the intellect and the soul will find a sphere in which their noble faculties will have full employ. The body has time and space to do all that it is able to perform. It can bring all its mysterious powers into complete action, and run its subtle machinery on till it wears out, and can do no more. Not so the intellect. At advanced age, the mind is in its infancy. The giants in the mysteries of nature are as Newton, a child on the sea-shore, playing with shells, while the great ocean unexplored lies before them.

Less than the intellect does the soul do the great work of which it is capable. It is a prisoner chained to a body of death. It dwells in a cramped and sickly mansion, which is decaying each hour, and destined to come down at last. This earthly house is not capacious enough for the soul's full work. It has not time to develop its rare traits; it only begins to act. Like David, it gathers materials for a princely house of the Lord, but leaves the accumulated treasures unused. Before even the fires of discipline cease to glow, the frail tabernacle that holds the soul begins to fall to pieces. Does the tenant share in the general ruin?

Reason demands a future life. God has planted a longing in the soul that he means to gratify, and this longing is universal. No temporal good, temporal success, can hush or satisfy this longing. One may master science, and grasp all the world, and still the soul cries out and is unblessed. Add house to house, pile up gold mountain high, still the soul cries: "Bread, water; I perish!" This intense desire for another life is read in the keen desire for novelty peculiar to the race; in its attempt to hew out cisterns for its comfort, and its readiness to follow strange gods; in its costly offerings for the sin of the soul, when the babe is thrown into the waters, or when men fall beneath the ponderous wheels of an idol's car to be crushed to death; in the universal faith in immortality, written on dome and minaret, on obelisk and altar, in the heathen world. As God has given full scope for all the faculties and desires that belong to earth, he will answer this universal longing for a better world, and will not doom the soul to disappointment.

Without a future life men live here in vain—the afflictions and discipline of life are lost, or become mere cruelty, as there is no chance to improve their power. Many are carried to the grave by their sufferings from the hand of God. If there be no life beyond, they have suffered in vain. The inanimate creation come to their full maturity ere they die. The beasts attain the full measure of their capacity at once. They never change—no better, no worse. So have they been for thousands of years. The bee, the beaver, and the horse, those most sagacious of animals, are the same now that they were before the flood. They have added nothing to the sagacity or ingenuity of their kind. They have skill, instinct, and ingenuity—no more, no less.

Not so with man. He is capable of infinite progress. Mark the boy of ten years and the same person at fifty. See how easily the rude boor can be transformed into a finished gentleman, and the savage Hottentot into a man of science. The infant, weeping and wailing in its helplessness, is not the complete man in the flush of power and strength, commanding senates or kingdoms. The mind of man could go on from improvement to improvement forever, did not death come in and arrest the work. Death comes often when the man is in full vigor; often when, like Moses, he has an undimmed eye; often his sun goes down while it is yet day; or he is arrested and cut off in the midst of plans and inventions calculated to bless the world.

Future life is reasonable, for it follows the analogy of life. "There is hope of a tree," that it will live though it be cut down. "Shall not man live again?" reason asks. The insect lives out its allotted time, weaves its own tomb, and dies. In the appointed hour the tomb breaks, and forth comes a new creation, in gorgeous attire, having put on a new body—with new tastes and company, wholly different from the poor worm that was wrapped in the casket in which it died, and from which the beautiful creation burst forth. "Nature dies and lives again," and may not man? If the blasted leaves of autumn are renewed by the return of spring, and the very corruption and decay of the earth add to the bloom and fruit of the new harvest, "why then should it be thought a thing incredible that God should raise the dead?" If the diamond comes forth from the dull, black, and invaluable carbon, and, by a change of the particles that compose its vile body, wears a new and glorious body, can not "God change our vile bodies, and fashion them like his own glorious body"? How universal is the language of faith in a future life! Men deny it; nations never. All feel that when a man closes his eyes in the sleep of death it is not "the last of earth." At the bedside of death we feel, "She is not dead, but sleepeth." This faith has run along the great highway of human life, with the atonement, the judgment, and the rewards of the good and bad beyond the grave. The hope of Job and the reasoning of Plato tell the same great truth.

That universal dread of death indicates the soul's immortality. No one has put this truth better than the immortal bard, when the would-be suicide balances the chances of the "dreams that may come in that sleep" to which all are summoned. Did not men have an innate fear of death, a belief that it is not the end of man, who would live and bear the whips and scorns of time, when one could end these sorrows with a bare bodkin? Once embrace the idea that death is an endless sleep, and who would live on a couch of agony when eternal repose was near? No one would accept the discipline of this life; be weary, disappointed, and sick; be outcast and downtrodden;

tread the path of want, woe, and infamy; be exiles and tenants of dungeons; be scourged and oppressed; meet and suffer the reverses of life, when the silence and quiet of the grave could be invoked. Men would embrace death as readily as a tired traveler would welcome the couch of repose. Now and then a Christian, weaned from the world by crosses and sorrows and afflictions, having laid in the grave nearly all he loves, such may sing, "I would not live alway." But most of our race choose life, and choose to bear the ills they have. The highest of authority teaches us that by the fear of death our race are "all their lifetime subject to bondage."

Nor can the mystery of the resurrection detract from its reasonable character. Nature has mysteries, as well as grace. Who can explain how the fallen and rotten leaf enters in the bloom of opening spring? Who can fathom that change of particles by which charcoal becomes the brilliant, worthy to adorn the imperial diadem? Moses, Elias, and Christ, on the mount, seemed to wear one garment, and it was radiant with the glory of heaven, indicating the body the saints shall wear in the Father's mansion. And is not death as unreasonable as the resurrection of the dead? To one who never saw his fellow die, it would seem as unreasonable to say that this active, reasoning, loving being, with his powers half developed, who really seems just ready to live, that he could be cold as ice and inanimate as marble, as it would be to say that a body cold in death could arise and walk. When we look at man; his gifts and powers; the capacity of his soul, which has no scope for action;

the analogy of nature in favor of a future life; the universal language of hope; the universal dread of death; and that change that is going on in man and nature—all these are reasons why death should not be an endless sleep.

2.—FUTURE LIFE CERTAIN.

> "Palms of glory, raiment bright,
>   Crowns that never fade away,
> Gird and deck the saints in light,
>   Priests and kings and conquerors they."

ALL the considerations that we have named, that make a future life reasonable, make it certain. Aided by revelation, they lead us to the great truth that "all who are in their graves shall hear the voice of the Son of Man, and come forth."

Conscience has given but one voice on this matter. We read her testimony in the omens and signs so universal; in the readiness to dwell on the dark side of things; in the disposition to interpret all mysterious and seemingly supernatural things as indicative of evil. Belshazzar, at the impious feast, could not read one word of the mysterious handwriting on the wall; but his terror sobered him, and he knew the flaming characters boded him no good, long before Daniel made the writing plain and the interpretation sure. Judas had every thing to live for. The government was on his side, and he had done a service that would not soon be forgotten. So far as this life was concerned, he was provided for. But such was the energy and terror of conscience, that he went out from confession to suicide, and hastened to his own place; telling how fearful a thing it is "to fall into the hands of the living God."

The providence of God makes future life certain. The aspect of this life is such as to make men doubt the justice of God. It troubled and saddened David. He obtained no relief till, in the sanctuary of God, he saw the end of the wicked. When we read of the providence of God, in the light of future life, we can say:

"Deem not that they are blessed alone,
    Whose days a peaceful tenor keep;
The God who loves our race has shown
    A blessing for the eyes that weep.

"The light of smiles shall fill again
    The lids that overflow with tears,
And weary hours of woe and pain
    Are earnests of serener years.

"Oh! there are days of hope and rest
    For every dark and troubled night;
And grief may bide an evening guest,
    But joy shall come with early light.

"And thou, who o'er thy friend's low bier
    Dost shed the bitter drops like rain,
Hope that a brighter, happier sphere
    Will give him to thy arms again.

"Nor let the good man's trust depart,
    Though life its common gifts deny;
Though, with a pierced and broken heart,
    And spurned of men, he goes to die.

> "For God hath marked each anguished day,
>   And numbered every secret tear;
>   And heaven's long age of bliss shall pay
>   For all his children suffer here."

The "Gospel brings light, life, and immortality." Jesus, our Lord, is the "first fruits of them that slept." Before him, men had been raised from the dead; but all died again. "Jesus dieth no more." "If the dead rise not, then is Christ not raised," men are yet in their sins, and those who preach a future life "are false witnesses of God." If man is not immortal, then there is no reason for the mission of Jesus to earth: he does not save men here; he redeems none in this life from pain and death; if man has no soul, he dies as the beast, and the Son of God is no Saviour. Man has wants in common with the beasts that perish. But, like them, he can not be satisfied when those wants are answered.

> "The beasts are happy;
>   They come forth and keep
>   Short watch on earth,
>   And then lie down to sleep."

The word of God makes up man of body and spirit. A separation takes place at death. "The dust shall return to the earth, as it was, and the spirit unto God that gave it." The Bible likens the soul to a tenant in a house which is to come down; but the occupant is not to share in the ruin. The soul is to have a new mansion in which to dwell, "not made with hands, eternal in the heavens."

Our attachment to the living is to the soul, and not

to the casement. Death comes, and you say, "She is gone;" yet the body remains. David, when he wept and mourned, and said of his dead son, "I shall go to him, he can not come to me," had the body near, for it had not been laid in the tomb. But who wishes to embrace the cold clay? We say with Abraham: "Give me ground to bury my dead out of my sight." All that binds us to the living departs when the soul takes its flight. If we love the body, it is for what once was connected with it.

How marked the changes in man from birth till he comes to the full stature of his manhood and the meridian of his powers! Webster sitting on his mother's knee, how unlike Webster shaking senates! Alexander in his nurse's arms, and Alexander, the world's conqueror, weeping that there was but one world to conquer, how unlike! With the marvelous changes that so affect the body and the intellect, the soul remains the same. We can relive our youth at any moment. In the maturity of our strength, we know that we are the same moral beings that laughed and cried in childhood. The man reels under the burdens cast upon him in his youth. In age, seared and withered, we feel the folly and wrongs of early and giddy years. The man who never saw water frozen will not believe that it can be solid as granite and make a highway for elephants. And if death were not the common event of life, no one would believe that man could sleep the sleep that knows no wakening on earth; that he could sleep unmoved on the bier, and be insensible to the cry of children and the agony of the bereaved; that he could know "neither love nor hatred" in that tomb where "their love, and their hatred, and their envy is perished."

We are permitted by that beneficent Father who, when sin made the race subject to vanity, made it also subject to hope, to feel and know through his word that death is not an endless sleep, and the grave is not our home. Man shall die, but he shall live again. "If our earthly house of this tabernacle be destroyed, we have a building of God, not made with hands, eternal in the heavens." Of the condition of those who have fallen asleep in Christ we are not ignorant, neither do we "sorrow as those who have no hope." "Christ is risen from the dead; those also who sleep in Jesus, God will bring with him." "Death is swallowed up in victory." "Death, the last enemy," is destroyed. Dark to a Christian the pathway may be, but the crown is sure. His home on earth may be as mean as the stable in which his Redeemer was born, but he has a mansion above. He may lie at the gate of the millionaire in this world, sore, sad, and perishing; but angels will convey him from his sickly bed to Abraham's bosom. He may suffer here from pain, woe, affliction; but beyond the grave he shall have rest in Jesus. Die when and where he may, be sepulchered in a mausoleum, or left neglected and dead on the field of carnage, or thrown into the sea to sleep among the coral, amid the surges of the ocean, he sleeps well who had "hope of the resurrection of the just." God knows his place of sepulcher, and will call him in the last day. We can bury our dead, and say:

"Thou art gone to the grave—but we will not deplore thee,
    Though sorrows and darkness encompass the tomb;
The Saviour has passed through its portals before thee,
    And the lamp of his love is thy guide through the gloom.

"Thou art gone to the grave—we no longer behold thee,
    Nor tread the rough paths of the world by thy side;
But the wide arms of mercy are spread to enfold thee,
    And sinners may hope, since the Sinless hath died.

"Thou art gone to the grave—but we will not deplore thee,
    Since God was thy ransom, thy guardian, thy guide;
He gave thee, he took thee, and he will restore thee,
    And death hath no sting, since the Saviour hath died."

3.—FUTURE RETRIBUTION REASONABLE.

"Be this my one great business here,
With holy diligence and fear
    To make my calling sure;
Thine utmost counsel to fulfill,
And suffer all thy righteous will,
    And to the end endure."

WE are not left in doubt how the world felt without the revelations of the Bible on the future life. We learn this from the eloquent statement of King David before God lifted the vail, and showed him the condition of the wicked after death. He saw the wicked in triumph, and was envious of their prosperity. Pride compassed them about as a chain, violence covered them as a garment, they had more than heart could wish, their eyes stood out with fatness, they were corrupt, and spake blasphemy against the Most High, yet they had success here, and neither trouble nor plague, as others, and no bands in their death. With such a comment on the divine justice, what use was there to serve God? What profit was there to pray to him? Why should his people tread the bitter way of duty, when a full cup of sorrow was wrung out to them? But when God instructed David about the terrible end of the wicked whom he envied, their short life and certain doom, the fact that their feet stood on slippery places, from which God would cast them down to destruction, he saw how foolish he had been, how ignorant, and how like a beast without reason before the Lord.

God, who has given us hope, has given us a sense of justice. We feel that bad men are not and can not be punished in this life. We want evil men punished. This is not a spirit of revenge, but justice which God has planted in our moral nature. Even the barbarians at Melita had it. When they saw the viper on the hand of St. Paul, they said: "No doubt this man is a murderer, whom, though he hath escaped the sea, yet vengeance suffereth him not to live." We wonder some men live.

We know that few men are adequately punished. We know God is just, and there must be a world in which they shall be rewarded for the deeds done in the body. It is common to the race. It is seen in that certain looking for of judgment, the expiations offered to Moloch, the widow on the funeral pile, and the child thrown into the waters, reveal the fear of future wrath, and show how constantly, though vainly, by the offering of the fruits of the body, men attempt to atone for the sin of the soul. Natural religion allows a future life and punishment, and intelligent deism can not hide or blot it out.

The merest glance at life shows that its distinctions are not according to merit; that woe, misfortune, and trouble come not according to desert. Unless God had intended the sanctions of another world to follow man in the present, he would not have allowed the whole creation, through fear of death, to be made subject to bondage—making life bitter, and death terrible. But as God is just, as men are not here truly rewarded, and yet are to be, that reward must be in some other life, and that life must be after the death of the body.

Such is the character of God's moral government in this life, that it is made impossible to reward men for what they do here, be it evil or be it good. Much of the woe of this life is shared by the innocent as well as the guilty.

The flood that took away the old world swallowed up children who had committed no wrong. The doom that hung over Nineveh would have fallen, and "threescore thousand persons, who could not discern between their right hand and their left." War falls with awful power on the helpless and the innocent, while the authors of national calamity often fatten on the carnage and reap golden harvests from the miseries of the land.

When men are punished in this life, they are punished for crimes against social order and law, and not for sins against God. Many are above law; giants in wickedness that the law can not reach. No man believes that Herod, Nero, Richard III., or Frederick the Great got through with the consequences of their acts—acts that run on for ages—when they were cold in death.

Men can, and do, evade the law. Property saves many. The skill of an advocate comes between a prisoner and his retribution. Men escape by flight to other lands, and live in splendor on their ill-gotten gain.

Conscience demands punishment. It is the candle of the Lord in man. But it may be put out. It can be hardened and made quiet; men are often past feeling. Paul, the mad persecutor, was on excellent terms with his conscience, and the more men sin the less they feel. How monstrous the idea of punishment, under the government of a holy God, that the more men sin the less they suffer!

As the present woe is not the result of merit, the end of justice can not be answered in this life. Are the good exempt from sorrow, and the evil the only ones who are plunged in woe? Do the good succeed, and the evil only fail? Are the good elevated to places of trust and power, and the evil walk solitary in the vale? Not so. Life is mapped out as it was when David wrote. The thought to us is too painful, as we see the wicked prosper and the good drink of the full bitter cup wrung out to them. The tower of Siloam does not fall on the greatest sinners in the city. The blood that Pilate mingled with the sacrifice was not the blood of the most desperate in Jerusalem.

Would God so govern this world if this was a state of retribution, and not of trial? Would God give us a sense of justice, and in no way answer it? Would a good ruler afflict his obedient and trusty servant, and lavish his rewards and honors only on the rebellious? Either there is no God and no justice, or there is a world where all that is dark in the providence of God will be made clear; in which we shall "discern between the righteous and the wicked, between him that serveth God and him that serveth him not." God's judgments here are mere arrests. The old world and Sodom, with the angels that sinned, are still held for trial at the judgment of the great day.

Men live after death. Abel, though dead, yet speaketh. Bad men, in books, traditions, songs, and deeds, live and destroy, long after their natural life is ended. Men relive in their children in the blindness, drunkenness, and madness, that marked their own character.

In this life we are on probation; in the next we shall be fully and adequately punished. And whatever reason or consideration demands a future existence, demands that that existence shall be one of retribution. From any stand-point that we look at this subject, a future retribution is reasonable.

4.—FUTURE RETRIBUTION CERTAIN.

"That day of wrath, that dreadful day
 When heaven and earth shall pass away;
 What power shall be the sinner's stay?
 How shall he meet that dreadful day?"

ALL the considerations that lead to the belief that future life is reasonable and certain, make future retribution reasonable and certain. The certainty of future retribution depends on no one argument, on no one text. It runs through the entire Scriptures. You read it in the preaching of John the Baptist, when he called men to repentance, and told his hearers that the august personage whom he came to announce would, in the last day, burn up the wicked life chaff, in an unquenchable fire. Our Saviour's preaching inspired doubt. Men who heard him asked, "Are there few that are saved?" The first sermon that fell from his lips was full of proof of future retribution. The sermon on the mount closes with that thrilling illustration of a houseless sinner in the day of storm. The Saviour nerved his disciples to suffer "persecution for righteousness' sake," for men could only kill the body; but God could "destroy both soul and body in hell." He warned his hearers against blasphemy against the Holy Ghost, for it "never could be forgiven," but would be punished with "eternal damnation." That sin Ananias and Sapphira committed. He taught his hearers that "the dead in their graves should hear his voice, and come forth" to a resurrection of life or a resurrection of death. He promised his followers, for all their trials and sufferings for his sake, "a recompense at the resurrection of the just." Paul, when he preached, affirmed his "hope of the resurrection both of the just and the unjust." Those who "have part in the first resurrection" are called blessed and holy who are to escape "the second death." That "cloud of witnesses" brought to view by St. Paul, from Abel to John, all lived, walked, suffered, counted not their life dear unto themselves, took joyfully the spoiling of their goods, were tortured, not accepting deliverance, endured scourgings and imprisonments, were stoned and sawn asunder, wandering about on the hillside and in the vales, clothed in the skin of animals, destitute, afflicted, tormented—all these walked by faith in a future retribution. They suffered that "they might obtain a better resurrection." The judgments of God accorded in the Old Testament are used in the New as admonitions, beacons, and warnings to us. They all are referred to a future life, and warn us that men and the "heavens are reserved unto the day of judgment and the perdition of ungodly men." The promises of the Gospel are coupled with conditions which must be kept if the blessings would be secured. Even Paul conceived the case, how even "himself, having warned others," would be a "castaway," and be found at the last "naked, and not clothed upon by the righteousness of Christ." The last sermon which fell from the lips of the Saviour is that recorded in the twenty-fifth chapter of St. Matthew's Gospel. In it we are told that the universe will be summoned to judgment; that Christ, the King of Glory, will sit on his throne, surrounded by his angels, and judge the universe. The judgment will be final, and its awards will be endless life or endless death. Men who read the Bible, and are not convinced that future retribution is certain, such would not be persuaded though one rose from the dead.

5.—PECULIAR FEATURES OF THE FINAL TRIAL.

> "Dread alarms shall shake the proud,
> Pale amazement, restless fear;
> And amid the thunder-cloud
> Shall the Judge of man appear."

THE judgment of "secret things," this will be the peculiar characteristic of the final trial. We read that "God shall bring every work into judgment with every *secret* thing, whether it be good or whether it be evil." St. Paul declares that God "shall judge the secrets of men by Jesus Christ, according to my Gospel." He further states that "there is nothing secret that shall not be revealed, and nothing hidden that shall not be made manifest."

No judgment would be just that had not this characteristic. Human judgment is imperfect, for we do not know men. They can dissemble, and do. God permits it here, else life's work could not be done. Men could not walk, act, or speak, if the secrets of their hearts were open. Many owe all their position to their duplicity, their power to seem to be what they are not. They live in honor, die in peace, are held up as patterns, and the chiseled marble perpetuates the lie to distant times. Education helps this deception. The eye is educated not to quail, the cheek not to blush, the brow to be clear and fair, the hand not to tremble, the nerves not to quiver, the whole man to be cool and self-possessed. The villain wears a comely form, and the sensualist a genteel exterior.

Strip this all off here, lay bare and lay open the real man, let the world know why men do their best things and their worst, and would not our estimate of men be more just, and very different? But who can abide such a revelation here? What families would be clothed in shame and households dishonored! Universal alarm and terror would prevail; business pause, life stand still. Let it be known that a full, complete, and universal exposure would attend the dawn of to-morrow; that all disguise would be stripped off; that the good from the bad would be known, the pure from the vile, the sincere from the hypocrite; all hidden things be read aloud, all secret things known, concealed purposes blazed, physicians' secret books be opened, and deeds of darkness shine as the sun at noonday; and the mere announcement of such a revelation would convulse and terrify this hollow world. Men would fly from the face of man, and call on rocks and mountains to fall upon and hide them. Yet such is to be the final trial. The disclosure is not to be made simply in the presence of men, but of God, of Christ, and of the angels.

Without such revelations men can not be judged

justly at the bar of God—not if they go as they go to human tribunals; not if judged by what men seem, and not by what they are. Here the ungodly seem pious; the sordid, beneficent; the knave, virtuous; the vile, liberal. Concealment here may be needful. It will not be allowed at the judgment. All must come out and be known—the false from the true.

Such a revelation will produce the reverses which we are told will attend a final trial. They will be great, and often where least expected. The least in the kingdom of heaven will be the greater. Martyrs will stand before warriors. Humble disciples will rank above kings. Many on the left, we are told, will be astonished at the place assigned them. Such reverses transpire in this life, as we know men. High in position, they fall; trusted in life, they are dishonored; honored in the church, their robes are stripped off. Their former good position only aggravates their guilt. It is nothing that, up to the moment of exposure, they were held in high repute—that men reposed in them. The revelation of secret things here makes the reversal just.

The judgment of the secrets of men will constitute much of the terror at the last day. Exposure here is terrible. Men abandon their homes and families, flee their country, or commit suicide, rather than endure it. "Spare me, don't expose me," they cry; "pity my family, do not disgrace my children." So, in the judgment, we are told men will cry out to the mountains and rocks, "Fall on us, and hide us from the face of him that sitteth on the throne, and from the wrath of the Lamb, for the great day of his wrath is come, and who shall be able to stand." Few boldly deny future judgment. But few realize what it is, or how they will stand the revelation of secret things before Christ and all his holy angels. This shakes the conscience, blanches the cheek, and makes the death-bed awful. It is the "terror of the Lord." Men are judged each day; they prepare for it, and are content. Could they go to the bar of God as they go to the bar of man, and they would fear it as little, it would be as imperfect. But this calling up and calling out all the hidden man, this blazing the secrets of the soul before the universe, this makes the pulse beat quick and the heart tremble. Standing before him who can read "the thoughts and intents of the heart," and who will "judge the secrets of men," men may well tremble. Now Judas is one of the twelve, then he will dwell in "his own place." Here, tares grow with the wheat, then they will be judged to the fire. Here, the goats graze with the sheep on the same hillside, then they will be separated from the fold. Here, hypocrites and believers walk hand in hand in the same church, then we shall "turn and discern between the righteous and the wicked, between him that serveth God, and him that serveth him not."

Even this terrible truth is not without comfort to the humble child of God, whom the judge has promised to remember and "spare in that day, as a man spareth his own son that serveth him." Tossed on life's stormy sea, misrepresenting and misunderstood, condemned by lying tongues, chained in dungeons, and on gibbets his "record is on high." Clear and bright shall his name shine when God shall judge the secrets of men.

Should this view of the final trial provoke the inquiry, "Who, then, can be saved?" What soul can pass this ordeal? Who can stand when the judge appears? We answer, perhaps but few. Your name and mine may be cast out. Sad reverses may take place where least expected, in the household, and in the church. But fall the blow where it may, "God will judge the secrets of men according to his Gospel." Let the results of this judgment be what they may, it will still be true in that day, that "the pure in heart shall see God."

XXVIII.—THE CITY OF EPHRAIM; OR, A CAKE NOT TURNED.

"Every day hath toil and trouble,
  Every heart hath care;
Meekly bear thine own full measure,
  And thy brother's share.
Fear not, shrink not, though the burden
  Heavy to thee prove;
God shall fill thy mouth with gladness,
  And thy heart with love."

THE city of Ephraim was located near the Jordan, and was famous for its fine flour. When Jesus could "walk no more openly among the Jews, he went into a country near to the wilderness, into a city called Ephraim." When the ten tribes revolted from the house of Rehoboam, and made themselves a distinct nation, they selected the city of Ephraim as their capital. The house of Israel is called Ephraim from this fact, and it is thus known in the Prophets. In the book of Hosea, we have a distinct description of the moral and religious character of Ephraim. One of the most graphic features is taken from the domestic customs of the people, and their mode of baking bread—"Ephraim is a cake not turned." It was the custom of this people to bake their bread on plates of iron heated hot. The dough was mixed and spread on the hot iron plates. To have good bread, it was not only needful to have good material, and to have it well mixed and well laid on, but it must be watched and tended, and when baked on one side the cake must be turned, else one side would be a bitter coal, the other side a sour paste, and neither side would be fit for use.

"Ephraim was a cake not turned." He had great excellencies and great defects. The mixture was good, but spoiled in the baking. There was no balance in his character—no proportion in his parts; and all that was really good was neutralized by much that was evil. It was a choice between a bitter coal and sour dough. His piety was evanescent, like the morning cloud "that passed without rain;" "like the grass on the housetop, that withered before it grew up." He was punctilious in small things, but was not just. He was exact in forms, but destitute of mercy. He was careful in his sacrifices, but he neglected to obey God. He supposed himself holy, but he was self-deceived; his strength was devoured; "yea, gray hairs were upon him, here and there, and he knew it not." Because he was a cake not turned, all his gifts, graces, tithes, and professions were in vain.

Ephraim is a type of men. It is safe to trace men as God traces them; to classify them as God classifies them. The leading sect in the time of our Lord was of this description. As formal men, of exact and punctual ritual service, they had no equal. In religious profession, public devotion, the giving of alms, and the paying of tithes, attendance at the temple, and an ostensible regard for the law of God, they are a model people. But they said and did not. They gave good counsel, but set a bad example.

"Do as they bid," said our Lord, "but do not as they do." It was not wrong for the Pharisees to clean the outside of the platter, for one side clean is better than both sides filthy. It was not a sin to make beautiful the outside of the sepulcher, for both sides need not be repulsive. But as they were both overdone and underdone, they were rejected of God, and called a generation of vipers.

Men now divorce doctrine from practice; and cling to the logic of argument rather than the logic of a good life. Their title to heaven is a sound creed; their acceptance hereafter is their orthodoxy. The Pharisees were sound in the faith, yet were rejected. There is no heresy in hell, for "devils believe and tremble." Men ought to be rooted and grounded in the faith. But a holy life will cause the world to give glory to God. Sound doctrine is indispensable to a good Christian character; so is a skeleton to a horse, and a foundation to a house. But a horse made up of nothing but a skeleton, would be "a vain thing for safety;" and a house with nothing but a foundation, would not be much of a refuge in a storm.

Another class divorce good works from evangelical faith. Many do not think much of "set people." They do not "like doctrinal preaching." "Action, action—good works, noble deeds, these are the great results to which all should look." But action and noble results come only from strong faith. As well refuse to lay well the foundation, and say the "house is the great thing." "Don't waste time in leveling mountains and bridging ravines—send along the train. Don't plant the posts and hang the wires—send along the news." Doctrines may be distorted, and so presented out of their connection as to grow the errors they were sent to root out—as the best of food, taken out of proper proportion, and not properly distributed, produces rickets, deformity, apoplexy, and death. The head of John the Baptist looked better on his shoulders than on the platter of Herodias.

One man wants religion all emotion; another is cold, formal, and without fervor. The standard of action with some is their feelings. They act as they feel like it. A sermon is good, if it stirs them up and makes them feel well. They give not on principle, not to carry on the Redeemer's kingdom, but as the fancy dictates. Some have their religion in their eyes. They weep easier than they act. Others have theirs on their tongue; they talk well, but, like Bunyan's Talkative, they are "saints abroad, and devils at home."

The great failures of life come from the defects that neutralize the good qualities of men. One of the Cunard steamers was on her way to Boston. She was laden with a valuable cargo, and a large number of passengers. The sea was smooth, and, according to the reckoning, the steamer was full two hundred miles from land. All at once the alarm was given, the steamer stopped, the paddles reversed, and it was found that she was not twice her length from sunken sands. The ship was close on to Nantucket Shoals, on which the keel of no vessel ever touched and escaped. The question was, "How came the steamer in that position?" It was found that a small nail, driven in the pilot-house as the steamer left the Mersey, had acted imperceptibly, but surely, on the compass, and turned the ship from her course. So the strength of the vessel, the ability of the commander, and the knowledge of the pilot were neutralized by an insignificant nail.

The want of turning has been the undoing of thousands. An artist has great skill, but small defects harm his success. A doctor is learned, but over against his ability he places some idiosyncrasy that holds him down. A minister may have splendid talents, but want of balance will destroy his usefulness. A mechanic may be a good workman, but so unreliable, so ready to promise, so uncertain to perform, that he can never get ahead. A warmhearted, zealous Christian may be a scourge to his brethren. A son may have talent, and make it void by small errors. A daughter may be brilliant, accomplished, and learned, yet win no friends.

Personal labor and toil may be made useless. A wife may overdo her "talking to her husband on religion," and fail on the side of a "meek and quiet spirit." A parent may say much to a son on the value of personal piety, a Christian merchant may seek by solemn appeals to lead his clerk into the way of wisdom, yet neither be converted, the excellent conversation being controlled by the logic of daily life.

Personal salvation is made difficult from the necessity of a balanced character. Much about religion is not difficult. Men have often professed faith in Christ to gain an end. The Church gathered by Christ and the Apostles held Judas, Ananias, and Simon Magus. Many have been baptized in the name of Christ who will come forth to a resurrection of shame and contempt. It is easy to be impulsive as a rocket, and to explode as gunpowder. It is easy to join in the acclaim of the multitude, and be religious on great occasions. But to be a whole-hearted Christian, well balanced, baked on both sides—to be consistent each day and in each place—to grow in grace as we grow in years, and in favor with God and man as we grow in stature—this makes the way narrow and the gate strait. But so walked those holy men who surround us as a cloud while we run our race. So walked that blessed company "through great tribulation," whom John saw grouped around the throne, having gotten the victory. So must we walk, if we would cross the flood joyfully, and sing with the redeemed around the throne.

XXIX.—THE OAKS OF EPHRAIM; OR, THE FRUITS OF BAD TRAINING.

> "O Lord Jesus! let me not
>   'Mid the ravening wolves e'er fall;
> Help me as a shepherd ought,
>   That I may escape them all.
> Bear me homeward in thy breast
> To thy fold of endless rest."

In a time of civil war in Jerusalem, when King David's life was in danger, and he fled from his capital, and, bareheaded and barefooted, with tears ascended the Mount of Olives, a man came to the captain of the king's host, and told him that the chief conspirator was hanging by his head in the thick boughs of one of the oaks in the woods of Ephraim. These woods were on the east side of Jordan, near to the city of Ephraim, and among these groves the Saviour walked during the week of his passion. The commander-in-chief took darts in his hand, and thrust them through the heart of the leader of the rebellion, and took the body and cast it into a deep pit in the woods, and threw upon it a heap of stones.

Absalom was a favorite son. His father, the king, was burdened with the rule of so mighty a kingdom. The king not only fought the battles of the people, but was also a judge, and the causes to be heard were brought before him. He was their king and their psalmist, their priest and their great captain.

David, for political reasons, made foreign domestic alliances, and did what it would not have been safe for Isaac or Jacob to have done; and in all his life he felt the power of his disobedience to the command of God, and the consequences of marrying heathen wives imbittered all his days.

Of a heathen mother Absalom was born. He had none of that home maternal training that marked Moses, Samuel, and Solomon; none that made the home memories of David so sweet; that implanted such noble principles in Joseph; created the symmetrical character of Nehemiah, and reared the godlike character of Daniel. Better a godly woman in a pagan court than a pagan woman in a religious house. The mother of Absalom in the palace of a king, was wild, gay, dissipated, and without religious fear; she brought with her the pomp, vanity, and pleasure of her father's court. She implanted in the early heart of her son that personal pride, love of display, and ambition that made him the scourge of the nation, and cost him so bitterly in the end, when he hung from one of the oaks of the forest. All the bad deeds so planted bore full ripe fruit, and worked not only his own ruin, but raised a conspiracy against the government, and filled the homes with sorrow and the land with blood.

The king was toiling beneath his burdens. The public weal and the service of God occupied his time and thoughts. His home and the boy were neglected, and he was left to himself, and brought his father to shame. Without the sanctions and restraints of religion, without discipline and firm rule, never broke to the curb or bridle, proud of himself and of his position, Absalom ran on swiftly to ruin.

All the great gifts he had became a curse. He was heir to the throne, but he could not wait for the lawful accession. His unbridled passions hurried him on to great crimes. He had never been made to obey. Why wait for the death of his father? With mad ambition he attempted to seize the crown. He stole away the hearts of the people, seduced them from their allegiance, formed a conspiracy, raised the standard of civil war, lifted his hand against his own father, chased him up the Mount of Olives and over the Jordan, and hunted him among the mountain caves of Judea as though he had been a beast of prey.

He had great personal beauty. "In all Israel there was none to be so much praised for his beauty; from the sole of his foot even to the crown of his head there was no blemish in him." He was a magnificent man—the idol of the nation; his hair was a wonder, and revelation records the care he took of it. But all these gifts hurried him on to the crime of rebellion, and to his death of dishonor in the woods. Beauty, generosity, large-heartedness, a splendid voice, talent, and position, have been the undoing of thousands. Sanctified by religion, they become an ornament of grace. Unrestrained, they sweep us on to destruction. In addition to all his pride, vanity, and ambition, Absalom had that fatal gift that works so much crime among the young of this day—bad company and bad counselors.

We find him a king's son, with rare personal

beauty and rare gifts; his hand early stained with the blood of a near relation; betraying the confidence his father reposed in him, by playing the demagogue and traitor, as he stood at the gate of the city, saying, "Oh that I were judge in the land: I would do justice." How like a demagogue of the nineteenth century is this sleek, smooth-faced, insinuating, handsome boy—creating disloyalty in the hearts of the people—going to Hebron to lift the standard of revolt, under the pretence of service to his God—holding his secret cabals with traitors—spreading treason like a pestilence—pulling down the national standard and raising his own treasonable flag—and, when the treason was ripe, sending spies through all the land saying, "As soon as ye hear the sound of the trumpet, then shall ye say, Absalom reigneth in Hebron." And the continuation of the story—the terror of the king; his sudden cowardice; his tender regard for his rebel son; the courage of the soldier Joab, and his indomitable resolution to crush out the rebellion; the hope of the king that Absalom would escape; his great love for the traitor, for whom he would have given up his government and his life—all this, and more, with slight emendations, will be read as our own history a thousand years hence. Let us devoutly pray that treason may always find as fitting an oak to hang upon as that which Absalom found, and our nation have a successor like Solomon, and a glory even as his kingdom.

Guilt is cowardly. Absalom had a presentiment of his fate. He knew he would be held in detestation by coming ages. "Now Absalom, in his lifetime, had taken and reared up for himself a pillar, which is in the king's dale; for he said, I have no son to keep my name in remembrance; and he called the pillar after his own name; and it is called unto this day Absalom's place." The tomb of the traitor is in the valley of Jehoshaphat. It stands to this day. Dishonor marks it. It is mutilated by the stones cast upon it, for treason and ingratitude are inscribed on its tablets.

Absalom began life wrong. She, who ought to have been the guide of his youth, led him to ruin, and rolled the great curse on those that loved him most. He was brilliant, brave, popular. Used aright, his gifts would have made him the rival of Solomon. What David said to Solomon, God says to all the race: "Know, Solomon, my son, the God of thy fathers; serve him with a perfect heart and a willing mind. If thou seek him, he will be found of thee; if thou forsake him, he will cast thee off forever."

XXX.—THE CRAFTY CONFOUNDED IN THE TEMPLE; OR, HARD THINGS IN THE BIBLE.

> "Thy word, a wondrous guiding star,
> On pilgrim hearts doth rise,
> Leads to their Lord, who dwells afar,
> And makes the simple wise.
> Let not its light
> E'er sink in night,
> But still in every spirit shine,
> That none may miss thy light divine."

A CONSPIRACY was formed against the Son of God. It embraced the chief men of the nation, of all parties. Questions of delicacy and difficulty were framed, with deep deliberation, to ensnare our Lord in his talk, embroil him with the government as a sower of sedition, or with the people as one who attempted to undermine the common faith. The conspirators met him in the temple, and were foiled in the presence of the people. The Saviour returned the attack, and entangled these conspirators, and hoisted these moral engineers with their own petard. Out of their own sacred books he suggested difficulties and apparent contradictions that they could not clear up. These tactics silenced his enemies, who were anxious for no more public discussions with the Prophet of Nazareth.

The conspirators professed to believe the prophets. They held the common faith, that the Messiah was to come, and come from the house of David. The problem proposed by the Lord was this: "As David, speaking by the Holy Ghost, called the Messiah Jehovah, how could he be David's son? How could the son of David be his Creator?" To the Saviour the solution was easy. The God of David "was made flesh, and dwelt among men." But the Saviour did not choose to lift the vail, but left the maligners of the Son of God discomforted and in alarm. He was willing to let men know that there were mysteries in revelation and grace that human reason could neither solve nor grasp.

And this is the spirit of the Bible. Its sacred authors take no pains to conceal the many things in the Scriptures that are above human reason. "The mystery of godliness," as set forth in the word of God, is really the same theme that shut the mouth of the revilers in the temple, is one of the hard things, viz.: that "God was manifest in the flesh, justified in the spirit, seen of angels, preached to the Gentiles, believed on in the world, received up into glory." Times, seasons, and events, which are unknown to the angels, must be so called.

> "Not Gabriel asks the reason why,
> Nor God the reason gives;
> Nor dare the favorite angel pry
> Between the folded leaves."

The Bible is put into our hands with the faults of good men written out in bold characters. It is filled with homely metaphors, so humbling to the so-called learned. It has statements that men call contradictions, with dark sayings, that carping critics detect. And, more than all, it affirms plainly that hard things will be found in the Bible, that men, unlearned and unstable, can, if they will, wrest to their own destruction and that of their followers.

The very need of a revelation presupposes that mysteries and hard things will make a part of it. New and momentous truths will be looked for, and much that is new to man. It was supposed that the proud and unlettered would stumble at these, as childhood stumbles up the difficult hill of science. How little of God or his providence can we understand at all! How poorly we comprehend the immortal soul! The memory, the imagination, the will, the sovereignty of God, and moral agency, who can grasp?

Of the mysteries of body and soul the Bible treats. As we contemplate ourselves, we realize that we are "fearfully and wonderfully made." How can we expect to find, all clear, in that book which treats of heaven and hell, our destiny and the endless life to which we are hastening? At best, we can only "see through a glass darkly." If the great master in Israel stumbled, and marveled at the truth of regeneration, need we wonder that some of the truths of revelation are above human wisdom? What can we know of the incarnation, but to believe and adore? What can we know of heaven and its glories? What can we know of that world where devils and wicked men dwell together, where the worm dieth not, and the fire is not quenched? And what can we know of him who in "the beginning was with God, and was God," and yet "humbled himself to be obedient unto the death of the cross"?

The Bible runs along the whole line of human life, till time shall end. It treats of the Church in all ages, till the end shall come. It talks of battles and victories thousands of years away. Much of it relates to nations yet unborn; to heresies, whose authors do not yet live; to deeds centuries ahead; to battles in which the soldiers that are to fight have not been born. It strikes the keynote of that anthem that shall be sung by uncounted millions on the spot where now the unbroken forest stands, and where the roar of the wild beast and the savage war-whoop only break the repose.

> "His providence unfolds his book,
> And makes his counsels shine;
> Each opening leaf and every stroke
> Fulfills some deep design."

Not alone in the Bible is the path of God one of mystery. All of life is full of it. The man who receives, in nature or grace, only what he knows, will have a short creed. God in nature is even less understood than in revelation. The connection between rain and a blade of grass—between the bloom of the rose and the dead leaves of autumn—between the medicine and the disease, who pretends to understand? We accept the mystery in nature, and say: "Secret things belong to God." How marvelous and past finding out are the mysteries that science set forth? Chemistry and electricity, who can grasp these? It is as easy to wrest nature as it is to wrest revelation. In nature there is no atonement. Obey, or be lost, is the law of natural life. The chemist can blow up his laboratory and himself. He can extract deadly poison from the most luscious fruit. The engineer often goes up with his own petard. The air that plays on the lungs of an infant can sink navies; and the combination of the element of intense flame with another agency gives the world its great boon of water. The mysteries of nature are large; they demand faith, humility, and obedience—as much so as revelation.

Much in the Bible is not hard, but plain, clear, and within the grasp even of a fool. All that relates to duty, and to the terms of salvation, are so plain that a child can "become wise unto salvation." Put the Bible into the hands of Jew or Greek, pagan or infidel, and ask them what it teaches about being saved, and all will return the same answer. One system, one way, is set forth in the Bible. Believe or hate the system of grace, all find that system in the Bible. Much is plain in nature. No matter how unread men may be in the mysteries of science, or the phenomena of the world, they can know enough, if they will, to answer the end of existence. Men ignorant of chemistry can plow, sow, and reap. No man may fold his hands, and refuse to take medicine till he can fathom the mysterious connection between his complaint and the remedy—or refuse to work till he understands the process by which the grain he sows enters into and produces the coming harvest—nor wait till God shall make plain to him all he has chosen to conceal. We have in nature and revelation all the light we need to guide us to-day, and compel us, at the last, to take as a harvest what we have sown. The way back to God, and the conditions of pardon, are so clear that the "wayfaring man, though a fool, need not err therein."

The light of the millennium will change no duty, alter no condition. The path to the throne, the cry of the soul for pardon, the fount in which we wash to become clean, will remain the same till probation ends. Could we analyze the sun, know of what it is composed, and how it shines, we would have to use it as now, and plow and sow to have a harvest. Could we know all the phenomena of nature, we would still have to obey her laws to live. We must keep from the precipice and from poison, or we die. Could we know all the mysteries of redemption, know all that was said and done in that council in which the incarnate Son of God proposed his mission of mercy to man, we would have to apply the blood of Jesus, as now, to be pardoned, and have our names written in the Lamb's book of life, to escape the second death. Could we have stood on Tabor, when Christ talked with Moses and Elias about "his death, to be accomplished at Jerusalem," or see what the angel saw in Gethsemane, who came and strengthened the divine Sufferer, no bond would be canceled, no duty lifted, and men would have to believe on the Lord as now. Till hard and mysterious things in nature arrest human duty; till men refuse to see and enjoy the sun till all is clear about its origin and the source of power; till men live in agony and go down to death, because they put back the kind hand of the physician, and refuse the cooling and healing draught till all the hidden things of medicine and disease are made plain; till hungry men refuse bread till they can comprehend how the sun, air, light, and rain unite in one grain to make food, and in another to make poison; until the mariner, on a dark and stormy sea, refuses to steer by the compass till the mystery of the needle and its attraction is understood; till the sufferer in agony refuses sleep till he can know all of the hidden things of nature's sweet restorer; or a man, falling into the sea, refuses the rope thrown to him till the law of tides is explained to his satisfaction;—till this takes place, no man can be excused or vindicated who refuses to believe and obey the Gospel, because it is full of the deep mysteries of God. No man can wrest the Bible without wresting it to his own destruction, as well as that of all who follow him. Unhallowed hands must not be laid on the Word of God. It is the sacred Mount of God; men die who touch its soil with unholy feet. Nor may men alter the divine law, and change the old light on the dangerous coast of life, or so change it that it ceases to be a guide. Such blind guides lead men surely to destruction.

> Within the sacred volume lies
> The mystery of mysteries;
> Better the man had ne'er been born
> Who reads to doubt, who reads to scorn.

XXXI.—THE SEA OF GALILEE; OR, A WELL-INSTRUCTED SCRIBE.

> "There is a book, who runs may read,
> Which heavenly truth imparts;
> And all the lore its scholars need—
> Pure eyes and loving heart"

Poets and historians join to praise the beauty of the "blue Galilee." It is about sixteen miles long and six wide. It lies in a deep basin surrounded with lofty hills, excepting only the narrow outlet of the Jordan at each extreme. It is subject to whirlwinds, squalls, and sudden gusts, from the hollow of the mountain. But the most furious gales are succeeded suddenly by a perfect calm. The appearance of the sea from Capernaum is peculiarly grand. To the Christian this lake has its highest interest, from its association with the history of our Lord. His youth was passed, and the toil of his manhood borne, within sight of its beautiful waters. The cities and towns that nestled on its shores were full of the presence and mighty works of the Son of God. Cana of Galilee, where he commenced his miracles by turning the water into wine, was in sight of the waters to be rendered so famous in the early history of the Church; with Chorazin and Bethsaida, where most of his mighty works were done. On the glassy bosom of Tiberias he preached many of his memorable discourses. Here he found Simon and Andrew, James and John, and with these formed the apostolic college, taking them from the fishing-boats, and from mending their nets, to be fishers of men. By the side of the sea demons confessed the divinity of Jesus, and, in the herd of swine, were plunged beneath its waters. Turning from the Gentile woman, whose faith wrung a blessing from the Lord, as dogs gather crumbs that fall from their master's table, he came near the sea of Galilee, and healed a great multitude of lame, blind, dumb, and maimed. Obedient to the laws of the land, from the bosom of the sea he drew the tribute-money, rendering to "Cæsar the things that are Cæsar's." When the multitude pressed upon him he left them on the land, while, in a boat, he put off on the sea, and taught them many things. Amid the tempest and the storm he walked on the water, entered the ship, and calmed the fears of his terrified disciples. After his resurrection he showed himself to them at the sea of Tiberias, and bade them cast the net on the right side of the ship. Much of his public ministry was at his home, in Capernaum, a city on the western shore of the sea of Galilee, on the borders of Zebulon and Naphtali.

Going out, as he was wont, to preach the Gospel of the kingdom, on one occasion he sat himself by the seaside. A great multitude were gathered together, and he went into a ship, and sat. The whole multitude stood on the shore. In the presence of his disciples, he spake the discourses contained in the seven parables recorded in St. Matthew's Gospel. Having finished the utterance of these parables, he turned to his disciples and said, "Have ye understood all these things?" He added, "Therefore every scribe which is instructed into the kingdom of heaven is like unto a man that is a householder, which bringeth forth out of his treasure things new and old."

The minister of the grace of God is a scribe who should be well instructed in the things of the kingdom of heaven. The things which he is to know and to teach are contained, in substance, in these seven parables of our Lord. Such a man is a householder, and, as a steward, he is to bring forth out of his treasure new things and old. To him is committed the great truths embraced in that compendium of doctrine spoken by the Saviour on the sea of Galilee, and called by him "these things." The group of parables alluded to contain the doctrine to be preached to men in the name of Christ, the class of hearers that will listen to the Word, its triumph among men, its power on the soul, the value that men will place upon it, the motives from which they would receive it, and the final disposition of those who, by it, were saved or lost.

The first parable is that of the sower. The common, familiar doings of daily life were selected by the Lord to illustrate divine truth. Lifting up his eyes from where he sat, he probably directed the attention of his hearers to a husbandman scattering his seed in the furrows. The relations of the teacher and the taught are set forth by a comparison between the sower and the soil. The design of the parable is to show how truth will be received, and why labor is so often lost. As the sower went forth to sow, so men will go forth to preach. The accidental hearer, or the hearer unprepared for the seed, or the hearer whose heart, like the unbroken glebe or the hard footpath or traveled grove, would not be benefited. The devil catches away that which was sown in his heart, or it is a prey to the birds. Flocks of birds follow the husbandman in the East to gather up, if they can, the seed-corn which he has scattered. The hearer represented by the stony ground is a superficial receiver of truth. His soul is like the soil spread thinly over a rock, without depth, impulsive, warm-hearted, and, for a time, happy. There is always much to try a Christian; tribulation and persecution will come, and the stony-ground Christian will fly from his steadfastness with the first blast of opposition. The hearer whose condition is likened to the seed among thorns, allows the world to strangle the Word. Poor, perhaps, when he heard the Gospel, he permits the cares of life to press, and the riches of the world to choke the seed. He don't apostatize openly, but acquisition is paramount. He has less and less time for God, till business wholly crowds religion out. The good hearer, like the good soil, is broken up in preparation for the seed. He is an honest receiver of the truth, and not a caviler. He receives the Word readily, and receives it with meekness. He stands in the way to get good from the ministry. He labors to understand the Word of God, and to practice it. He will not escape temptation, but temptation will not overcome him. Persecution will assail him, but adversity can not move him. The waves of tribulation will dash over him, but he will be steadfast, and possess his soul in patience. Cares of the world will surround him, but he will keep them, as thorns and weeds, under his feet. The fascinations of wealth will endanger him, but he will make them subservient to his Christian profession.

The second parable is that of the tares. This our Lord himself explains. He is the sower, and the good seed are the children of the kingdom. There is no contradiction between this parable and that of the sower, for the good seed received into the heart constitute the children of the kingdom. Men become the children of God by the reception of truth; by its rejection they become the children of the devil. The field is the world, i. e., the men in the world. The Son of Man goes forth personally, or by his chosen ambassadors, to occupy this field, and make men the children of God. To defeat this purpose is the work of the devil. He can not catch away the Word, but he can corrupt it. He does not do his work openly, but, like a coward, steals stealthily into the field, and, while the tired husbandmen rest at noon, according to custom, he flings in the tares among the wheat, and goes his way. This treacherous custom, this form of malice, was not unknown in the East. Tares resemble wheat, are of rapid growth, and can not be detected till the fruit come. So men will mingle heresies with the seed of the kingdom, and false spirits will appear in the Church. Men will privily bring in damnable heresies, and in the name of Christ preach another Gospel. Sleeping husbandmen often allow this to be done; but, at the last, the great householder will come forth, and separate the tares from the wheat, gathering the wheat into the barn, and burning the tares in the fire.

The parable of the mustard-seed naturally follows the preceding. The mustard-seed is the smallest grain that becomes a tree. This it does, and often so tall that men can ride under it. The fowls like the seed, and lodge in the branches. This emblem is chosen to indicate how great a thing the kingdom of God shall be from so insignificant a beginning. A peasant, born in a small and despised province of Rome, is to give his religion to the world, and rule all the nations of the earth. The power of his truth is to be in the soul—to renovate, restrain, and console. It is to pervade all nations, to control all law, government, and trade, till the very bells of the horses have inscribed on them, "Holiness to the Lord."

The parable of the leaven is unlike the three preceding ones: they speak of the outside or palpable growth of the kingdom; the leaven indicates the secret growth and transforming power in the soul and in the world. There are various kinds of leaven —good and bad—and these indicate the principles which govern men, whether they be the old leaven of malice, or the leaven of truth. It sets forth the power of the Gospel in the heart, as it touches each particle, and in the end leavens the whole lump.

The parable of the hidden treasure introduces us to the intrinsic value of the Gospel. It is a treasure hid in the field, of more worth than all things else. The "topaz of Ethiopia shall not equal it. It can not be gotten for gold, neither shall silver be weighed for the price thereof. It can not be valued with the gold of Ophir, with the precious onyx, or the sapphire. The gold and the crystal can not equal it; and the exchange of it shall not be for jewels of fine gold. No mention shall be made of coral or of pearls." The doctrine of this parable is, that all that seek the Gospel, yield all that stand in the way of its acceptance. If a man can not abandon father and mother, wife and home, if need be, and even life itself, he does not value the Gospel sufficiently to attain it. The parable represents a class of men who are not directly seeking salvation. The husbandman working in his field, and accidentally, as it were, turns up a treasure. So Nathanael found him whom Moses and the prophets did write. The woman of Samaria did not leave her home with the expectation of finding that water of which if she drank she would never thirst. The centurion, at the cross, did not marshal the hundred men to guard Christ to his death, with the expectation of confessing that Christ as the Messiah before the world. Zaccheus, in his zeal to see the Lord, when he climbed the tree, had no expectation that Jesus would be his guest, and come with the blessing of salvation to his own house. But all who desire the Gospel will regard it as the chief good of life, and will sell all that they have to buy it. As the angel said to the Church of Laodicea, the Gospel says to all the world: "I counsel thee buy of me gold tried in the fire, that thou mayst be rich."

The parable of the merchantman seeking goodly

pearls differs from the hid treasure, in that the husbandman found the treasure unexpectedly in the field, recognized its value, and immediately secured it. In the parable of the pearls, the merchantman represents a class who are searching for pearls, the value of which they know. He had a distinct purpose in going out, and resolved to search until he found a treasure. He wanted goodly pearls, and these represent that truth which men are to seek, and which they are to buy, but may not sell. With an earnest desire to accomplish the purpose for which he had left his home, the merchantman "found one pearl of great price, went and sold all that he had, and bought it." How plainly the Saviour is set forth, in this parable, as the great treasure to be secured, to obtain which every other treasure is to be sacrificed.

The parable of the draw-net is unlike the parable of the tares. That of the tares represent the present mixture of the Church; that of the draw-net, the final separation. Men must not root up the tares. God will do so in the day he has appointed. The hauling-nets of the East were of an immense length, some nearly half a mile long, leaded below and corked at the top. These represent the Gospel, which was to go into all the world and sweep the whole earth. The net would embrace all who heard the Gospel, and all grades and all characters. The separation is represented as being made, and made with great deliberation—the good separated from the bad, the clean from the unclean. As our Lord applies it, "So shall it be at the end of the world;

the angels shall come forth, and sever the wicked from among the just, and shall cast them into the furnace of fire: there shall be wailing and gnashing of teeth."

XXXII.—FOOTSTEPS ON THE MOUNTAINS; OR, PREACHING CONSIDERED AS A PROFESSION.

> "Bid the trumpet of redemption
>   Greet our country's farthest shore,
> Boldly claim our Lord's pre-emption
>   For the agonies he bore.
> On the prairie and the mountain,
>   In the valley rich and fair,
> By the river and the fountain,
>   Plant the Rose of Sharon there."

ISAIAH, wrapt in vision, saw the Messiah's day, and spoke of him. On the distant mountains he caught sight of the coming messengers laden with the tidings of salvation. Kings sent couriers, trained to running, who bore messages of importance to distant parts of the realm. The dress of the envoy indicated the character of the message. Black foretold calamity; red indicated war; white promised that the coming herald bore tidings of peace, with the favor of the king. As the herald came from mountain to valley, his very feet appeared beautiful on the hilltop, when his dress told both that he was the king's servant, and that he brought tidings of peace and joy. Applying this to the coming ministry of the kingdom of our Lord, the prophet says: "How beautiful upon the mountains are the feet of him that bringeth good tidings, that publisheth peace; that bringeth good tidings of good, that publisheth salvation; that saith unto Zion, Thy God reigneth!"

St. Paul, in allusion to the office work of the ministry, cites this prophecy, and to the Romans affirms that without the ministry men can not be saved. "Faith cometh by hearing, and hearing by the word of God." "Whosoever shall call upon the name of the Lord shall be saved." But men can not " call on him in whom they have not believed." They can not " believe in him of whom they have not heard." They can not " hear without a preacher." They can not " preach except they are sent." And he states that it was to the ministers who are " called of God as was Aaron," who are put into the ministry as was he himself when God called him by his grace, that these poetic words belong: "How beautiful are the feet of them that preach the gospel of peace, and bring glad tidings of good things."

Preaching is God's great instrumentality to save the world, and preaching was the subject of prophecy. So came the Gospel to men. It was the favorite term by which God's holy servants are designated. Noah is called a preacher of righteousness. Prophets were appointed in the time of Nehemiah to preach in the city of Jerusalem. Jonah was sent to Nineveh to preach the preaching God bade. Moses was preached in every city in the time of Christ. John, the forerunner of our Lord, came preaching the kingdom, and died because of words of faithful rebuke uttered to the ruler. Our Lord began his ministry by quoting the words of Isaiah, that the spirit of God had anointed him to preach the Gospel to the poor. This was his great work till his death. His prayers were few, and those mostly breathed out alone with

God. In all the cities and villages, during all his life, he "preached the Word." The Apostles did the same, as the Acts prove. Paul was so earnest and constant in this, that he would not allow time to baptize; others could do that. He was sent ' to preach the Gospel." His charge to the Elders of Ephesus, and to Timothy and Titus, show the great prominence he gave to the ministry of the grace of God. Warning men, dividing the Word, proving himself a workman not to be ashamed, was this great work. Its importance and his love for it created the strait in which he did not know whether to go to Christ, or abide in the flesh and be of further service as a preacher to the downtrodden Church of his Lord and Master.

Jesus gave his ministers peculiar and honored names. He called them angels, bishops, ambassadors. He called them to follow him; do as he had done; speak by his authority; and, as if he was on earth, beseech men to be reconciled to God. He told them that men would treat them as they treated him, and that it was "enough for the disciple to be as his Master." He promised to magnify his grace in their weakness; and for this purpose he put the sacred "treasures in earthen vessels," that if at any time they felt they were not fit to preach, they should remember that "their suffering was for God." In all things he instructed them to be true to their position. Be finished workmen, and no botch, was the order. With books, with prayer, and with study; with sound and holy converse; laying all the world under contribution; using well the gift God gave them; with tact, talent, and ability; first approving themselves unto God, next to be workmen that need not to be ashamed, in the mode of handling and dividing the word of God.

That small success should seem to attend the profession is not strange. As men count success, our Lord's ministry was not brilliant. The voice of discouragement was put into his lips centuries before he was born. "Who hath believed our report?" The ministry is a success, and has been for eighteen hundred years, tried by any test. With some men all spiritual things are familiar: the Bible is effete, the Church is behind the age, and the world is not yet converted.

Men want immediate results. Break up the soil, plow, sow, and reap in the same day! Men must wait till the millennium comes before "the plowman shall overtake the reaper, and the treader of grapes him that soweth the seed." God's order in nature and grace is that one shall sow and another reap—Paul plant and Apollos water. "Other men labored, and we enter into their labors." So all gifts aid the Church, and each blow struck at the heart of the old serpent, from Abel till now, tells.

Who succeeds in any calling? Thousands fail in trade; and in the so-called learned professions, where one succeeds, one hundred fail. Success is the exception, failure is the general rule. Look at trade—how few go steadily on to fortune from the start! Look at the law—her advocates are many, how few make a name! Look at medicine—in the path of eminence we find only here and there a traveler. Such statesmen as Webster and Clay appear only in a century.

Men talk of the talent there is in Congress. A member need not make but one speech in the session. He can sit in his seat, hear the debates, read, reflect, select his subject and his side; commit what he writes, or print it without commitment or delivery; be goaded on to do his best by rivalry, interest, or fame; and that one speech will make him famous. It is a well-known historical fact that Mr. Webster was aided in his great speech in his debate with Hayne by the talent on his side of the Senate. He made excellent use of all the material he found at his hand. Now give the preacher a theme that will rock continents and command the attention of the world, and let all civilized nations look on as the encounter takes place; put all the ministry at work to aid in the preparation; call on poets and philosophers, antiquarians, orators, and professors; make them all hewers of wood and drawers of water to the preacher, and if he had brains he would make a fair sermon.

A minister has but one theme. His sermons must be many, and delivered in the hearing of men who come up from the fierce warfare of life, and who are accustomed to sharp debate and good oratory. Sick or well, in funds or out, with his own infirmities or woe pressing on him, he must do his duty, prepare the weekly sermon, and present something ever fresh and novel. Let the Congressman, lawyer, or orator be put in such a position, and how eloquent would they be?

To all the trials incident to the ministry men are called. They are peculiar to each sect. As with the individual so with the preacher, "each heart knoweth its own bitterness." A man who visits California must round the Cape or cross the plains. One who would visit London must cross the seas. The question of going is for each to consider; but all who go must take all the burden that attends the journey. So is it with the ministry. To change denominations is to change the place and keep the pain. What our Lord and his Apostles endured must be the common lot of all who preach. We wish human nature was better; but it is not. It is hard to feel the want of appreciation—a whole week spent on a good sermon, at which men nod and women go to sleep. But Paul preached to drowsy hearers. The trump of doom would not keep some people awake. We are told that one sleepy hearer under a sermon of St. Paul's fell from a window and broke his neck. We have the apostolic gift of putting people to sleep, but not the gift to mend broken necks. I have seen men asleep on the jury under the impassioned eloquence of Rufus Choate. I saw a man fast asleep during the singing of Jenny Lind, and he paid twenty-five dollars for the choice of seats.

The ministry, as a profession, has its advantages. It gives a noble social position from the start. What the merchant, the lawyer, the doctor obtain by years of toil, the student of divinity takes at a bound. With his first sermon he has his social status, and he at once takes rank with the highest in the land. While the pay of the preacher is not large, its average is far beyond that of any other profession. A few merchants make fortunes; the mass live on moderate incomes. Men in the medical profession work their way up, and live for years, most of them, on less than the average of pay given to the ministry. Few lawyers live on their profession. In that overcrowded calling a few have splendid fees, but the great mass get small pay, and are indebted to outside labor for support and competence. The support of the minister is not always what it should be. But it more than averages with the incomes of the people, while the children of the preacher rise, generally, to position and wealth, and have a name among the merchant princes of the land. The character, discipline, and education of the parsonage is an inheritance of value among men.

The preacher is one of a great army that is to conquer the world. He is called to a work for which the blessed Son of God laid down his life. How godlike his theme—what blessed fruit his eye is permitted to see—what comfort he imparts! He is an ambassador from the King of kings. He has friends among the noblest and the best of the race. He has the confidence of men in their happiest and saddest hours. He is called in to bless the cradle, hallow the bridal altar, and weep over the bier. He knows men in their best and worst estate. He knows how hollow the world is—how little gold and crimson can do for a wounded spirit. He knows what it is to point an alarmed sinner to the cross, and catch the death-song of a soul saved by grace. And, more than all, he knows that if he is faithful in his calling, "when the Chief Shepherd shall appear, he shall receive a crown of glory that fadeth not away."

XXXIII.—THE CORINTHIAN REVILERS; OR, THE GUILT OF IGNORANCE.

> " Ambition, stop thy panting breath!
> Pride, sink thy lifted eye!
> Behold the caverns, dark with death,
> Before you open lie;
> The heavenly warning now obey,
> Ye sons of pride, go watch and pray."

THE city of Corinth was the capital of Achaia. It was populous and rich beyond that of any other city in Greece. Its worship was vile; its people, full of pride, effeminacy, and lasciviousness. Into this city St. Paul came to preach the Gospel. He abode with a Jew named Aquila, and wrought with him in the same craft, for, by occupation, both Aquila and Paul were tent-makers. The Jewish synagogues being opened, Paul reasoned in them every Sabbath, and persuaded the Jews and the Greeks. Some believed on Christ; and marked reforms attended the ministry of the word. Out of a corrupt, dissolute people, Paul gathered an humble and devout Church, who were washed and sanctified in the name of the Lord Jesus and the spirit of God. In his letter from Philippi to the Church in Corinth, he alludes to a few disturbers of the peace and revilers of authority in that Church, who turned the grace of God into lasciviousness, the communion into a bacchanalian revel, and introduced disorder into the assembly of the saints. These smarted under the rebuke of those in authority. They were contumelious and restless. They denied even the authority of Paul to rebuke them, and expressed a doubt whether he were really an Apostle. But St. Paul was not shaken in his purpose to enforce wholesome discipline. "The things I write unto you," he said, "are the commandments of the Lord. But if any man be ignorant, let him be ignorant." He would not condescend to enlighten such ignorance, for it was willful. He would not attempt to guide such erring, for the persons of whom he wrote had opportunities to know, and yet would not learn. Light was given, but they closed their eyes and pretended they could not see. He was an Apostle; his commission was ample. He was an ambassador; his credentials bore the signet of the King. They could reject him, but at their peril, for they must settle for such rejection with God. Men unreasonably ignorant must be so, and take the consequences.

God deals with us as rational creatures. He reasons with men on momentous things. Redemption and pardon are commended to us with the invitation: "Come, now, let us reason together with the Lord." St. Paul, when addressing Felix, on the solemn themes of eternity, "reasoned of judgment to come." There is a point beyond which reason and argument do not go. If men resist the light they have, and demand an unreasonable amount of proof, God does not gratify them. He says, "If any man be ignorant, let him be ignorant."

Our Saviour so conducted. Sometimes he answered men, sometimes he did not. He was tenderly solicitous to make Nicodemus understand the terms of admission into the new kingdom; but to his foes, on another occasion, he stooped down and wrote in the sand, deigning no other reply. Full of affectionate words to Martha, about the resurrection of the dead; at the bar of Pilate, he was dumb, insomuch that the governor marveled. Silent, when adjured to speak; then overwhelming his foes, so that no man durst ask him a question.

Governments are bound to give a fair publicity to the laws of the land. Some mode must be adopted by which men may know what is law and what is not. Governments are not bound to accumulate proofs till all the vile and all the carping are satisfied. They are not bound to see that all the people know the law. It is enough that all may know what is right and what is wrong. On each person, then, the responsibility is thrown. Nations act on the maxim, old as civilization, and printed for ages on the fly-leaf of statute books: " Ignorance of law, which all are bound to know, is no excuse to any man." Suppose a robber should plead, at the bar, that he never read the law by which he is arraigned; or the incendiary, that he did not see the law made that forbids the crime of which he is charged; or the person arrested for assault and battery assert that he was not convinced that the statute which forbid his beating his fellow-men was really binding on him; or the murderer set up as a defence his conscientious scruples to the law. Would such pleas be allowed? Would the trial be stayed? Would pardon be issued on such a plea? The answer would be that of Paul to the Corinthian revilers: "If any man be ignorant, let him be ignorant." If men will not know the law that is within their reach, they must take the penalty.

Men can not hold their own unless they hold it legally. To make a contract that can be enforced, a deed that will convey title, or a will that will protect widows and orphans, men must do it according to law. No matter how sincere the parties may be, nor how much better their own way may appear, they must act legally, or not at all. If they do not know, "the law is open, and there are deputies."

This rule holds in religion. For the instruction and the salvation of men, the ministry and the Church are, to a degree, responsible. But not to the extent that scoffers suppose. The world has a responsibility in this matter as well as the Church. It is not the duty of the ministry to track cavilers around the globe, satisfy all their scruples, answer all their quibbles, and make truth clear to those who will not come to the light lest they should be reproved. If one class must take heed how they preach, the other must take heed how they hear. On the unfaithful watchman the blood of souls will be found; but a faithful minister may say, "I am pure of the blood of all men." When all that reason and grace demands is done, those that are ignorant must be ignorant.

No other and no higher proof can be given of God's existence and sovereignty than are found in nature and revelation. If a man has studied these honestly and fairly, he must remain ignorant if he is not convinced. The same is true of the class that reject the system of grace in the Gospel. Such a system all find who read the Word of God. And men who wish to hold to the Bible, and yet reject what it teaches, have to alter it. Men who disbelieve the incarnation, find fault with St. Luke. Those who deny the deity of the Saviour, want a new translation of the first chapter of John. Those who deny endless punishment, are troubled with the twenty-fifth chapter of Matthew. If the system of grace held by the Church is not taught in the Bible, it can not be taught. A new revelation, expressly given, could not teach it. If men can dispose of the proof that revelation present, they could dispose of more. If they can alter, and make meaningless the words of Holy Writ, they could, in like manner, dispose of a new revelation.

Saul of Tarsus was, probably, as honest an enemy of the Gospel as ever existed. He affirms that all he did as a persecutor was done through ignorance and unbelief. Yet he regarded his ignorance as a crime. He calls himself a blasphemer—unfit for the ministry—the chief of sinners—not worthy to be an Apostle, because he persecuted the Church. There was light in the world, and he ought to have seen. The Jews did not know the Son of God. Paul says, "Had they have known him they would not have crucified the Lord of glory." But did their ignorance save them from the doom pronounced by their King, whom they crucified? The Jews demanded a sign; pretending to want evidence that Jesus was the Messiah; promising to believe, if a genuine miracle by him was wrought. They were not satisfied, they said, with any thing he had done. They looked on the miracles he wrought on the sea and the land, on the dead and on demons, on the sick and in nature, and they were still ignorant, these miracles not convincing them. A man well known to the Jews was taken sick and died. He was laid in a tomb, in the presence of his friends, and remained in the grave four days. In that hot and sultry clime the work of corruption soon began. The Saviour came from Jerusalem to the house where the dead man had lived. In the presence of neighbors and kindred, the voice of the Son of God called the dead from the tomb, bound hand and foot, with his grave-clothes on. The foes of Christ ate, drank, and talked with him. To deny the reality of this miracle, no one dared. To ascribe it to the devil, no one ventured. The bitter enemies of Christ, in council, with the high priest at their head, admitted that "an open and noted miracle had been wrought," and that no one "could deny it." They added, "if we let him alone, all men will believe on him." They did not accept Christ because of this miracle which he wrought; they did not intend to. From the grave of Lazarus they went to the hill of evil council, to plot the death of Jesus, to make the bargain with Judas, and send the Saviour to Calvary. Their guilt was the guilt of ignorance; they did not "know the Prince of Life," because they rejected the evidence that would have led them to believe. God puts responsibility where it belongs. There is a limit to all labor and all warning. Noah did his duty toward the race, and then entered the ark to escape the flood. Abraham pleaded for Sodom, and then turned and offered his evening sacrifice for his own household. Jesus gave ample warning to Jerusalem, wept over its obduracy, and left it to its fate. Paul wept and warned for the space of three years, and could then say, "I am pure of the blood of all men." The Word of God makes ignorance a crime. Jesus was the great witness, and testified to the truth. God sent him, and commanded men to hear and believe on the Son. So great was the guilt of rejecting him, so wicked and unreasonable was unbelief, that on all such rejecters the "wrath of God shall abide." The declaration of Jehovah is, "If thou art wise, thou shalt be wise for thyself; but if thou scornest, thou alone shalt bear it."

XXXIV.—MOUNT HERMON; OR, CHRISTIAN UNION.

"One family, we dwell in him,
  One church above, beneath,
Though now divided by the stream,
  The narrow stream of death.

"One army of the living God,
  To his command we bow;
Part of the host have crossed the flood,
  And part are crossing now."

LOCATED about fifty miles from the Sea of Galilee is the mountain of Hermon. It is celebrated for its perpetual dews, which are thus explained:—The Sea of Galilee sends forth a continuous vapor. This is wafted northward by the wind. The vapor, coming in contact with the snow-crowned summit of Hermon, is condensed, and flows down the sides in perpetual supplies of moisture. From May to August the dews fall in showers. The tent of the traveler will be drenched. The great plain of Palestine is not far from this mountain, on which great battles have been fought, and the banners of all nations have been wet with Hermon's dew. Hermon is rendered poetically immortal by the sweet psalmist of Israel. He makes it a type of the blessedness of brotherly love: "Behold how good and how pleasant it is for brethren to dwell together in unity! It is like the precious ointment upon the head, that ran down upon the beard, even Aaron's beard, that went down to the skirts of his garments, as the dew of Hermon, and as the dew that descended upon the mountains of Zion; for there the Lord commanded the blessing, even life for evermore." The history of nations and of men is but a comment on these words. Moses sinned at the waters of strife, and spake unadvisedly with his lips. The Apostles, who had the example of our blessed Saviour before them, contended who should be greatest. Nations have had their deep foundations sapped, and been blotted out from the earth, by its power. The beast of the field has made its lair in the palace, wild men have pitched their tents in the solitude of a city, and where the mighty trod silence perpetual reigns, because strife held dominion over the land. The Greeks had one language and one glory. But when they became divided, they fell like the trees of the plain before the Roman tornado. The Swiss were firm as their native hills, which buffeted and defied the storms of a thousand winters. Discord and civil feuds, like a pestilence, spread among them, and they fell like one of their own villages beneath the avalanche. Strife dashes out the cheerful glow of home. A biting word rankles like a poisoned arrow. An hour of contention can destroy the peace of a lifetime. Refinement, elegance, wealth are no compensation where strife is. The bonds of wedded life, under its power, become an iron collar, a chain, a ball on the limbs of a serf. Men of business, in the anxiety and peril common to all, have been stricken down by that insidious foe, that throws down all barriers, and runs, among men who should live in peace, lines of alienation that even death can not remove. It crushes out all the finer sensibilities of our nature. It withers with a touch the ties of brotherhood. The power of a united Church, moving on to conquest and walking in love, in contrast with a rent and contending people, all can understand.

There is much to unite the Church of God, and much real union among the followers of the Lamb. God has given to the Church varied gifts, that all may be suited and all be satisfied. As the landscape is varied, the seasons unlike, each beautiful in its time, so is there variety in the Church. At a public table, one "can eat all things, another eateth herbs." No hungry man would refuse to eat because some things on the bill of fare suit not his taste. Union is the boast of Rome, but nowhere is there less. The Pontiff is annoyed with divisions and strifes that the Protestant Church knows not of. Orders, sects, clans, rivalries, and parties assail his peace. He can not trust his own children, whom, by the lifting of a finger, he can send to hell; for he is guarded to his prayers by foreign bayonets.

On the side of the Church there is union in essentials, and in all things liberty. The Bible is the rule of faith, the judge

> "That ends the strife
> Where wit and reason fail."

The Church is the army of the Lord. Not all cavalry, nor infantry, nor artillery; not the same uniform, not the same regimental flag. But, in time of common peril all rally around the great national banner of the tribe of Judah, and strike for the common cause. Like the billows, many; yet one, as the sea. Like Israel, numerous in families and many in tribes, but one nation before the Lord.

The literature of the Church is vast, varied, incomparable. To what sect does the proud roll belong? What denomination can point to this peculiar treasure of the Church, and say, "This is mine"? Who can claim the men and women, heroes, martyrs, and defenders of the faith before kings, in dungeons, and at the stake, who have died on heathen grounds and on the battle-field of truth? What sect can stand alone, and say, "Behold my trophies, the seal that God is with us, and not with you." Did Bunyan, the glorious old dreamer, suffer for the Baptist or for the Church in all ages? In a quiet village on the Merrimac, a delicate and fragile girl heard the heathen call for help. It cost something to be a missionary in that day. She obeyed the call, and laid her life down at her Master's feet. The Hopia-tree under which she rests is a prouder monument than the mausoleum that holds the ashes of Napoleon the Great. Can you hedge up such a life within the bounds of any sect? As well confine the sun to your garden plot, or keep the dew from your neighbor's field. To whom does that haystack belong, on the Berkshire hills, at the side of which Mills and his companions knelt to consecrate themselves to the work of missions, a consecration the Church feels to-day?

But Christian union is not Fourierism. Blending all sects in one would damage, and not promote the cause of true union. Two can not walk together, except they agree. He is the best Christian who has his own church at home, and serves Christ at his own altar, as he is the best husband who is most faithful to his own fireside. A man's bones are best in his own body, and the head of John the Baptist was more useful on his own shoulders than on a platter. When Abraham and Lot could not agree, their friendship was promoted by a separation. We can be hospitable, be friendly, and invite friends to our board. But to our dearest associates there are some things that we do not open to them, there are sacred services to which they are not invited. Men can be bigoted or liberal in any sect. When we love Jesus, we love all that bear his name. But when the devil gets into men, lean or fat, conservative or radical, high Church or low, new school or old, Calvinist or Arminian, open communion or close, down they run the steep hill, at the same gait, into the same sea to be choked. "Let brotherly love continue."

XXXV.—HEBRON; OR, THE MISSION OF CHILDHOOD.

> "Wake, parents in Israel! Oh, wrestle and pray
> That grace to our youth may be given!
> For the hands that in faith are uplifted to-day,
> Shall prevail with our Father in heaven."

HEBRON is one of the oldest and best-preserved cities in the Holy Land, situated about thirty miles south from Jerusalem. It was of note and fame long before Joshua conquered Palestine. It was a citadel in itself, and has been the theater of memorable events. It occupies the site of the ancient Mamre. It holds, in all fidelity, the sepulcher of Machpelah, where the ashes of Abraham and Sarah repose. It formed one of the cities of refuge. David here set up the standard of revolt, and found, in the tough, turbulent, and brave people who flocked to his banner, and in the strength of his position, a defense against Saul. Amid its fortresses Absalom, for a time, defied the armies of his sovereign and father. In later times, it was one of the sacred cities, and the residence of the priests when their services were not demanded at the temple.

Long the oracle had been dumb. God had ceased to commune with men. No outward symbol indicated the Divine presence. Earnestly men prayed and waited for the coming of Elijah, whose advent should precede the expected Messiah. God put honor on two lonely homes. He appeared at the altar of sacrifice to indicate the mission of childhood, its place in the better covenant. He selected the spotless virgin of Nazareth and the aged saint of the order of Aaron—in both instances he reversed the order of nature, and gave the Gospel in the child of Hebron and in the babe in a manger. We place a low estimate on children—on their value and their power. When the things of yesterday pass from the memory of old men, the things of childhood are fresh. In age, sere, yellow, and withered, man feels the power of early and thoughtless days. To no saint, however pure and ripe for heaven, are such words spoken as God has spoken to children. Their mansion is safe. Their song will swell around the throne. In the blood of Calvary they will have a part. To the Christian heart it is a welcome truth, that both John and Jesus come to us, not in the form of men, as the angel came to the disciple on Patmos, but in the form of weak and wailing infancy—weeping tears of childhood, within a manger's mean recess. So near God comes to men. We handle the word of life. We take the Saviour in our arms, as did Simeon, and shout: "I have seen thy salvation, Lord."

The child John had a sacred ancestry. His father was a priest of the order of Aaron, and his mother, also, was of the same holy lineage. Pious were this holy pair, walking in the ordinances of the Lord blameless. Into that otherwise blessed home no child had entered, to cry, "My father," or "My mother." Eighty years had passed over the head of

Elisabeth, and no infant had pressed her bosom. No wail of childhood had been heard in the home of Hebron. Like all Hebrew women, she had longed for a son; had prayed, "Let the Messiah's day be in my day, let him spring from my house." "Come, Elijah, and bring the promised redemption." Her earnest prayer was heard. In a manner little expected by this saint, well stricken in years, God came to her house. At the time of evening sacrifice, while the multitude of the people were praying without, while Zacharias was executing the priest's office, he went into the temple to burn incense. Gabriel stood on the right side of the altar of incense, and the priest was sore afraid. The august visitant calmed his fears, revealed the great mission to which himself and Elisabeth were called, gave him a sign, and departed. The waiting multitude marveled that he tarried so long. As he came out, they "perceived that he had seen a vision." He left the temple and hastened to his home, to prepare his house for the great gift that was soon to cheer and make glad the heart of his wife. As was foretold, the forerunner of our Lord came. The glad news ran through all the hill country. "Neighbors and kinsfolks heard that God had showed mercy to Elisabeth." They crowded into Hebron to look on the unwonted and affecting sight—an infant in those aged arms. A mother's love coursed through that withered frame. Men marveled, and said: "What manner of child shall this be?" So God put honor on this child, for as a little child came the promised Elijah! A few months later, on the straw, in a public stable, weary and alone, with none to comfort her in her great sorrow, the virgin maiden of Nazareth, the last of the royal line, laid herself down in that lowly place, where the babe of Bethlehem was born.

The coming of a child to a young mother is a great event, as great as the coming of the child John to the home in Hebron. It lays all the house under contribution. It sweeps the soul as by celestial fingers. It creates maternal love—a love stronger than death. A little child is a thing of mystery. Bone of your bone, flesh of your flesh. You relive in the eye, the brow, the complexion, and the constitution and temper. Its wail stirs your life-blood. Its coming changes home. It sobers the thoughtless, and tones down the lovers of pleasure; and what sermons, judgments, promises, and entreaties can not do, God often does by the birth of the first-born and only son. "God help me, and that right early," is the mother's prayer, as the responsibility of training an immortal soul presses on her young heart.

The influence of childhood pervades all life. How its confidence, reverence, faith, and love rebuke! How eager to hear! How touching its early devotion! How charmed with the story of the angels, and the child among the stalled oxen! How it fills the ear of an unbelieving parent with strange questions about the unseen world to which the little babe-brother has gone, or some friend has been carried! How it fills the house at early dawn with the sweet hymns about the time "When Jesus was here among men"! Few parents understand their children. If pious, it is expected that they will give up petulance and play, and be at once sedate men and women. The little one has been thinking of the blessed Saviour, and wants to love him. But the idea that children can be Christians and be children still, is one the Church is hard to learn. So the chilling reception their emotions receive, induces them often to hide or suppress them.

Doddridge's mother has been praised for teaching him the great truths of the Word of God from the tiles on her hearthstone. But the mother was quite as much indebted to the son. He would be taught. He compelled the mother to explain and repeat the wonderful stories of the holy men of God, till all were imprinted on his tender memory. President Edwards had his place of prayer at the early age of five years. But the little sympathy he got from home induced him to place his closet of prayer away from the house, where, unseen, he could wrestle with God, and bow his will to his word. In the great revival at North Hampton, in the time of President Edwards, a little girl was converted. No one had any confidence in the reality of that conversion. She was opposed. Her request to be admitted to the Church and the communion was denied—a series of tests applied to her, of years' duration, that would have induced many a mature mind to stumble. But she held on. At last she was admitted, but with great apprehension. Fifty-four years after, she was a true and faithful disciple of the Lord.

During a revival of religion in one of our large cities, a little girl was quite anxious to attend an evening meeting; but it was stormy, and her mother thought it not best that she should go out. A stranger present, noticing the disappointment of the child, said to her as he went out: "My dear, if you can not go to church to-night, you can give your heart to the Saviour at home. Will you do it?" "Yes, sir," said the child, as the company went out. No attention was given to the response, as it was regarded as a childish expression of the little girl. At the close of the meeting the mother found her daughter up. On remonstrating with her, the child said that she had given her heart to the Saviour that evening—that, now she was a Christian, she could not go to bed without family worship, and that she was sitting up for prayers. The next morning she arose quite early, and spent the time in arranging her affairs for the new life on which she had entered—putting away such of her toys as she thought were not consistent with the duty of a Christian, and placing in a conspicuous position her Bible and hymn-book. From the pulpit, a notice was given of a meeting for all who wished to be examined for admission to the Church. Our little convert resolved to go. She out-argued her mother, and put herself on the call from the pulpit to all who wanted to make a profession of the Saviour. She was one of that number. She wanted to celebrate his dying love. But whether she was worthy or not was a question for the Church to decide. So she came into the assembly of the elders. Her answers were clear, and she asserted that on the evening mentioned she gave her heart to Christ. It was suggested that she was quite young to profess Christ, and it might be well for her to wait a little while. Her reply to her pastor was: "You come into our Sunday-school and urge us children to love the Saviour, and to do so at once; and when we do love the Saviour, you tell us we are too young. Will you please tell me how old a little girl must be before she can love Christ?" Her views of Divine truth were clear, and when asked how often she prayed, she answered: "Every time I can get a chance." It was thought best to delay the admission for a while. But on each call for candidates for admission to the Church she appeared. Her importunity at length got the better of the fears of the grave fathers, who thought a little lamb would be safer outside the fold than in it. She was admitted, still asserting that on that night, alone in her room, when a little child, she settled the great question, and gave herself to Jesus. For years, among the humble and earnest workers for the Lord, she has kept in the front rank, and honored her profession by a consistent walk.

Mrs. Van Lennup, the bright, beautiful, and talented daughter of Dr. Hawes, of Hartford, was converted in childhood. Earnestly she longed to confess Christ before men. Impassioned and with tears were her pleadings that she too might celebrate the dying love of her Redeemer. But twelve years of age was regarded as the youngest period at which a child should be admitted to the Church, and she mourned away the years that intervened between her and the table of the Lord. The reality of her conversion was seen in her early consecration to the cause of Missions, and her heroic and untimely death, afar from home, among the people whom she sought to save.

Crowds came for miles around, to see the unusual sight of a lad baptized. For full seventy-three years afterward he witnessed a good confession, and has now a world-wide fame as Dr. Gill, the commentator. Bishop Heber, at five years of age, at sea, was able to comfort his widowed mother, in a storm, by reading from the Word of God and leading in prayer. The piety, literature, and biography of the Church, all pay tribute to the power of childhood.

The soul closed to nearly all tender and good influences, can often be entered by a little child. When eloquent appeals are made in vain, the still small voice of an infant commands attention. Coming home from the place of song, the little songster preaches Jesus in the home of blasphemy and dens of infamy. His impassioned plea: "Don't swear, father, it is wicked;" "Don't bring any more rum into the house;" "Oh! please don't beat mother," tells, often, on the brutal man. "Won't you please go to our Sunday-school, mother, and hear our sweet songs?" has power. Many an outcast has had occasion to bless the teachings of a little child that took them to a place of rest. The lion and tiger yield—a "little child" can lead them. It is the mission of childhood to open the heart, and change the sordid and churlish to open-handed liberality. What no appeal can do, the call of childhood commands. The young parent may seem to need no church, no pew, no Gospel. But the child must be cared for. That must not run wild, and grow up as a heathen. In the gay circle the young bride is the gayest. In the rounds of pleasure, in the largest expenditure, she leads, nor heeds the grave admonition. But the voice of a babe on her arm she hears and obeys.

Great lessons come from the dying cradle of a child. Clear its faith, fearless its tread, and to it the Babe of Bethlehem often gives sweet views of its home in heaven. "It is well with the child." So all feel who love the Saviour. Sweet and safe it sleeps. A clear light shines on its pathway across the dark river, and we almost hear the melody of angels as its soul wings itself away. All that is repulsive, dark, and terrible in death is removed—our children live—and earth has one cord less to hold us. Unspeakable boon! A child in heaven. Heaven seems more real to us—we long to be there. In death, as in life, we may become as little children, and so be sure of the kingdom of heaven.

> "She is not dead, the child of our affection—
> But gone unto that school
> Where she no longer needs our poor protection,
> And Christ himself doth rule.
>
> "In that great cloister's stillness and seclusion,
> By guardian angels led,
> Safe from temptation, safe from sin's pollution,
> She lives whom we call dead."

XXXVI.—NAZARETH; OR, THE HOME OF THE CHILD JESUS.

"Jesus, who reigns above the sky,
And keeps the world in awe,
Once was a child, as young as I,
And kept his Father's law.

"At twelve years old he talked with men:
The Jews in wonder stand;
Yet he obeyed his mother then,
And came at her command."

NAZARETH is situated on the northern part of Palestine, about fifty miles from Jerusalem. The town is built on the western slope of the hills which give their name to the place. From the sharp eminence on which the city stands, the view is magnificent. A panorama of great beauty opens to the eye, embracing the summits of Tabor and Hermon, the bold promontory of Carmel, the Great Sea, and the verdant battle-plain of Esdraelon, and the blue Galilee. Nazareth was the home of Mary, the "Mother of our Lord." In humble circumstances, she lived with Anna, her mother. She was affianced to a man of low estate, but a just man, and one that feared God. Here Gabriel announced to her the high mission to which she was called, in which she should be "blessed among women." From this city she took her toilsome way to Bethlehem, to fulfill the Holy Scriptures, as the place where Christ must be born. From the time of the circumcision till his baptism by John, our Lord was a resident of Nazareth. Here he "grew in wisdom and in stature, and in favor with God and man."

It was not without a purpose that the Son of God had a home among men, and was led by his pure and gentle mother in the ways of the Lord. True, was he God. So was he man. He was taught, he was guided, he was restrained, he was trained, and so became for us an example. As he was led, so we may lead our households in the fear of God. How gladly would we have looked in upon that home—with what interest have read that chapter that held all his child's acts from his birth to the scene among the doctors in the temple—and how, as he was "subject to his parents," we would gladly have followed him, step by step, till he went into the synagogue on the Sabbath, and stood up to read! Untold interest would have clustered about the hearthstone of that cottage home in Nazareth; around the virgin and that Holy Child; about his pastimes, his plays, and companions; and, more than all, about that face on which anger cast no shade, and sin plowed no furrows. God gratifies no idle curiosity. Few are the pencil-strokes that indicate the home-training at Nazareth. Few are the facts that we can gather that throw light on the inner life of that holy household. But how suggestive these hints! They tell us how he grew in favor with God and man.

Both Mary and Joseph were eminently pious. Joseph was a just man—just to his own home, just to his own wife. Many are pious abroad. "Talkative was a saint abroad, but a devil at home." A piety that will bear the undress of life and the searching eye of kindred will do for both worlds. Mary was a spotless virgin. Submission to God's will, looking along the dark path she was to tread, led to the reply to Gabriel: "Behold the handmaid of the Lord. Be it unto me according to thy word."

The Sabbath was hallowed in that home. On the opening of his ministry at Nazareth, we are told that Jesus went into the synagogue on the Sabbath day, as "his custom was." If any family could have dispensed with the Sabbath, it was that of Joseph. Their Son was wise in the Scriptures; he astonished the doctors of the law. Both Mary and her husband were learned in the Word of God. Yet the Sabbath was kept. Public worship was attended—not only the great festivals of the nation, but the ordinary ministration of synagogue worship. Personal holiness, knowledge of God's Word, the wisdom and spotless purity of the child Jesus, made social worship and public prayer and praise a necessity and a privilege. It is easy to be religious on great occasions. But true piety walks the lowly paths of duty, and is faithful in that which is least.

Joseph and Mary put value and honor on the altar service by supporting public worship. The altar and the temple looked to the people for support. The family at Nazareth were poor, yet gave they out of their penury. At the circumcision the offering was small, but it was made. Jesus knew well the sacrifices of the lowly; and it touched his heart, and called up the sacrifices of his own blessed mother, when the widow threw in her two mites as an offering. David would not accept from Ornan the Jebusite the gift of Mount Moriah, nor the cattle, nor the implements of labor on the threshing-floor, for sacrifice. He made the purchase of all, declaring that he would not offer "unto the Lord of that which cost him nothing."

> "That man may last, but never lives,
> Who much receives but nothing gives;
> Whom none can love, whom none can thank,
> Creation's blot, creation's blank.
> But he who marks, from day to day,
> In generous acts his radiant way,
> Treads the same path the Saviour trod,
> The path to glory and to God."

Subjection to authority and submission to just restraint was an element of the training under which the child Jesus was brought. From the presence of the Elders of Israel, where he was found after a three days' search, he went to Nazareth, and "became subject to his parents." He obeyed his mother at once, without hesitation or debate. Mary knew all that Gabriel had said about the future of her son; she knew his divine paternity; yet she commanded him, and he obeyed. "He learned obedience as a son." What a contrast between this home and that of Eli, whose "sons made themselves vile, and he restrained them not." We have little of the government of Mary. So we have more Absaloms than Samuels, more Phineases than Timothies in our religious homes. "A child left to himself bringeth his mother to shame."

How will our homes compare with that of Nazareth—in personal piety and fitness to train those whom God has put in trust? Do we pray, with Manoah, "How shall we order the child, and how shall we do unto him?" How are our observance, with our households, of the Sabbath and the regular worship of God? The support we yield to the cause of Christ? The unbending rule of submission, as a principle, in our homes? In the rich, ripe, and glorious fruits as, under such training, the children will grow good as they grow old, wise as they grow tall, and in favor with God and man. Under the sacred power of personal consecration and prayer, the worship of God and the Bible, the bright vision, seen by the Word of God, of a prosperous commonwealth, will dawn on our homes and our nation. "Our sons are as plants grown up in their youth, our daughters as corner-stones polished after the similitude of a palace," and garlands of strength, beauty, and grace will be combined, in elegance and strength, in the national fabric.

XXXVII.—MOUNT OF OLIVES; OR, PASSAGES IN THE LIFE OF OUR LORD.

"Thou sweet gliding Kedron, by thy silver streams
Our Saviour, at midnight, when moonlight's pale beams
Shone bright on the waters, would frequently stray,
And lose in thy murmurs the toils of the day.
O garden of Olivet! thou dear, honored spot,
The fame of thy wonders shall ne'er be forgot;
The theme most transporting to seraphs above,
The triumph of sorrow—the triumph of love."

OLIVET lies on the east of the city of the great king. It derives its name from a forest of olive-trees that once adorned its sides. A few, of great age, still remain. Beneath some of them, it is supposed, the Redeemer oft reposed while he dwelt with men. Olivet was at one time terraced to its very summit, and clothed with fruit and foliage.

It shares with Calvary in the great transactions connected with redemption. The one is identified with the life of the Son of God; the other, with his death. All along the pathway of the Church, from the day that Abel and Cain rambled on its grassy sides till the present, it has been an honored spot.

In full view of the sacred localities around the city, it rises in great beauty, and is full of the life of Jesus. Do we wish to visit Bethany, and look on the tomb of Lazarus? on the eastern slope of Olivet, about halfway down, we find this endeared city.

Would we repose within the inclosure of Gethsemane, and meditate on the agony of the Saviour as the sins of the world felled him to the earth? we shall find the consecrated inclosure at the base of Olivet. Would we recall the days of Solomon's glory and shame—or know him, when in the royal gardens he wandered among the "lilies, the myrrh, the roses of Sharon, and trod walks perfumed with myrrh and frankincense," or meditated on him who was "fairer than the children of men," the one who "dwelt in the garden, the chief among the ten thousand of the children of men"—or behold him over against the temple he built and consecrated in his youth, presiding at pagan altars? we shall find all on Olivet. Here Solomon walked and meditated in the royal gardens, and on one of the high peaks of the mountain committed his great sin against Jehovah.

Olivet was the chosen retreat of the Saviour. At the close of the day he sought its grottos and groves, to be alone with God. Crowds pressed on his pathway, and oft, with his disciples, when he would be away from men, he retired to this mountain. With no home among men, he found his closet of prayer on the hillside; and in the grotto, where oft his ancestors had found refuge, or sought the help of the Almighty, he passed "whole nights in prayer." He could not live without devotion. The multitude, in their zeal to be near him, followed him from place to place, and gave him little time for secret communion. Olivet bore witness to his fidelity to personal duty, when, "arising a great while before day, he went into this mountain to pray." With no roof but the blue dome of heaven, on the mountain sides where his ancestors led their flocks as sheppards, where Abraham worshiped and David sang, David's Son had his bower of prayer. Before the busy world were awake, or the crowd had left their couches of rest, Jesus, "rising a great while before day, went out into this solitary place, and there prayed." The groves of Olivet sheltered his blessed head, while his garments were wet with the dew of the morning. What an example, and what an admonition! We live in a crowded age. The world presses hard on religion. The tide of business surges around our homes, and often puts out the fire on the household altar. Family prayer is neglected, or hurried. The busy Christian has no place and no time for private devotion. The demon of business enters the empty soul, and brings with him seven spirits more earnest than he. In a crowded city, away from home, living amid the multitude, with business and domestic care crowding, how can any one find an hour for private devotion? So pleads the worldly Christian. But let Olivet speak. Let those nights "passed in prayer"—that secret, hallowed spot, visited for divine aid—that "rising a great while before day," plead the necessity and the possibility of prayer amid the most trying circumstances. Jesus never had a home. He was ever on the march after he began his ministry. He, too, could have pleaded business, the pressure of the great work he came to do, and the difficulty of being alone. He could live without private daily communion with God as well, surely, as any one of his disciples. But, brushing sleep from his eyes, arising from his couch tired and wayworn with the fatigues of the day, "while it was yet night," long before the earliest pencil of light gilded dome or minaret or mountain peak, while the dew was yet on the grass, and his disciples were hushed in repose, then he trod the glittering pearls beneath his feet, to find the altar of prayer and to be alone with God.

> "Cold mountains and the midnight air
> Witnessed the fervor of thy prayer;
> The desert thy temptations knew,
> Thy conflict, and thy vict'ry too."

At the base of Olivet lies the garden of Gethsemane. A solid wall, old as Solomon's time, incloses the sacred ground. Olive-trees, that flourished when David worshiped on Zion, invite the traveler to repose. Trees, beneath which the Redeemer sat on that dark and fearful night in which he was betrayed, still remain. The clinging vine, hanging to the boughs of the old olive-trees, recall the tender words of Jesus spoken on that spot: "I am the true vine; abide in me."

> "He so far thy good did plot,
> That his own self he forgot:
> Did he die, or did he not?

> "He that loseth gold, though dross,
> Tells to all he meets his cross:
> He that sins, hath he no loss?

> "He that finds a silver vein,
> Thinks on it, and thinks again:
> Brings thy Saviour's death no gain?"

Precious to the Christian is Gethsemane, because a greater than Solomon lay his head beneath the olive-trees that, in extreme age, still stand in the garden. The inclosure is nearly square, trodden by no human foot without deep and solemn awe. The base of Olivet witnessed the deep abasement of the Son of God, as the summit did his exaltation. The one saw the craven and timid band betray, deny, and shrink away. The other marked the martial and heroic bearing of the same band, bidding adieu to their ascended Lord with transport, and marching to the city of David as men come to whom victory is certain, as men who draw the sword, under the command of the Captain of their salvation, never to sheathe it till the conquest was complete, till over all the world Jesus reigns as King of kings and Lord of lords.

We can not leave the Mount of Olives without pausing on the center summit, known as the Mount of Ascension. "Christ died for our sins, according to the Scriptures," and the Prince of Life, like common mortals, slept the sleep of death in the tomb. In shame, ignominy, and desertion, guarded by the Roman soldiers, he lay in Joseph's tomb. The three days and three nights in which the Son of Man must be in the tomb drew their leaden steps along, till at last rays of light penciled the horizon and told of coming day. Holy women, who, "according to the commandment, rested on the Sabbath," came early to the tomb, to take and embalm the body of one whom they loved in life, and would not desert in death. Early as they came, they were not early enough to see the great sight. The tread of the king had been heard. Heaven was moved. "This is the day the Lord has made." An angel of the noblest rank came to the sepulcher. His countenance was like lightning, his raiment white as snow. Before him the Roman guard became as dead men. The Roman seal was broken, the stone rolled back, and on it the angel sat, to attend his Sovereign as he came forth, conqueror, from the realm of death. With infinite composure the Redeemer unrobed himself. No haste, no confusion. All the cerements of the grave were taken off one by one, and "laid in order," on that couch, to be hallowed in all ages. As he passed from the tomb, Gabriel bowed low to the Prince of Life, now the first fruits of them that slept.

Onward came the women to the tomb. Accepted will be their offering—told to men and angels at the last day—though Jesus needed it not. Fear and astonishment seized hold of them. The stone was rolled back, even at that early hour. Jesus was gone, and the sepulcher occupied by "young men in shining array." "Seek ye the living among the dead?" they asked. "Come see the place where the Lord lay." They understood him not. All they knew was this, that the Lord was gone. Malice had done its work, lest he should be tenderly cared for by his friends, they said, and this poor consolation was denied.

So the women departed, all but one. She lingered near the empty sepulcher. She had watched its door, during long and weary hours, when the guard surrounded the tomb. But all this watching had been in vain. Yet the place was dear to her still, and she bedewed the soil with her tears. So deep was her sorrow, that she knew not that a form was near her. A voice said: "Woman, why weepest thou?" It was a tender voice, full of compassion. It called forth the affectionate response: "They have taken away my Lord. I know not where they have laid him." Affection is quick in its perceptions. A new light dawned on Mary. This is the keeper of the tomb, she thought. "It was needed. The body had been removed to another spot. The friends of the Crucified will still possess and embalm it, and lay it away in some hallowed grave." Eloquent with love she approached the stranger, and uttered the wishes of her heart in tones of earnest entreaty: "Oh, sir, tell me where you have laid that blessed form! He shall be no trouble to you. He does not lack friends. He shall have a fitting burial, if you will tell me where you have laid him. He was my Lord and Redeemer. I was a poor, outcast woman. He found me in shame. He touched me, and I was clean. He called me, and in mercy pardoned my sevenfold sins. He led me to God. O gardener! tell me where you have laid him, and I will take him away." "Mary!" the stranger replied, in those well-known tones. It was enough. "Rabboni!" is all she can say, as she falls at his feet. Such tidings could not long be withheld from friends or foes. The terrified soldiers spread dismay by the news that Jesus had left the tomb. The Apostles were told that Christ had appeared unto Mary. Two disciples, on their way to Emmaus, had their hearts warmed and their eyes opened, as Jesus "communed with them out of the Scriptures." The eleven met to consider the strange events. In the midst of their company the Lord appeared. In tones that thrilled their souls he said, "Peace be unto you."

Short was the tarry of the Son of God among men. The work he came on earth to do was done. He now took a final leave of the City of David. From Moriah's heights he looked down on coming ages. On Zion's heights he relaid the foundations of David's throne. His army was to be gathered by other hands, and by chosen leaders. Invested with full authority, the conquest of the world was to be achieved. The handful of corn was to shake as Lebanon, and his domain to stretch from sea to sea. All nations shall serve him. Once more he went out of the city of his fathers by the gate of Benjamin, attended by the little band whom he left to conquer the earth. He trod on the spot where the young, bold persecutor would soon hold the garments of them that stoned Stephen. His pathway was through Gethsemane, near the betrayal, and near the site of the agony and bloody sweat. He looked on the ground where, alone, he trod the wine-press for a guilty world. Reaching the place where he wept over the guilty city, he paused and took one long, lingering look, sad, tearful, over the doomed city of his fathers. The pathway trodden by that long cloud of witnesses who, from Abel, preached to and warned the world, lay before him. That lowly grotto, how dear to his heart; how fragrant with precious memories; where he passed whole nights in prayer, and arose a great while before it was day, to be alone with God! Nor did he forget the humble roof of the sisters of Bethany, on which he gazed fondly. Full of choice recollections that cottage-home; fragrant with holy friendships and Christian memories; where so oft he rested and was refreshed. On the middle summit of Olivet he stood, with his disciples around him. To them he gave the great commission to "Go, and preach the Gospel to every creature." He stretched out his hands in blessing, and overshadowed them with the divine favor. And while his hands were lifted over them, while the tones of his seraphic voice lingered in their ears, bodily he went up from them into that bright cloud that received him out of their sight. Jesus, Redeemer, Ascended! bless us with the blessing promised to those who have not seen thee, yet have believed.

XXXVIII.—GADARA; OR, THE PERISHING CLASSES.

"Still near the lake, with weary tread,
 Lingers a form of human kind;
And on his lone, unsheltered head
 Flows the chill night-damp of the wind.

"Why seeks he not a home of rest?
 Why seeks he not a pillowed bed?
Beasts have their dens, the bird its nest,
 He hath not where to lay his head."

GADARA was a city of some renown and importance, lying east of the Sea of Galilee. The name, however, was applied to a large, wild track bounded by Tiberias. The country was inhabited by a wild and turbulent people, and the power of our Lord was demonstrated over one of the wildest and most turbulent of all his class. The Redeemer closed his instructions contained in the seven parables, and, to avoid the multitude, sailed for the country of the Gadarenes. His reception was not auspicious. A madman, possessed with a ferocious spirit, met him near the tombs, where he had his dwelling. He was a fierce, untamed man. He was often bound with fetters and chains; but the chains he plucked asunder, the fetters he broke in pieces. Night and day he was on the mountains and in the vales, making the plains hideous with his crying. He was a sight most terrible, for he cut himself with stones, and lacerated his body with bruises.

The Jews knew not the Son of God. But demons knew him, acknowledged his Godhead, and bowed before him. Afar off the maddened fugitive saw the Son of God approach. How strange the encounter! For he who was denied in the holy temple by priest and people, was, in the wilds of Gadara, acknowledged by a man filled with demons. He shouted the name of Jesus. He uttered his titles and office, saying: "What have I to do with thee, Jesus, thou Son of the most high God? I adjure thee, by God, that thou torment me not." Rejected by men, he was hailed as the divine Son of God by devils. How august the scene! On the shores of the blue Galilee stands the madman of Gadara, one whom none can bind or tame. The splashing oars attract his attention, and he comes forth from the abode of dead men to see who it is that disturbs the solitude of his abode, or who dares set foot on his domain. He comes out mangled and bleeding. His eye rests on the majestic form of the Son of God, and he shouts out his name and titles. Jesus pronounces those divine utterances that bid the legion of demons depart. The madman becomes as a little child under the voice of the Great Teacher. People crowd around to look on the demoniac clothed and in his right mind.

So, in our time, perishing, abandoned, and hopeless classes hear the voice of the Son of God, and live. He came to seek and save such. He was the friend of the lowly and outcast. The woman whose sins were many was forgiven and cleansed, and sat at his fect repentant and forgiven. No person is so maddened by sin that he does not at times have gleams of sanity, in which his wretched dwelling, fare, and dress are seen. Bound by chains of evil, that cut into his very soul; clogged by fetters, that hinder his advance in all right ways; dwelling among the skulls of dead men slain by the hands of strange women and bad men, he knows how sad, how terrible, how infamous his condition is. The prodigal "came to himself," when he cried: "I perish with hunger. The servants in my father's house have bread enough, and to spare." Mary Magdalene, under such gleams of sanity, sought the presence of the Great Physician. How radical her cure! How steadfast her faith! How faithful her watch at the sepulcher! How affectionate her tarry at the empty tomb, where she addressed the gardener, and found in the stranger her Lord and Redeemer!

Into the company of the dissolute and hardened, among men and women past feeling, for whom the people of God have no hope, Jesus comes, as at Gadara, rebuking the demon within, cleansing the soul, and making the abandoned new creatures. The bad song gives way to praises to the Lamb. A sweet solace takes the place of the poisonous bowl. A new passion drives out the demons of gaming and vice. So was it with the noble church at Corinth. It was composed of men who had been, some of them, among the most desperate of their race—thieves, drunkards, extortioners, and idolaters. But, called by Jesus, they were reformed, washed, cleansed, and became trophies of infinite mercy and grace. Saul was one of these desperate cases. So desperate, so far beyond the reach of mercy was he thought to be, that the sainted Ananias argued the point of his conversion with the Lord. This disciple thought that Saul, in his mad attempt to destroy the Church, had feigned conversion to get Christians into his power; and in so doing had even deceived the Great Head of the Church, who commanded Ananias to visit Saul at Damascus.

Jesus alone can cast out demons, break chains and fetters, and clothe the desperate men of the world in their right mind, and place them at his feet. If their sins be as scarlet, he can make them white as snow. The triumphs of the cross are seen in this, that in all ages and climes men mangled and desperate are saved. The world looks on with wonder, as did the people of Gadara, to see such wrecks of humanity restored. No longer a foe to themselves, or a terror and shame to their friends, but happy in their homes, happy in God, and happy in salvation.

How difficult it is to reform, all can tell. Impossible is it without divine aid. The soul must be occupied from which the demon is temporarily driven. If not, and the house is left empty, the exorcised demon will return with sevenfold force, and the "last state of that man will be worse than the first." The reformed man must take unto himself a ruling principle, or he will be repossessed by the great passion he thought was conquered. The demon of gambling goes not out by the power of mere resolution. Let the sudden, the exact temptation come on him, and the man will fall. But if Jesus, the Son of the most high God, commands the demon to depart, he goes out never to return, for Jesus comes into the soul to abide. Down the steep declivity the demon is hurled, and he is choked in the sea. Men may throw down the cup, but the demon lurks around, knowing but too well that, unless Jesus keeps the citadel, the hour will come when vigilance from within will cease, and his opportunity to retake possession will come. He can bide his time. But let divine grace enter the soul, and the tempter departs, never to come back, as when Jesus resisted him on the mountain; and, as then, the angels of God will sustain the tempted one. Men who are victims to lusts, to intense passion, or other strong impulses, resolve to reform. But the master power within them will not loose their hold, nor down at their bidding.

Gadara gives us hope when we labor for the good and the salvation of the so-called desperate and perishing classes. The Holy Spirit can go, and does go, where man will not. No eye but that of the Omniscient can tell when the soul is tender, and where lies the soil in which the seed of truth can be lodged, and not be lost. Not only in the palaces of the great, nor in the homes of plenty, among families educated, refined, and moral, does Jesus walk to heal, to scatter blessings, and save souls. He often leaves the favored homes of men, where truth and ordinances are fragrant and abundant, where men hear with willing ears the words of truth, and, as at Gadara, he seeks the lost, the abandoned, and desperate; he finds them in the wilds of the world, amid the habitations of cruelty and the abodes of death, and, taking souls from the depths of infamy, vice, and despair, bids them go and "tell what great things God has done for them."

> "Oh! methinks I hear him praising,
> Publishing to all around,—
> 'Friends, is not my case amazing?
> What a Saviour I have found!'"

XXXIX.—HOME OF THE LORDLY; OR, HELL A REALITY.

> "Can you stand in that dread day
>   When he judgment shall proclaim,
> And the earth shall melt away
>   Like wax before the flame?
> Sinners then in vain will call,
>   Though they now despise his grace:
> 'Rocks and mountains, on us fall,
>   And hide us from his face.'"

In the closing part of the sixteenth chapter of St. Luke's Gospel there is a narrative of impressive brevity. Drawing near to the close of his public ministry among men, the Divine Teacher, for the first and last time, lifted the curtain that hides eternity from man, and bade the world look on the agony of a lost soul. It is a view that few contemplate and feel at ease. It was presented by one who knew the height of heaven and the depth and horror of hell. He uncovered the dark world of the lost, to teach what it is that makes death to the sinner awful. The picture is drawn by the pencil of a celestial artist. The story told is brief and graphic.

Two men lived in one city. One was very rich; the other, very poor. One was in full and robust health; the other, full of sores. One lived in a palace; the other lay on the rocky pavement, without bed or roof. One sat daily at a sumptuous table;

the other took, thankfully, of the crumbs that fell from the table of the full-fed rich man.

Both died. In the halls of splendor, amid tokens of opulence and grandeur, the rich man laid himself down to sleep his last sleep. He had lived amid purple, fine linen, and abundance. He was sordid and hard-hearted. But all his wealth and magnificence could not keep death from his couch, nor woo angels to bear his departing soul to the paradise of God. The beggar died; died at the gate of the rich man; died in destitution and suffering; but not unknown at the court of the blessed, for angels stood at his dying couch to carry his soul to God.

Both the beggar and the rich man beheld each other in the region beyond the grave. Both had a conscious memory of their life on earth. The rich man knew the beggar as he lay in Abraham's bosom, as well as when he lay at his gate asking a few crumbs of food. Lazarus knew the rich man as well as when he spurned his petition, and laughed to see the vile dogs of the street cool with their tongue the burning fever of his sores. The change of condition between those men was great. Both felt it.

Selfish still, the rich man first of all asks relief from torment. He fed Lazarus with crumbs. He asks at the hands of Lazarus a drop of water. In stern tones justice awakes the conscience of the sufferer by that impassioned sentence: "Son, remember." Relief for himself is impossible. He invokes aid for those dear to him at his father's house, that in their lifetime they may repent, and so avoid that place of torment. But justice again replies that all the living have ample warning and ample space for repentance, and men who will not be persuaded by the warning God has given in this world, would "not repent though one went to them from the dead." And, more than all, the wide gulf that separates the abode of the good from that of the evil forbids escape from hell, or the visitations of mercy from the abode of the happy. The curtain falls, teaching that the doom of the good and bad are irrevocably fixed at death.

This is a history, and not a parable—clear, concise, fearful. I have no doubt that both of the parties named in the narrative were known to those to whom Jesus spake. It has about it none of the marks that attend or distinguish the parables of the Lord. The narrative was told to teach that this life is the only probation of sinners—that their doom is fixed at death—that there is no change of moral character after death—that repentance in one's lifetime, alone, can save from hell—that sinners have memory, consciousness, feeling, and reason, beyond the grave. Our Lord, in whose lips deceit and guile were never found, states that "there was a certain rich man"—that "there was a certain beggar"—that the rich man died and went to hell—that he was in torment—wanted relief—wanted to escape, and could not. And who shall contradict him, and say that his words were not true?

It is a small matter to attempt to show that the primitive meaning of the word translated hell does not mean a world of torment. We have to do with it as it was used in the time of the Saviour, and so it was used. Our word heaven meant the atmosphere —is there no abode of the blessed? Paradise meant a garden—was it to some inclosure on earth the Lord promised to take the penitent thief? Imagery does not change the great truth that runs along the narrative. Heaven has no golden gates, literal stones of diamond and pearl, pavements of real sapphire and gold, walls, rivers, trees, monthly fruits, flowing founts, and harps of gold. But does the imagery of the Bible destroy the home of the saints?

There are two conditions after death—joy and woe, peace and torment. To those conditions went the rich man and the beggar at death. "If one went from the *dead* they would repent." "In thy *lifetime* thou receivedst thy good things." The punishment of the lost is admitted to be just. "Have mercy on me." None but a guilty soul can have mercy shown to it. Punishment to the soul is what flame is to the body. All that we do for man must be done in this life, as there is no passing from the one world to the other, and no messenger comes back from the dead to do the living good.

Around the blessed, clusters in heaven all that is lovely—around the lost, all that is fearful and repulsive. Heaven is the home of the saved, the abode of God, of Jesus, of angels, of the noble men and women of the earth—holy, happy. Hell is the home of lost souls, and is full of rebels; there is found the congregated guilt of the universe, demons, blasphemers, the abominable, and all liars.

Heaven is full of light and joy, glory and song. Hell is full of sadness, woe, and despair. It holds the crime of the world. There the waves of the river of death roll their fearful surges through the dark caverns of despair. There hope comes not, that comes to all, and there sin has no restraint. From that world no voice comes but that of warning—"lest they come to this place of torment"—"send and warn my brethren." It is a call to repentance from hell. It is a warning not to waste the lifetime of probation. It dissipates all hope of relief from future woe. It annihilates the dream of annihilation, for men are tormented in the abode of the lost.

We have Moses and the Prophets, and the added testimony of Jesus, the Sabbath, the Gospel, and the ordinances. We have Sinai and Calvary; Horeb and Bethlehem; the cross and the sepulcher; the pillar of fire and the advent of the Holy Ghost. How much deeper our guilt than that of the rich man, if we repent not in our lifetime, but take up our abode, at the last, in the world of lost spirits!

In this narrative God shows us what estimate he puts on the pomp and circumstance of life. The rich man lay on his stately couch, covered with fine linen, under a canopy of purple, attended by servants impatient to do his bidding. Near his gate, on the hard pavement, festering corruption covering his body—a deformity and a reproach—lay one of God's noble ones. Neglected of men, ragged, hungry, outcast, denied crumbs to which the dogs were welcome, he was known in heaven and honored of God, and an angel sent to bear his soul to Abraham's bosom.

This narrative identifies itself with Gethsemane and Calvary, teaching what it is to be saved, and what it is to be lost—teaches why Jesus made his "soul an offering for sin," and what that agony was in the garden that wrung out the life-blood of the Saviour, and why he was deserted of God on the cross. It was to save men from hell that "he drank the wine of the wrath of God without mixture."

Count not the blood of the covenant an unholy thing. Do not despite to the spirit of grace.

XL.—THE MOUNT OF TEMPTATION; OR, WARNINGS TO YOUTH.

> "Here I live in sore distress,
>   Careful, timid, every hour;
> For my foes around me press,
>   Hem me in with craft and power.
> Not one moment safe can be,
> Lord, thy Lamb away from thee."

THE Mount of Temptation is unknown. For wise purposes it has been kept secret from man, with the times and seasons that the Father hath in his own power. General tradition points to the high summit near the preaching ground of John the Baptist as the scene of the temptation. Our Lord did not throw himself in the way of the tempter. The tempter sought him. He was tempted of the devil, tempted in all points as we are. He had no evil thoughts that could lead him into the wilderness. He had no bad passions to tempt from God. He had no wrong impulses. His bosom never heaved with sinful emotions. The tempest and tornado of temper never coursed through his soul. Crime and secret sins never consumed his spirit. They cast no shade on his holy features. Had our Lord been tempted with evil thoughts, bad passions, or wrong impulses, he would not have fasted forty days to prepare for a conflict he had endured thirty years of his life, which would end only when his natural life should cease. He need not have gone away from home or from men to be tempted at an exact time, when he was so tempted in all places and at all times. He was called to a new and awful conflict, one which, like his death, was not to be repeated, and which demanded intense preparation, and such a control of his own spirit as long days of prayer and fasting would only afford.

Our Lord came to dominion when he came into this world. The god of this world was to be destroyed: he was to be met at the beginning of His conquest: He met him at the close in the garden. If the transactions connected with the temptation are an allegory, then Gethsemane, Calvary, and the scenes of the ascension are allegories, and nothing remains to us: the whole scheme of redemption is as hollow and empty as the sepulcher to Mary when her Lord was gone.

The three great temptations to which Jesus was subject on the mountain comprise the great temptations of life. The first was the unlawful use of power for personal ends. He was hungry. He had power to turn stones into bread, as he had power to turn the rocks of Jerusalem into living sons of Abraham. In later times, he fed the multitude with a morsel of bread, and had a large supply remaining. So he need not have wanted food while this power was at command. Nature called for its exercise, a noble excuse was at hand; why suffer, why starve, when one word could create bread? But so it was not to be. The path he was to tread, the cup he was to drink, all forbade its use for personal relief. Not by bread alone, but by obedience to God, man must be sustained. Impatient at God's plans, an attempt to reach positions by improper ends, a passion for gain or bread that urges one from the honest path, success by unlawful means, all indicate the temptation through which the Saviour walked when Satan said: "Command that these stones be made bread."

Ambition and pride constituted the second temptation—that of the pinnacle. It was a temptation involving great craft. The Jews expected a king—one that should come, as Elijah went, in fire and splendor. Would our Lord accommodate himself to this expectation, meet the excited state of the nation, and dash himself from the pinnacle down to the pavement on which the daily sacrifice was smoking, appear unharmed in the midst of the crowd of worshipers, he would be hailed king by acclamation. In the first temptation, our Lord threw himself on the Word of God. To this the crafty tempter appeals, to show that in such a fall Jesus could meet no harm, as the "angels of God would bear him up, lest his foot should be dashed against a stone." In this temptation Satan puts on the garb of an angel of light. He quotes from the Word of God to make his success complete. The end promised by yielding on the part of the Messiah is his reception by the whole nation. So he would prove himself the Messiah, in that he was unharmed by his fall. The long and almost barren ministry of years unknown, the thorny and bloody pathway of Gethsemane and Calvary avoided, long ages of unbelief spared. "Had they known the Lord of glory," said Paul, "they would not have put him to death." By this descent they would know and receive Christ. The shame and agony of the cross would be unknown. A subtle temptation, worthy of its author! The flesh was weak. But Jesus prevailed. We must do God's work in his way. All attempts to serve God by violating his word, reading the Bible to make it suit our faith or ends, all neglect of his commands, impatience under his yoke, lowering the standard and sinking the cross to hide or excuse its shame, come under the temptation on the pinnacle. Men want heaven, but not holiness; the crown of glory, but not the crown of thorns; the palm of the victor, but not the preparation and toil of the race. All that can turn us from duty repeats this trial.

The pleasures and rewards of sin enter into the temptations on that great and exceedingly high mountain. "Bend the pliant knee, and acknowledge the lord of this world, and all the glory of kings and crowns and dominion below shall be thine." "Get thee behind me, Satan," was the stern rebuke. Satan has many devices. None so fascinating and successful as the promises of good held out to his victims. No realm so fair as that his finger points out. No charm so alluring. His waters are sweet and bread pleasant. His wine is red, and his bed soft. The paths in which he leads seem broad and pleasant and fragrant. Wrecks of men and women in infamy, sons vile and daughters named only with tears, the chains of the prisoners, groans from the dungeons, men in high positions fleeing in the darkness to be exiles among strangers, the saloons of the gambler, the dens of infamy and chambers of the desolate, crowds of lost men and lost women in our streets, tell how successful this temptation is, and what the promise of Satan is worth. In the hour of bitter sorrow that comes to all such, these victims will tell of the hour when, on that giddy Mount of Temptation, the good of this world was pointed out to their excited gaze by the glittering finger of the tempter. How bright and broad the way seemed; how pleasant and exhilarating the secret conference; how as a pleasant dream the flattering story fell on their ear; how, one by one, the barriers fell, and the tempter came nearer the citadel; how promises flattered till the fatal consent was given and the knee bent in homage to the great destroyer; how gorgeous the hue the world wore; its dazzing glory that for a moment flashed before the eye; the hilarity of the new friends created: all seemed to fulfill that which was promised. How soon the dream ended! The sun darkened at noonday. Alone on the dark Mountain of Temptation, and no friend near. How the sin, the shame, and the ruin came suddenly as an armed man!—with no refuge but the grave, and that leading to the judgment and to hell.

The Bible is full of warnings against the wiles of Satan. If he assailed the spotless Son of God, he will all of our race. No man is safe, no home secure. He knows all too well—what weak points we have, what temptations will avail with us, what secret faults are concealed under a bland exterior—and the right book or companion will be placed near us at the right time. Even in the house of God, where divine seed is sown, he flings in the tares and goes on his way. Few realize how mighty for evil is this enemy of souls—how vast his resources—how powerful in his secret workings. His stealth, his godly aspect oft put on, his holy logic, his aptness in using the Word of God, his ability to cover up the bones in his path with roses, all aid him in his conquest. As in the temptation of our Lord, he passes rapidly from one seduction to another. Often, as in this instance, these follow great privileges or especial blessings. From the august announcement thundered in the ears of thousands at the waters of Jordan, " Thou art my Son," Jesus goes forth to be tempted of the devil! From the transfiguration Peter goes down to deny his Master. No one can stand alone. His aid alone can avail us who met and conquered the god of this world, and who, by his holy Apostle, has bid us put on the " whole armor of God, that we may withstand the wiles of the devil."

XLI.—THE PINNACLE OF THE TEMPLE; OR, SATAN NOT A FICTION

> " With names of virtue he deceives
> The aged and the young;
> And while the heedless soul believes,
> He makes his fetters strong."

CHRIST was crucified on Calvary, that "he might destroy him that had the power of death—that is, the devil." "For this purpose the Son of God was manifested, that he might destroy the works of the devil." The existence, power, and talent of the devil is a doctrine of revelation, which teaches that in this world are two antagonistic powers—Christ and Satan. Around these personages center the angels of light and the angels of darkness. The aim of the one is to lead souls to heaven; the purpose of the other, to lead souls to hell. The success of the one gives joy to heaven; the triumph of the other, shoutings in hell. We are not responsible for what men have written or poets sung about the devil. All we know about this personage the Bible tells us. Its account is brief, decisive, clear.

In the Book of God we are told that spirits exist, good and bad; that above us are celestial beings, below us are fiends; that the fiends are legion, and are led by a chief, who has many names, among them the "Prince of this World." His concentration, power, and deadly hate justify the Bible term, "your Adversary." His resolute will, determined opposition, cunning, vast resources, and fatal success in peopling his dark domain, justify his ancient title of "old Serpent," "the Devil." Jesus pronounced him "a liar from the beginning." Paul affirms that he deceived and beguiled Eve by his subtlety, and the Church is in danger from the same wiles that brought woe on Eden. Jude tells that he kept not his first estate in heaven, but was cast down to hell. We are assured that when he will he can "transform himself into an angel of light," and almost "deceive the very elect." He is called a spirit, and works the works of horror, crime, and woe, in the children of disobedience. He is the most industrious of beings, "going up and down the earth" continually, "seeking whom he may destroy." The brief story in the Bible about this satanic being is this: He was an "angel of light" in heaven, the "Son of the Morning," and "Lucifer" was his name. Pride was the sin through which he fell, for St. Paul states that "pride was the condemnation of the devil." He was in Eden, and brought death into the world, and all our woe. He tempted Job and David. He took the Son of God into his power for a moment, and led him into the Mount of Temptation. He laid his hand on Peter, and made him speak the devil's own language. He entered into Judas, guided him as he made the bargain of blood, and he betrayed his Lord, and hastened him to confession, suicide, and hell. He is a spirit. He can assume any garb—that of an angel of light—a man—or a reptile. He is finally to be cast into hell, with whom and his angels wicked men are to dwell, when assigned to the left hand by the final Judge. Because we have such an adversary, who is omnipotent, seeking our ruin when least expected, like a venomous serpent in a bed of roses, we are exhorted to sobriety and vigilance, commanded to put on the whole armor of God, that we may escape the wiles of the devil, and evade him who goeth about seeking our ruin like a roaring lion.

This view of the devil is philosophical. There are good spirits; there may be bad. We can not grasp the great mystery of the being of God, as a spirit, without revelation. As plainly the existence of the devil is taught. There are beings above us, there may be beings below us. There are good men and bad. Bad men tempt the good and seek to destroy them. So may it be with bad spirits. We can not see the devil; we can not hear his footfall; we can not look on his awful deformity. But all this makes him more terrible, and our souls an easier prey.

The Bible view of the devil is reasonable. It contradicts no law. It conforms to our reasoning of God. We trace all good to one great agent, why not all bad? We can not grasp the omnipotence and omnipresence of God, nor can we those attributes found in the devil. Reason demands a God as the author of all good; so a devil, as the author of all evil. God has a home in heaven; Satan, one in hell. Make the devil a figure of speech, and the same reasoning will remove the being of God from the universe, and give the world up to atheism.

Reference made in the Bible to Satan must be to a person, and not a principle. That a principle could beguile Eve through his subtlety—talk with God and with Job—go up and down the earth—lead Christ into the wilderness, and tempt one who knew no sin—is simply absurd, and turns the truth of God into a lie. Nor can we escape the truth by calling the devil a disease, for disease could not ask the Son of God, who knew him when men did not, permission to go out into the swine.

A denial of the existence of the devil impeaches the mission and integrity of the Son of God. He came on a mission that was mythical, if there be no devil; for he came to destroy the devil, and bind and overthrow him that had the power of death. He found the faith in evil spirits universal. Demoniacal possessions were as firmly held as faith in the Divine Being. One who could cast out devils, was allowed by the Jews to act by the power of God. He met those demons in the public presence. He talked with them, commanded them, cast them out, and appealed to this power to do so to prove that he was divine. "If I, by Beelzebub, cast out devils, by whom do your sons cast them out? They shall be your judges." When his Apostles said to him, "Lord, even devils are subject to us through thy name," he replied, "In this rejoice not that spirits are subject to you, but rather rejoice because your names are written in heaven." He did cast out devils and control evil spirits as the Son of God, or he did not. If he only accommodated himself to the age, and seemed to do what he did not, he was simply a charlatan, a necromancer, a juggler, and, like Jannes and Jambres, who withstood Moses, he was, what his enemies claimed for him, a "deceiver of the people."

Could we see the devil—know how terrible he is—look on his demoniacal glare—his awful radiance—we should be appalled. Few would be taken captive by him at his will. But his terrible secrecy—his power to transform himself into a being of holiness—his knowledge of the human heart, make him the great enemy of souls. He strews the path of sin with roses. He gilds the ways that lead to death with fascinating brightness. He is around us and within us. For our feet he lays snares, with which he seduces the race. He laughs away our fears. He makes the fatal glass red with beauty. He writes over the doors that lead to hell: "Ye shall not surely die." He promises men good in sin. He stifles conviction, catches away the Word of God from the soul, drives away serious thought, and allures men into the broad road of death. "Be not ignorant of his devices," is the caution of inspiration.

XLII.—THE CITY OF DAVID; OR, THE NIGHT INTERVIEW WITH CHRIST.

> "Abide with me! Fast falls the eventide,
> The darkness deepens—Lord, with me abide!
> When other helpers fail, and comforts flee,
> Help of the helpless, oh, abide with me!
>
> "I need thy presence every passing hour:
> What but thy grace can foil the tempter's power?
> Who like thyself my guide and stay can be?
> On to the close, O Lord, abide with me!

As the time drew near for our Lord to begin his ministry, he attended the great festivals in Jerusalem that brought the nation together. By speech, or by act, he usually called the attention of the people to himself. His mother and kinsfolk, a few neighbors from the fishing villages and boats around the Sea of Galilee, a handful of fishermen and sailors, really regarded him as a prophet of the Lord. He was too harmless and blameless in his life; of too little account to attract either the reproof or attention of the grand council at Jerusalem, to whom all such matters belonged, and by whose permission prophets, real or pretended, spake by authority.

Our Lord introduced his public life with the miracle at Cana of Galilee, and ran along a line of deeds that attested his divine power. Up to the city "at the passover on the feast-day," in open light, before ruler and worshiper, within the sacred inclosure he announced his claim to be the Son of God. In the midst of the solemnities of the feast he stood up and cried: "If any man thirst, let him come unto me and drink." He daily wrought miracles in the presence of all the people. "Many Jews believed on him when they saw the miracles which he did." But to all outward view, the humble and unlettered were the only parties who accepted the new Messiah. The learned men of the nation, who "knew the law," "who sat in Moses's seat," and were competent to pass on the claims of men, rejected him, after hearing him speak and looking on the miracles which he did. It was their comfort to know that "none of the rulers believed on him," and that the Sanhedrim did not account him to be a prophet.

The Sanhedrim was an imposing body. It was the high secular and ecclesiastical court of the Jews. The Jewish nation was a religious one. The civil was subordinate to the sacred. He who held the highest sacred authority was the highest civil ruler. Seventy-one men of rank and learning, priests, elders, and scribes, composed this council. The high-priest of the nation was its president. The high council sat at Jerusalem. But local courts were held in the chief cities and towns in the land, composed of persons of the same class. Its power with the people was unquestionable. Its robes, on which flaunted portions of the law—its ostentation and sanctity—its professed holiness—gained from the people profound respect. They saluted the members in the public places, and yielded to their authority in all things. Whom the Sanhedrim honored, the people welcomed.

Whom the Sanhedrim denounced, the people derided.

The appearance of the Son of Mary was not welcome to the grand council. The claims of the Great Teacher could not be overlooked. In the secret sessions of that august body, it was conceded that no one could do the miracles that Jesus did unless God was with him. Among the members of the Sanhedrim was a man named Nicodemus. He was attracted by the public life of the Son of God. As one qualified to sit in Moses's seat he knew the prophets, and knew that the fullness of time had come. He was familiar with the events that attended the birth of the remarkable personage who was now filling all the land with his fame—the visit of angels at Bethlehem, the wise men at the manger, Simeon's and Anna's prediction, and the scene at the waters of Jordan. He was probably present at the miracle in Cana of Galilee. He was among the number who believed in his name when they saw the miracles which he did. He was no open disciple. He knew the intense hate that the chief men of his nation bore to the Divine Teacher. He sought an interview with him, and selected the night. He chose this time from "fear of the Jews." Even he would not be spared if his private conference with Jesus was known.

So he came to Jesus by night. He speaks not alone for himself. He represents the chief rulers and teachers of his people when he makes the full and frank confession—" Rabbi, we (all of the Sanhedrim) know that thou art a teacher come from God, for no man can do the miracles that thou doest except God be with him." To the Saviour this confession must have been peculiarly gratifying. To the people, and in the chief seats of instruction, these men professed to hold Jesus in contempt, as one unworthy serious notice, at best as a madman, working miracles, if at all, by the power of Satan. But in their own hearts they knew him to be from God, and so confessed, the one to the other, that no man could do the deeds Jesus did unless God aided him.

But our Lord came not to earth to receive honor from men. The great work of salvation was his, and at once he passes from the confession to the theme of personal salvation. "Am I a teacher from God? Listen then, and obey my word. I have set up a new kingdom on earth. Each man must enter it for himself, as each man must come into this world for himself. No old allegiance, no old submission to any other or former government will suffice. Nicodemus, you yourself, a master in Israel, holy, pious, and devout in the law as you are esteemed, you must be born again, and so come into my kingdom, or you can not be saved." Sovereigns make their own terms for citizenship in the kingdoms of earth. Men pass into the bounds of the sovereignties on such conditions as the governments please to impose. To these terms all must conform, or they can not enter, and can not be citizens of the land. As God spake by the mouth of his holy prophets, he has now set up a kingdom among men. No one has a natural right to enter, for "the unclean shall not pass over it." Aliens and strangers are not citizens of this kingdom, and God has concluded all in unbelief. All are aliens from this new commonwealth—Jews as well as Gentiles. He offers mercy to all. One door is open to all, through which each may enter, and "except a man be born again he can not enter the kingdom of God."

It is quite clear that the new birth is not simple morality—a life outwardly pure and correct—for Nicodemus had this when he came to Jesus by night. His position, as a ruler of the Jews, shows that he was not only a good man, in the common use of that term, but that he was one of the holy men of that day. Besides, it was no new thing to teach the common or higher forms of morality. Moses, in the Law and Prophets, did write of this. There was nothing in this to marvel or to be astonished at. It would be an absurdity to suppose that Nicodemus did not know the duty of morality, or that he would cry out, "How can these things be? How can a man be born when he is old?" If the Saviour indicated that a pure and moral life, and that alone, was all that was needed to enter into the new kingdom and be a subject of the same, Nicodemus had this at that moment. Natural religion taught it. Pagan philosophers had written splendidly on the beauty and power of virtue. On this theory, the conditions on which a sinner could enter the kingdom were already complied with by this master in Israel. But the terms for the new kingdom astonished him. He marveled at them. He could not understand them. Including morality, a pure and spotless life, they held more than this. A man could be a moral man by the code of his fellows, and be an alien from God and be lost! With all the good a natural man could show forth, he would not be saved unless he was born again.

Neither did the new birth consist in an intellectual reception of Christ as the Son of God. Nicodemus had that when the Great Teacher brought home to his own soul the searching truth, "Ye must be born again." This confession of the Sonship of Jesus was on the lip of Nicodemus when he crossed the threshold of the Saviour's abode: "We know that thou art a teacher come from God." It was the avowal of the Saviour as a divine teacher that called out the condition uttered under the solemnities of an oath: "Verily, verily I say unto you, ye must be born again." If this comprehended only a belief in Christ, an intellectual reception of him as a teacher and an exemplar, there was no sense in telling Nicodemus that he must become just what he was at that exact moment, to be saved. The new birth includes a reception of Christ as a teacher. But it includes more.

Neither was it a simple regard for sacred forms—the outward worship of God. In all these matters the Pharisees led the world. The Jews gloried in their punctilious observance of the law. They paid tithes of all they possessed. A master in Israel was complete in the ceremonial services, and in the times and seasons and forms of divine worship. But he was not created anew in Christ Jesus. The law must be put in his heart, not on his garments. He must worship God in spirit, and not in the letter only. The new birth included the forms of worship. It included more.

Nor was this condition a progressive education, the starting a child right, and then aiding by good lessons and good influences, till he come to manhood in the faith. The benefits of early and good training could not be new to Nicodemus, yet he knew nothing of the new birth. Moses, Samuel, Solomon, all taught its value and its power. Years before, Solomon had said, "Train up a child in the way he should go, and when he is old he will not depart from it." All that was taught in the Holy Scriptures on this matter Nicodemus knew. He was a subject of its power. In his own home the law had been taught to him, by the way, in the lying down and rising up, according to the commands of God. But, in regard to the new birth, he could still ask, "How can these things be?"

Pure morality, an intellectual reception of Christ, a regard for sacred ordinances, the progressive power of a sound and good religious training, not only were not new in the time of the Saviour, contained nothing at which men need marvel or account to be impossible, but were wholly unlike the fitness demanded as conditions to enter the new kingdom. All these were gradual, while the new birth was sudden as the coming of the wind, no man telling from whence it cometh. The changes taught by education and kindred instrumentalities were of man; but the new birth was not of man, but of the spirit of God. The coming of those results could be watched, marked, and traced; but the coming of the new birth would be heralded by no sign. The new birth was mysterious in its coming, and marvelous in the fruits. As the twig from the wild olive-tree could bear fruit according to the vine in which it is grafted, and so act "contrary to nature," so was every one that is "born of the spirit."

The Church of God is a kingdom. It has its laws and ordinances, and its own terms of admission. Men need not be citizens of this kingdom unless they choose. But they can be so only on the condition the sovereign appoints. When the Dutch owned the Island of Manhattan they made their own terms of admission. If men did not like them they need not remain. Penn laid down his rules of citizenship to Pennsylvania, and Calvert did the same for Maryland. The Puritans left home, kindred, and the dear graves of their sires, to find a home where they could sing their own songs, have their own customs, and serve God as their consciences dictated. They wanted a holy colony. No man could hold office among them unless he was a member of the visible Church. They came three thousand miles away from men to do as they pleased. The world was wide, and all who disliked their customs could found a colony for themselves. In all this they acted on the principle that they had a right to dictate their own terms of citizenship for their own country.

The sovereigns do the like. Men are banished from some kingdoms, and, without passports, are refused admittance into others. In some nations the conditions of citizenship are quite distasteful. The restlessness of colonies, and the uprising of one part of a nation against the other, all show that the nation will assert its authority over its subjects. Men may call the conditions harsh, absurd, unjust, or unnecessary; yet to enter those kingdoms men must comply with the terms. A man not a citizen of England, Russia, France, or Italy, can be made a citizen; but it must be on the terms the governments impose. Suppose a man who is an alien should attempt to vote. He refuses to be naturalized, to tread the path to citizenship provided by the laws. The officers in charge would say, "You can not vote. You are not a citizen." The alien replies, "I am a loyal man. I obey the laws. I keep out of the state prison. I am better than thousands of men who are citizens. I don't get naturalized, for I don't think much of forms; I am liberal, and allow men to do just as they please. If a man wants to be a citizen, it is well; if not, it is as well. I have no political creed. I stand alone. I don't think much of set people." To all this the stern executors of the laws reply, "You can not vote unless you are a citizen." A man born in one of the British Isles wishes to run for the Presidency. The Constitution demands that the occupant of the highest office in the land must be a native-born citizen. Naturalization could not help him. We make our own conditions. We have a right to do so. So does God's King, who has set up his throne on the hill of Zion.

The new birth is a necessity. No man could be blest in the new kingdom without that change demanded as a condition. Men in sin can not be happy in any state or condition. Men need not be told this.

As well argue that fever consumes and pain racks. Natural religion teaches this, and deism can not hide it. What natural religion and deism can not teach, Jesus does: how men can get rid of the curse and be happy. We have not in us the elements of good. We scramble for the world—wrangle and fight for its honors and wealth—work as a galley-slave, and be mean, hard, unjust, to gain what are apples of Sodom to us, dust and ashes to the touch: we gain faded leaves as the crown for the panting runner, and a sepulcher for the conquering hero. Fitful are our joys, while revenge, malice, hate, and envy blend with all earthly joy. Some Mordecai sits at our gate, and we cry, "All this availeth me nothing." The soul is empty, and bliss we do not know. So let men lie down and sleep the sleep of death, so let them rise and enter the eternal state unchanged, and what would heaven be to them? Who could dwell on this earth with the congregated guilt of this universe? Wake up Sodom, Nineveh, Babylon, and the cities of sin, and bid them stand together, clothe them with immortal vigor, lift up all restraint, and who could live with this mighty congregation of bad men, even in heaven? Who would dwell with the aggregated crime of a large city, on earth. Parts of our city, men dare not tread at night; places in which a moral man would not live with his household for millions, even with all the restraint that law can afford. But remove all restraint from bad men and bad passions, give them the power of an endless life, power to bear an eternal weight of infamy, and who would dwell among them? If heaven is to be an abode of the blessed, in which there shall be nothing that can annoy or hurt, then men must be changed to enter and enjoy it.

The new birth is a change of heart by the Spirit of God. By this agency men believe right, feel right, and act right; the sacred doctrines of the cross are accepted; the affections are turned to God, and the life is pure, prayerful, and holy; haters of God become pious, the impure are cleansed, and the service of God becomes a delight. Men may have a form of godliness; keep the Sabbath and attend worship as men take medicine; walk in the commands of God as pilgrims take to the scourge; do as little as possible, and escape as soon as they can. But to the soul on which God's spirit has operated, the worship is a delight; and wisdom's ways, though straight and narrow, are ways of pleasantness and paths of peace. A new creation is wrought, and to the redeemed soul all things become new.

The children of the kingdom know that the work is of God. Like Saul, they resisted. In a degree, they were mad against the Church, detested the truth, and desired none of its promises. Brought to the light that convicts, and to the Saviour that pardons, each cries out in wonder:

> "Why was I made to hear thy voice, and enter while there's room,
> When thousands make a wretched choice, and rather starve than come?"

How we, each of us, resisted the Spirit's call, and plunged into folly, and sometimes into sin, to drive away the gentle agency that was wooing us to heaven!

Still the Spirit hovered over us. He gently forced us along. We saw a pleading Saviour. Calvary and its sacrifices were too much. The heart broke, and the gentle arms of Jesus took us at the fall. We could only say:

> "Lord, thou hast won; at length I yield;
> My heart, by mighty grace compelled,
>   Surrenders all to thee.
> Against thy terror long I strove;
> But who can stand against thy love?
>   Love conquers even me."

The operations of the Spirit are diversified, but the results are the same. All are not called in the same way. One call Mary heard, and accepted; another, Andrew; and quite another, Nicodemus. Some fly to Jesus in terror, as Sinai's smoke terrifies and the thunder sounds in their ears. Some hear the tender call from Calvary, and run to its grassy sides. Some, like John, in his Hebron home, seem consecrated from their birth. Others, like Obadiah, are servants of God from their youth.

Two forces are at work among us. The one to draw men to heaven, the other to hell. All that calls us to God, that convinces us that we are sinners, that creates within us new desires, that fastens the mind on some great truth, that makes us know that we have a soul to save, that would bid us fly to Jesus and have life, come from the Spirit. How sad it is that so many resist and quench the Holy One, till he depart from the soul! How full of peril the condition of many who have had their summer-day, who have felt their guilt, and been not far from the kingdom! They have passed through revivals and judgments; been afflicted, their idols taken from them, and their hopes dashed to the ground. But in vain! They resist the Holy Spirit till past feeling, and pass on to the judgment.

It was not thus with Nicodemus. A silent, a secret searcher for truth; honestly avowing the difficulties in the way of accepting the great truths of the kingdom; confessing fully all he believed of Jesus in the interview he sought; we find him, at the last, a hearty and bold disciple, who had obtained the great gift of God, and become a child of the kingdom. In the council of his nation that adjudged our Lord to the cross, he was not consenting to his death. He bore the taunt of his associates, as being a disciple of the "Deceiver," because he demanded, "Doth our law judge any man before it hear him and know what he doeth?" And when, at the last, that the holy Prophets might be true, and Jesus laid "with the rich in his death," Joseph, that just and honorable councilor, who had waited for the kingdom of God, "went boldly to Pilate, and craved the body of Jesus." At the cross he was joined with Nicodemus, who in this hour of shame openly avowed the Lord, and jointly they "took the body of Jesus and wound it in linen clothes, with the spices, and placed it in a new sepulcher, wherein was man never yet laid."

XLIII.—THE WELL OF SYCHAR; OR, SECTARIANISM REBUKED.

"See, from Zion's sacred mountain,
 Streams of living water flow;
God has opened there a fountain,
 That supplies the world below.
  They are blessed
 Who its sovereign virtues know.

"Through ten thousand channels flowing,
 Streams of mercy find their way;
Life and health and joy bestowing,
 Waking beauty from decay.
  O ye nations!
 Hail the long-expected day."

BETWEEN the mountains of Ebal and Gerizim lies the valley of Sychar. It was that parcel of ground which Jacob added to the inheritance of Joseph; "I have given thee one portion above thy brethren, which I took out of the hand of the Amorites with my sword and bow." The valley is located a short distance from the city of Samaria, about forty miles north from Jerusalem. Sychar was fertile, sheltered, and well watered. Here the shepherds led their flocks into fertile fields. This valley suggested the beautiful figures introduced into the twenty-third psalm: "The Lord is my shepherd; I shall not want. He maketh me to lie down in green pastures. He leadeth me beside the still waters." The custom of the shepherds to go before and lead their flocks induced the Great Shepherd to say, that the "shepherd, when he putteth forth his own sheep, he goeth before them, and the sheep follow him; for they know his voice, and a stranger they will not follow."

The whole region around Sychar is one of matchless beauty. Above the valley rises Mount Gerizim, the sacred mountain of the Samaritans. Here Abraham halted under the oaks of Moriah; Simeon and Levi completed their terrible revenge; the twelve sons of Jacob were buried; and Jacob dug the well of which he drank and his cattle, on the side of which Jacob's nobler son rested from the noonday fatigue. It was in this valley that Joseph sought his brethren, to ask for their welfare; and from Sychar he was carried into Egypt as a bond-child. Few spots have changed as little. The valley is fertile, and sheltered, as in the olden time. On all the hills around men tend their flocks, in garb and manners not unlike the sons of the patriarch. Jacob's well still remains. Women come from the city to draw water for the noontide meal. The Ishmaelite merchants pass along, ready to buy another Joseph. And to-day, men going from Judea to Galilee "must needs go through Samaria."

Great truths come to us from Sychar. Jacob's well was there. It was a gift of great value to men whose wealth consisted in flocks and herds. Men relied on cisterns to keep their cattle alive in the time of drought. But often these were broken, and the flock perished. But a well of water was a great boon, and it was especially so of the well at Sychar.

It was deep, dug out of a firm rock, and held many feet of water, and was never dry. How impressive a type of him who gave men "that living water of which when men drank they thirsted no more"!

It was the site of Joseph's sepulcher. He died in a royal palace, at the age of one hundred and ten years. But he loved Sychar and the rural home of his fathers. Its green vales and its fertile mountains floated before his eye as he sat beneath the crimson canopy in the palace in Egypt. He loved it to the last. "God will appear to you in good time," said the dying ruler. "He will bring you out of this land; and when you depart, ye shall carry up my bones from hence," and he took an oath of his brethren. One hundred and forty-four years after, God redeemed the seed of Jacob with a mighty arm from the bondage of Egypt. The bones of Joseph were not forgotten. Moses took them sacredly into his own care. He carried them through the Red Sea. He bore them carefully on during the long march of years in the desert, and gave them in charge to Joshua, when the lawgiver went up on Nebo to die. Joshua bore them to the promised land. And when the enemy had been conquered, so that the dead should not be disturbed, two hundred and eight years after Joseph's death, his bones were religiously sepulchered in the valley of Sychar.

On either side of Sychar stand Gerizim and Ebal. On these mountains Israel ratified the law that God gave them, and took the oath of obedience as the blessings and the curses of the law were read in their hearing.

Gerizim is the holy mountain of the Samaritans. Near Samaria it rises fertile and commanding. It is separated from Ebal by the narrow valley, and the strong voice of a man can be heard from one mountain to the other. The mountains of Ebal and Gerizim, with the valley that divides them, was the scene of that magnificent national spectacle when the law was publicly accepted by the tribes of Israel. Joshua moved on to Sychar with the people he had led through the waters of Jordan. The ark of the covenant, with all the symbols of Divine presence, attended by the priest, the elders, the officers of Israel, with banners and with music, assembled in the valley of Sychar, near Jacob's well, and near the sepulchers of those holy men whom the people so revered. Six of the tribes went up on Mount Gerizim, six on Mount Ebal. The blessings of the law from Sinai were read from Gerazim, and all the people shouted, " Amen." The curses of the law were read from Mount Ebal, and to them also the people responded. Thus the law was publicly ratified by the nation.

At the base of Gerizim, Israel assembled to make Jeroboam a king. Ten tribes revolted from the house of Solomon. They broke the covenant they made on Gerizim, and broke it within sight of the spot that witnessed their vows of allegiance. They abandoned the union which God gave them, which had been a wall of fire to them, trampled down the national banner under which they had marched to victory, and went out to found a confederacy of their own, and to better their condition. Their end is enveloped in an oblivion as profound as that which hides from mortal eyes the tomb of Moses. The guilt was made the more damning in that they accepted the law, and bound themselves to obedience.

On Gerizim, Manasseh reared his temple when the nation became twain, and blended the worship of idols with that of the true God. The Samaritans contended that Isaac was offered on their mountain, and not on Moriah, and that, as the blessings of the law were all pronounced on Gerizim, the fathers worshiped in that mountain.

Bigotry and exclusiveness have a rebuke at the well of Jacob. A Jew asks water at the hand of a Samaritan. No idle quarrels or sectarian disputes could engage the attention of him who came to save the souls of men. It was immaterial to him where the fathers worshiped, if men have in them that well of water springing up into everlasting life. Men need not rely on mountain or altar, if destitute of living faith. Neither in Gerizim nor at Jerusalem could men miss of acceptance, if they worshiped God in spirit and in truth. To this great truth let the Churches bow, and honor and walk with all who are united to the great Head of the Church.

XLIV.—THE RIVER-SIDE PRAYER-MEETING.

"God of the pure in heart,
　Here by the river
Gladness to us impart,
　Thou the kind Giver.
Under no lofty tower
　Bow we to thee;
Hear from our leafy bower,
　Thou Holy Three."

St. Paul was on his way to Europe to preach the Gospel in the British Isles. A vision called him to Macedonia. He sailed to "Philippi, which is the chief city of that part of Macedonia, and abode in the city certain days." He heard of a river-side prayer-meeting held on the Sabbath, and resolved to attend it. The story of that meeting is touchingly told by the Apostle himself. "On the Sabbath day we went out of the city by the river-side, where prayer was wont to be made; and we sat down and spake to the women which resorted thither." Those few holy women held the germ of a noble Church. Seldom was a sermon preached to a more unpromising audience; seldom one with greater results. A woman of wealth was among the company at the river-side. God opened her heart, and she opened her house to St. Paul, and made him welcome under her roof.

A significant introduction had the Gospel into Philippi. Its success aroused the enmity of bad men. St. Paul and his companion were arrested, beaten with many stripes, cast into prison, their feet made fast in the stocks, and the jailer charged to "keep them safely." But God was with his servants in the dark, inner prison-cell. Joy welled up in their hearts, songs of praise enlivened their captive hours, and the unwonted sound of prayer and song within that abode of guilt and woe rang through the corridors, and the "prisoners heard them sing." But, more than all, God came for their release. Earthquakes shook the "foundation of the prison;" "all the doors" were flung wide open; "every one's bonds were loosed," and all could go where they pleased. "The keeper of the prison, awaking out of his sleep, and seeing the prison-doors open," "supposing that the prisoners had fled," would have killed himself. But he was saved. He believed on the Lord Jesus Christ. He took from the jail those servants of Jesus, washed their stripes, and would have borne them himself, if he could. He set meat before them, was baptized that same hour of the night, and "rejoiced, believing in God with all his house."

From a few women at a river-side prayer-meeting a vigorous Church arose—one not ashamed of the Gospel, one not ashamed of St. Paul, a prisoner, a felon in a cell, in woe, want, and sorrow. How dear that little company of devoted women were to the heart of the Apostle, his letter to them, written from his prison at Rome, bears witness. He knew that his days were numbered. He went to Rome to lay down his life for Jesus as a sacrifice on the altar. But the blessed Church at Philippi did not forget him in his cell. Oft they had refreshed him, and were not ashamed of his chains. His prison-home was full of precious memories that he was not forgotten by the company whom he first met at the river-side; and the "things which were sent had the odor of a sweet smell, a sacrifice acceptable, well pleasing to God."

To these steadfast and loving friends he details, as seldom he chose to do, his private grief and personal sufferings for Jesus's sake. He knew he would find sympathy among the devout women, as his Saviour had found tender and enduring friendship from the sisters of Bethany.

But lest the Church, full of sympathy and love, should unduly grieve, he turns away from the matter of personal trial and persecution to the glory and humiliation of Christ, and what it cost him to redeem a world. Lest they should too much mourn over the privations and trials of St. Paul, and so become disheartened in the great race on which they had set out, he caused them to know that he would not have it otherwise than it was with him. He knew that he could never again see their dear faces in the flesh, but he would cheer them in their sorrow with the truth that life and death were one to him; for to live was Christ, to die was gain.

A doomed man, in chains and in disgrace, with the sands of his life counted, and soon to run out, yet of cheerful and heroic courage, living only for Christ, and anxious only that his dear children should not be cast down, a noble character was St. Paul. The same in disgrace and honor, in prison and in palaces, in want and in abundance, in shipwreck and on land, among treacherous brethren and warm-hearted friends, in stripes and in woe—one aim was his, to live for Christ; one end, death, and that gain.

How strong his Christian principle, how glorious his hope, that could lead to the debate whether he would live or die! How complete his consecration, when he could wish not to end the warfare, and end the conflict by endless joy and endless life; when he could elect to abide in the flesh to do longer the work his Master gave him to do, and to comfort his poor saints with his presence and eloquence!

St. Paul had preached the Gospel in many cities. Kings and nobles had waited on his eloquence, and counted him a man mad with knowledge. His bearing and eloquence had swayed the hearts of his royal auditors, as the tempest sways the lofty pines. To audiences composed of the most subtle, learned, and refined of all the earth, he had spoken of the things of the kingdom, as well as to women of reputation and men of renown and position. But none of these were so dear to St. Paul as the Church that came forth from that river-side prayer-meeting, and to these he unfolds his character, aim, and purpose as he does to no others.

He informed them that as no one excelled him as an enemy, so no one ought to as a friend; that personally he wanted to quit this rugged warfare, for to him death was gain; but such was his love for them and the feeble and despised Church of God, that he wished to abide in the flesh.

How brilliantly shines out his great motto, "The love of Christ constraineth us"! He loved the Church because Jesus loved it and bought it with his precious blood. He was willing to live to serve it. What a blessed consecration! "It is more needful for you that I abide in the flesh." And this incomparable man could hesitate between honor and infamy, wealth and deep poverty, freedom and heavy captivity, that he might wait on the Church of the Lord.

What other than this could we expect from such a man? When God called him, his answer was: "Lord, what wilt thou have me to do?" It was an honest question, put with an honest purpose. His submission, when made, was whole-hearted. To the end of his eventful life he kept the aim steadily in view. He had much to give to the Church when he joined it. He was a man of renown before his conversion, of the order of nobility in his nation, a Hebrew of the Hebrews, a scholar brought up at the feet of Gamaliel, and his future was brilliant. He gave all he had to give to Christ, and henceforth his life was hid with Christ. His hope was never dim. He could say everywhere: "I know in whom I have believed; he will keep what I have committed to him till that day." All the work he could do for his Master or his Church must be done in this life. Here Christ was traduced, and here alone human testimony would avail to honor the Son. Here Jesus was abased, and here only could men exalt him. Men had power in their rejection to influence others; here the power of example for good could alone be felt. Men have an opportunity to take sides in this life, and put themselves under the banner of the Lord of Hosts. Beyond this world such testimony would not avail. Men then could not change sides, if they would. No such example would be needed. Demons knew and bowed to the Son of God when he was vailed in his humanity; and the public sentiment of heaven is all right, and the inhabitants of that bright world know full well who Jesus of Nazareth is.

Nor can men do good to the Church when it has passed the flood. We can minister to Jesus in this life, in the person of his suffering saints. We can visit prisons, give the needy aid and relief, lift the cup of cold water to the parched lips of the perishing, and fill the cell or the dungeon of those in chains for Jesus's sake with a sweet-smelling sacrifice, well pleasing to God. To the suffering child of God, as well as to St. Paul, "death is gain." He will find no prisons, no scourges, no chains in his Father's mansions. He will not beg for a cup of cold water, for in that world men never thirst. No homeless ones will be there, for each will have a home in the palace of God. None will be hungry, for the redeemed feed on angels' food. No tears will be shed, no trials borne by those who stand on the sea of glass, having gotten the victory. There will be no decaying bodies to support, no feeble knees to be confirmed, for all will be strong, and able to "bear an eternal weight of glory."

> "No cloud those regions know,
> Forever bright and fair;
> For sin, the cause of mortal woe,
> Can never enter there."

Paul knew this. He was willing, for a season, to

abide in the flesh, to do the great work for which he was called and put into the ministry. He was willing to be separate from Christ. Believing that in this life, only, men could write their names in the Lamb's book of life, he labored to reconcile men to God. He preached, he warned, he wept from house to house and from city to city. Earnest, faithful, tender, he could close his ministry with the belief that, if men perished in their sins, he was guiltless. "I am pure from the blood of all men," he could say.

Such a life we may all lead. Such a life alone is worth living. It is consistent with the highest good of this existence, and its end is peace. Beauty, melody, taste, and song may attend the Christian pathway to the tomb. Talent, position, wealth, and honor can be consecrated at the cross. Without such consecration, gain all that men strive and battle for, few will find the world what they expected. The lofty mountain-peak may tempt the ambition and strength of the dweller in the lowly vale. Arid rocks, sparse vegetation, no flower or fruit, and cold winds, often repay the toil of the climber. Thousands have gained the world, only to find how fearful the price they paid —nothing less than their own soul. Men have arisen from the lowest walks of life to stand among the peers of the land, have built palaces and outshone kings, only to say, as they lay beneath their crimson canopy: "Oh, had I but served my God as I have my king, he would not have left me naked to my enemies." Men have gone out from a rural home, started for the goal that was in the dim future, sacrificed all that was fine, generous, and noble to attain the end, lived a life of strenuous warfare, gained their point, and stood among the great men of the land and age, only to repeat on their death-pillow, and have it read aloud: "The path of glory leads but to the grave." Such was not the end of Paul. As a steward, he was ready for his account. As a warrior, he had fought the good fight. As a panting runner, the goal was near, the crown sure. "For me to live is Christ, to die is gain."

What a blessed record the women, both in the elder and later dispensation, of the Bible, enjoy! And of these the devout women who received Paul and his message at the river-side are good examples. The women of the Bible have an honorable mention in that record of heroic saints, who, as a cloud of witnesses, attend the Christian in his race for glory, and who obtained a good report through faith. How fragrant the memory of Sarah, Rebecca, and Rachel—the mother of Moses, and Samuel—Elisabeth and the Marys—the woman at the well of Jacob, whose attention was arrested and whose soul saved by the great Preacher! How mysterious and gracious the providence of God that made the Moabitish maiden the mother of a long line of kings, from whom the Messiah should come! How striking the coincidence that a humble Gentile maiden, choosing the God of Israel above the gods of her fathers, and cleaving with intense affection to one who had guided her in the path of peace, should originate a line of kings which should be closed by the peasant maiden of Nazareth, who was elected to be "the mother of our Lord," and in all time to be "blessed among women"!

So has it ever been that the blessed Gospel has found its earliest and its fastest friends and its most self-denying workers among the women of the land. The cause of missions in modern times was not fully consecrated in the great heart of the Church, till the graceful and beautiful Christian girl from the banks of the Merrimac consecrated herself to the holy cause; and her honored grave under the hopia-tree in India is a prouder mausoleum than any that can be found beneath the arches of Westminster. The Gospel is the fast friend of women. They owe all that they have to its tender and blessed power; and the piety, devotion, and steady faith of the women of the Church are its proudest memorials.

As the demoniac at Gadara teaches that no condition is hopeless under the power of the Gospel; as the poor penitent who brake the precious ointment on the feet of Jesus shows us that no class are hopeless to whom Jesus speaks; as the woman to whom the Lord said, "Go, and sin no more," bids us look for trophies among all to whom the grace of God shall come—so shall the river-side prayer-meeting bid us look for fruits among the most unpromising assemblies, and from the most hardened soils, stimulating us to sow beside all waters, as we know not which shall prosper—"whether this or that."

"Sow in the morn thy seed,
At eve hold not thy hand,
To doubt and fear give thou no heed,
Broadcast it o'er the land.

"And duly shall appear,
　In verdure, beauty, strength,
The tender blade, the stalk, the ear,
　And the full corn at length.

"Thou canst not toil in vain;
　Cold, heat, and moist, and dry
Shall foster and mature the grain
　For garners in the sky."

XLV.—THE CITY OF THE GREAT KING; OR, THE CORONATION OF CHRIST.

"Enter, incarnate God!
 No feet but thine have trod
  The serpent down:
 Blow the full trumpets, blow!
 Wider yon portals throw!
 Saviour, triumphant, go
  And take thy crown!

"Lion of Judah—hail!
 And let thy name prevail
  From age to age:
 Lord of the rolling years,
 Claim for thine own the spheres,
 For thou hast bought with tears
  Thy heritage."

THE sovereignty of Israel sat on the holy hill of Zion. From the earlier times kings reigned in Salem, the city of peace. Melchisedek, to whom Abraham paid tithes, reigned on Zion's summit before the covenant of God was made with Abraham. With regal splendor the throne of David was here set. After him, in all his glory, Solomon held his court. In that dramatic psalm, the second, David, speaking by the Holy Ghost, said that God has set the throne of his Son on the holy hill of Zion, and declared the decree—made proclamation to all the world—that the throne of the Divine Son was established forever, that all his enemies shall be dashed in pieces like a potter's vessel.

It is the custom of nations to hold a coronation, and, in a public manner, and with imposing rites, place the scepter of government in the hands of the new sovereign. Men are living among us who saw the Father of his Country invested with authority as Chief Magistrate of this nation. Near the site on which the Treasury building now stands, opposite Broad Street, on the balcony of the then City Hall, in New York, Washington stood to take the oath of office. The crowd filled all the streets below. Chancellor Livingston administered the oath, which Washington took in a most reverent manner. The Chancellor added, "Long live George Washington, President of the United States." The assembled thousands caught up the strain and shouted, "Long live George Washington," amid eyes swimming with tears, and the waving of hats and handkerchiefs, and the shouts and huzzas of free men. And this was the first coronation of a sovereign ruler over the United States of America. Kings are crowned. Emperors are enthroned. Presidents are inaugurated. All indicating to the world the setting up of governments that must be obeyed.

In harmony with this custom, God gives notice to all the world, by royal proclamation, to kings and rulers, that his Son is the rightful sovereign of this world, and must be obeyed, that God has set him king on his holy hill of Zion, and rulers no less than subjects are called upon to kiss the Son in token of allegiance, else he will dash all the defiant in pieces.

This regal style is kept up in the Gospels. As a king, Jesus made his entry into his capital. As a king, he, by royal decrees, "proclaimed liberty to the captive." He commanded the prison doors to be thrown wide open. As a king he pardoned offenses against his government, when he pronounced the forgiveness of sins. And of the Son the Father said: "Thy throne, O God, is forever; a scepter of righteousness is the scepter of thy kingdom." The domain of Zion's King is from sea to sea, and from the rivers unto the ends of the earth. All nations shall serve him—the heathen are his inheritance, the uttermost parts of the earth are his possessions—all kings shall fall before him, and he will reign till he has put all enemies under his feet.

Some men are born kings. So was Christ. "This day have I begotten thee King on my holy hill of Zion." The wise men asked: "Where is he that is born King of the Jews?" Some have a kingdom given to them. Charles V. resigned his throne, and gave his crown to his son. God, the Sovereign of the universe, gave the kingdom of this world to his Son. "Ask of me, and I will give thee the heathen for thy inheritance, and the uttermost parts of the earth for thy possessions." Some sovereigns hold their scepters by election. William of Orange was crowned king of England by the decree of the nobles and peers of the realm, who elected him ruler of the land. Christ reigns in the soul, and comes in when invited, and takes his abode with men. Others obtain power and a throne by conquest. So God's King in Zion will rule this fallen world. All his enemies will be put

16*

under his feet. All kings shall fall before him. He shall ride on from conquering to conquer, and overturn kingdoms and nations, till he whose right it is to reign shall subdue all his foes, and his kingdom, like Daniel's rock, "cut out of the mountain without hands," shall break in pieces and consume all other kingdoms—shall fill the whole earth, and stand forever. By birth, by gift, by election, by conquest, God's holy Son is king in Zion.

It is a common thing for bold, bad, resolute men to usurp a crown that is not their own. And this the god of this world has done. We know of sovereigns in exile who claim the throne on which another sits, and who send out a protest, and demand the scepter, from time to time, that their rights may not be lost to them by a seeming acquiescence in the reign of the usurper. Rulers who have a right to the throne are often excluded. Jesus "came to his own, and his own received him not." As a ruler, man rejected him, saying, "We will not have this man to reign over us." And, on assuming the throne, the King will say, "Bring hither those, mine enemies, that would not I should reign over them, and slay them before me." Rulers are changed, deposed, and die. A decree goes forth, giving the world official notice that a sovereign has died and another enthroned in his stead. God thus sends out official notice to all the rulers, kings, and usurpers, that Jesus is king, that to him all must bow the knee or be destroyed.

How would the rulers of the world relish such a decree? Suppose a man in exile should demand the throne of Victoria, Napoleon, or Alexander? We know the Bourbons demand the throne of France, and men contest with Maximilian the sovereignty of Mexico; so men dispute and resist the claims of Jesus as king. The Word of God represents the kings and rulers of the earth in conclave, setting themselves, and taking counsel, against Zion's King; threatening to break his bands asunder, and cast away his cords from them—defying God and his anointed. God looks on that conclave, that defiant resistance to the scepter of his Son, that rage, that insult, that malice, and the resolve of that confederacy, not with fear and alarm—trembling for the safety of Zion's King—but with derision and laughter. The concentration of hate and defiance is not deemed worthy of a serious thought: "He that sitteth in the heavens laughs; the Lord has them in derision."

Zion's King was crowned for conquest. His kingdom has been on the increase since the angel of God broke Pilate's seal and rolled back the stone. "Of the increase of his government and peace there shall be no end." "The stone cut out of the mountain without hands" is swelling with gigantic proportions, and will fill all the earth. The handful of corn on the top of the mountain has taken root, and will soon be a forest, "which shall shake like Lebanon." The leaven is in the meal, and in due time will leaven the whole lump. The wrath of man can hasten the universal spread of the Gospel, but can not delay it.

Resistance to the rule of Zion's King is presented

to us under the most favorable circumstances for success. Kings, rulers, nobles, with strength, greatness, and power combine. These band together, and concentrate their hate and might against the young King, whose kingdom, weak and small, seems an easy prey, while these foes have all the appliances of success. Suppose many powers should combine to attack the throne of France, what conclaves, councils, combinations, alliances, and concentrations would be made!

Men and kingdoms have combined against the Lord, and against his anointed, since the coronation of the Son of God was proclaimed—combined when they were mighty and the friends of Jesus were a feeble flock. More than once they supposed King Jesus and his cause were overthrown. The Jews "set themselves," as St. Peter puts it, "for a truth against thy holy child, Jesus, whom thou hast anointed, both Herod and Pilate, with the Gentiles and the people of Israel, were gathered together." What an array against a child a few days old—a carpenter's son—the peasant of Nazareth—a prophet "followed about by a dozen fishermen or sailors," as Celsus states—one who had no name, no home, not one spear to defend his claims—not an ally. How this confederacy hated him—thirsted for his blood—watched him—lied about him—suborned men to convict him of crime—sent him to the cross surrounded by all possible marks of infamy, amid the exulting shouts of priest and people, Herod and the Gentiles. Eighteen hundred years have passed since the great spectacle was seen. Where are the Jews to-day? With no home, no temple, no national name, Zion a waste, the temple of the usurper stands on the site of the holy of holies, and Israel worships God in the city of her fathers only by permission of those who defy the religion of the Jew. And where is Zion's King? His name is honored in all lands. The sun shines on no part of the earth where his friends do not erect altars to his praise.

The Romans "set themselves," and did so at a time when the Roman Government was the imperial mistress of the world. Her temple at Rome, open or shut, told of war or peace in all parts of the world. She was a warlike empire, and the sun did not set on her domain. At that time there was no room for Zion's King in the inn. In a humble habitation, with the stalled oxen, the Prince of Life was born. He was cradled in a manger. During all his life he had not where to lay his head. Rome put Zion's King to death. Not content with this, she persecuted the infant Church for two hundred years. She inflicted on the followers of Jesus the most atrocious cruelties; sewed them in skins, and then threw them to the wild beasts; confined them in dungeons, and sent them to the stake. Where now is that proud mistress of the world? No land so poor, no people so mean, as those who dwell amid the ruins of the imperial greatness of Rome. Her decline began with the hour that she put the Son of God to death. While Zion's King leads the foremost nations of the world, the great commercial and political centers are under his control. Civilization, discoveries, inventions, and the march of humanity, attest his power.

The papacy "set itself." It attempted to do what Herod, Pontius Pilate, the rulers, the Jews, and the Romans could not do. It allied the kingdom of Christ to the State. It treated Jesus as Pilate, Herod, and the Jews treated him; put on him a mock royal robe, bowed the knee to him in derision, hailed him as king, and delivered him to his enemies. They tracked missions round the globe, and landed French priests and French brandy, where truth was taking root, under the cannons of men-of-war. God sent confusion among the followers. Women and men are now living who saw the Roman Pontiff fly from Rome on a coach-box, disguised as a lackey; and even now he is guarded to his prayers by foreign soldiers. He dare not trust his own dear children.

Infidels "set themselves." Giants in intellect, a whole nation threw off the binding force of religion, insulted Jesus, and dethroned God by a deliberate vote of its National Assembly. Voltaire boasted that it took twelve men to write up the religion of Jesus, but he would show that one man could write it down. But so terrible were the results of atheism to the state, that religion was recalled by the voice of the nation. The goddess of reason became a penitent. In the room where Paine wrote the "Age of Reason" a Christian Church has been formed.

God has his ark in his own sacred keeping. He oversees and overrules all. He sent his Gospel to the race, and made his Son King over all nations. This Gospel of the kingdom must go round the world. Devils may oppose and rend, but they will be exorcised. No man or nation can defy Zion's King and succeed. All his enemies will be overcome and dashed in pieces as a potter's vessel. Bow the knee to Zion's King, for "blessed are all they that put their trust in him."

XLVI.—MOUNT CARMEL AND THE SEA.

"Sweet to the troubled mariner, aloft on quivering shrouds,
It is to look in confidence beyond the warring clouds,
And know, when by deceitful winds at starless midnight driven,
There shineth down upon his path the guiding ray of heaven."

Mount Carmel is the only promontory in the Holy Land. The Carmel range is eight miles long, and terminates in a bold promontory twelve hundred feet above the Great Sea. It takes its name from its luxuriant beauty. It is made a symbol of the verdure, bloom, and undying vigor of the Gospel, for "the glory of Carmel shall be given unto it." It is in full view of Nazareth. Elisha the prophet, in Gilead, beyond Jordan, had his home in Carmel. He arose in the time of Ahab, a bad man and wicked. Judah was full of idols. Altars smoked from every hill-top. Groves were made sacred. Valleys were consecrated to Baal, a name given to the chief whom men worshiped. Eminences were crowded with worshipers. Incense went up from the summits, and house-tops were made the seat of sacrifice. But the God of Israel was despised. Thousands of prophets stood at the altar of Baal. But one prophet named the name of the Lord, and his life was not safe.

From his cavern home on Carmel, Elijah came forth to speak in the ears of Ahab the ominous prediction that God was God, and that on the land no rain nor dew should fall for full three years and six months—that the gaunt form of famine should stalk in the land, leading pestilence by the hand, till king and people knew that the Most High ruled among men. In his rough garment, his rural home, and simple fare, Elijah on Carmel was the type of John the Baptist. As he went up to heaven, so was he expected to come in person as the forerunner of the Great Shiloah. The Jews knew not the man who came in the spirit and power of Elijah. But the two had much in common. In his dress, mode of life, and tone of his ministry, the son of Elisabeth had much in common with the prophet of Carmel. He came in an age of great religious declension, and called, with trumpet-tones, the people to repentance. He avoided the great cities, and preached repentance to the neglected ones in the sparse settlements of the land. Men deserted the walled towns, and went out to him in great numbers. Even the rulers, the scribes, and Pharisees were among his auditors. At the fords of Jordan he baptized the repentant people, on the confession of their sins.

Carmel is full of interest. It stands, as of old, sacred to Jew, Turk, and Christian. The cavern called Elijah's still abides, and men look into the humble home of the prophet. The probable site where the prophet stood and looked toward the sea, is pointed out. A Carmelite convent stands near the altar on which the great trial took place, when Elijah mocked the prophets of Baal on the morning of his triumph. Here pilgrims are lodged and fed, and waited on by friars who claim to have descended from Elijah. Near the convent is one of the most beautiful views in all the Holy Land. Carmel is still fertile as the garden of the Lord.

Carmel is made the type of the millennial glory of the kingdom of God. Elevated, that all may see it—terraced to its summit with verdure, and clothed on all sides with fruit—its roots laved with water, so that its leaves shall never wither, it is to be an abiding memorial of the mercy of God, as full, as fresh, as free as when proclaimed by its divine Author. All that the Gospel did for men when Christ was on earth, it can do for men now. Its blood cleansed from all sin. He who presides over the treasury of grace is the friend of man, as when he was on earth. His promises support, his word comforts. He is the wisdom of God and the power of God unto salvation, and ever will be. It can never change. It can never lose its power while time shall endure. All who call on the Lord shall be saved. The tree of life shows no signs of decay. Its leaf can not wither, for God hath said that "the glory of Lebanon shall be given unto it, the excellency of Carmel and Sharon."

In the dark hour of famine, the prophet gave the command: "Look toward the sea." So shall Carmel teach us.

For three years and six months there had been no rain in all the land. The rivers failed—the springs dried up in their fountains—the grass withered, and the famine was sore in Samaria. On Carmel the prophet stood, looking toward the sea, when not a gleam of hope penciled the stricken earth. To the wicked Ahab, God sent the word: "I will send rain upon the earth." "At the time of the offering of the evening sacrifice," God vindicated his name and honor, and among the people it was "known that he was God in Israel." One man, "subject to like passions" with us, stood, in the name of God, against five hundred prophets, who came forth at the name of Baal. The great work of God, done through Elijah, felled the face of the people to the earth in awe, while they shouted, "The Lord he is God."

The nation brought to repentance, God was ready to lift his judgments from the land, and send rain on the grass and showers in the valleys. And the time came that God should send rain. "Elijah went up to the top of Carmel; and he cast himself down upon the earth, and put his face between his knees, and said to his servant, Go up now, look toward the sea." He looked, and said, "There is nothing." Seven times he went and looked toward the sea. At the seventh time he said, "Behold, there ariseth a little cloud out of the sea, like a man's hand." There was in it an abundance of rain. Soon "the heaven was black with clouds and wind, and there was a great rain."

The Bible makes much of the sea. It is made the type of God's omnipotence. "They that go down to the sea in ships, that do business on the great waters, see the works of the Lord, and his wonders in the deep." See it in the storm that he raiseth and calms; in the frail barriers of sand, that say to the sea, "Thus far, and no farther; here shall thy proud waves be stayed;" in the power that holds the ocean in its bed; in the constant restraint, that each storm prove not a deluge; in that God has set his bow in the clouds, in token that there shall be no more flood to destroy the earth—that how high soever the "stormy winds may lift up the waves thereof," God commandeth and maketh the storm a calm. There is no atheist on shipboard in a storm. God

> "Plants his footsteps in the sea,
> And rides upon the storm."

"Go look toward the sea," and we shall behold the sovereignty of God. God is king on the ocean, at least. Men are willing to concede so much. No one disobeys the law of the ocean, and lives. All men know this. But no less absolute is he on the earth. "Fear ye not me?" saith the Lord. "Will ye not tremble at my presence, which have placed the sand for the bound of the sea by a perpetual decree, that it can not pass it? And though the waves thereof toss themselves, yet can they not prevail; though they roar, yet can they not pass over it."

"Go look toward the sea," and we shall behold the wisdom of God. We find three times the amount of water to that of the land. "Why this waste!" the wisdom of man cries. The wisdom of God replies, "Is there too much moisture now? Do not the deserts and waste places ask for more?" Were there less expanse of water, and more land parched from drought, how soon would famine spread its wing, and brood eternally over all the earth? There is no chance in all this. God made the world to answer a great and grand design. He made it exactly. "He measured the waters." "He meeted out the heavens." "He weighed the hills in scales, and the mountains in balances." He knew how much of each material was needed to make just such a world as this. There is an abundance, but no waste. No part of sky, ocean, or earth can be lost. Men may use or abuse, but they can destroy nothing that God has made.

"Go look toward the sea," and we shall behold the mysteries of God. "The thunder of his power who can understand?" The earth and sea, providence and grace, are full of the mystery of God. One of the elements of which the sea is composed is an element of intense flame. God, if he pleased, could separate these properties, and girdle the world with fire and consume it, with no other agency than to allow the mysterious and subtle power that enters so largely into this great highway of nations to act on its original law. The color of the sea and its saltness who can explain? Its perpetual motion, without which its vast surface would girdle the globe with pestilence? Its regular tides, and phenomena that man sees, but can not explain?

"Look toward the sea," and we shall behold the goodness of God. So cries out the psalmist: "Oh, that men would praise the Lord for his goodness (as seen on the sea), and for his wonderful works to the children of men!" It is seen in that decree that holds the ocean in its bed, and fixes its bounds that it can not pass—in making the sea a storehouse of food for God's poor and needy ones—in the motion that gives comfort and health to the sons of men—in making it the highway of nations, and on it carrying the blessings of civilization, commerce, and religion to the race—in enabling the swift ships of commerce to bear the Gospel to the ends of the earth. The "sea is full of the goodness of the Lord."

"Look toward the sea," and we shall behold the providence of God. So men were taught when David sang of mercy and judgment. Men who do business on the great waters, we are told, tossed on the angry waves, mounting to heaven and sinking down to the depths, reeling to and fro, and at their wit's end, "cry unto God in their distress. His voice rules the winds and waves." "He bringeth them out of their distresses." Men who call on God at no other time, call on him in a storm at sea, when there is only a plank between them and death. How the providence of God looms up on the sea; in time of peril and fear, when all seems to be lost, what prayers, what vows are breathed to God; what promises are recorded against men who have met a storm on the ocean! What hair-breadth escapes has the sea been witness to! A ship on fire, or near the breakers in a storm on a lee shore! Often has life hung on a brittle thread, on the fidelity of a seam, or the honest nailing on of a plank. How sad the memories of the sea as connected with the providence of God! How many countless thousands have gone down to sleep in mid-ocean! The sailor-boy comes not home again. The young husband sleeps among the coral. How the eye dims as we read the record of a ship home from a long voyage! "Lost," "washed overboard," "killed," "left at such a port," stand against many names. Who can foresee how soon the clear sky will blacken, the quiet sea be roused to fury amid the artillery of the sky, or the glassy surface of the ocean, treacherous and uncertain, open to engulf navies? The providence of God is on the sea.

"Look toward the sea," and we shall behold its solemn revelations. In the vision of the last great day "the sea gave up the dead which were in it." How terrible will be the revelations of the sea when the millions slain in battle come forth from their watery bed; when the thousands that have gone down in tempest and storm, with their death-cry ascending to God, shall awake and come forth; when that great army, killed in cold blood, slain by the treacherous arm, and flung into the sea, shall meet their murderers face to face; when the cargoes of bondmen, stolen from their native shores, and thrown overboard that their captors may escape, shall tell the story of their wrongs! What revelations will come forth from the great waters of the earth—the Red Sea, the Irrawaddy, the Seine, the Thames, the Mississippi! The red blood of man has colored the sea; and men been killed and thrown into the water to hide the crime. What victims of jealousy, revenge, and hate—what deeds of darkness and cruelty, rapine and murder, the waters have borne to the ocean! What missing men will be found—what tales dead men, dead women, and little children will tell, when the sea shall give up its dead!

We are told that nothing is more common in some of the great cities of the Old World than for a traveler near a great river to hear a scream, an appalling death-cry, a splash, and then all will be still. "Dead men tell no tales!" Wait till the revelations of the sea are made; wait till the victim and the murderer stand side by side at that bar where exact justice is meted to all, and from whose decision there is no appeal! Let the St. Lawrence and the Great Lakes, the Rio Grande and the Amazon, Jordan, the Nile, and the Euphrates, the Danube, the Tiber, and the Ganges give up their dead, and the most dreadful book that will be opened in the day of judgment will be that which holds the revelations of the sea.

XLVII.—THE FIRST AND LAST SUPPER.

> "This was compassion like a God,
>   That when the Saviour knew
> The price of pardon was his blood,
>   His pity ne'er withdrew.
>
> "Now, though he reigns exalted high,
>   His love is still as great;
> Well he remembers Calvary,
>   Nor let his saints forget."

The ordinance called the Last Supper was instituted in that black hour called by our Lord the "hour of darkness." In an upper room, at the hands of her Great Head, in a time of fear and desertion, denied and betrayed by his own friends, the Church received the enduring memorials of a Saviour's love.

The public life of Jesus was closed. For man he had become poor; for him he had walked in woe and ignominy on earth. Insulted by those he came to redeem, he made his soul an offering for sin. His form bent with suffering, his visage more marred than the sons of men, his eventful life was to close in disgrace. Still the great purpose for which he came from heaven was incomplete. The hour for which he took on him flesh and blood was near, but had not yet come. He was yet to taste death for man. He was yet to be made a curse for sin, and to tread the wine-press alone, with his garments dyed in his own blood, like him that treadeth in the wine-vat. He was yet to know the bitterness of banishment from God; to be alone, deserted, forsaken, and send the thrilling death-cry down to the abyss of hell and up to the throne of God—a spectacle to angels and men. From that chamber he must go out to meet, once more, the prince of this world; be in agony in the garden; climb up the rugged sides of Calvary; sink beneath the cross; tread the dreadful *via doloroso* over the flinty road; and, amid fiendish shouts of exultation, amid ungodly jeers, forsaken by his own Father, whom he loved best, Jesus was to offer himself, on the cross, in expiation for the sins of the world.

Peculiarities of the First Supper.

1. It was instituted in the feeblest hour of the Church. In human estimation, the prospects of the Church had never been brilliant. There was much to attract in the person of Jesus. But his cause seemed a forlorn one. It was a grain of mustard in the earth; a handful of corn thrown broadcast on the mountains. What little hope those had that clung to him was soon to expire. The combinations against him were only to be too successful. The small room that held the little flock, held those among them that were not faithful. The Shepherd was to be smitten, the sheep scattered, and a few women at the sepulcher to be, seemingly, all who were true to the last to him, in whom so many trusted as the redeemer of Israel.

2. The Supper was instituted in the darkest hour

of the Church. Much had been hoped. But all was to end in disappointment. How sharp, the mournful language of the disciples on their way to Emmaus tells us: "We trusted that it had been he which should redeem Israel." Left as lambs in the midst of wolves, who would protect them? On whom could they rely? Great disgrace was to be thrown on the cause and on them, from the manner of their Master's death. It was to be to the Church a legacy of perpetual shame. The death of the cross was the last mark of detestation on the vilest of men—so shameful, so ignominious, so terrible, that no Roman could be subject to it. A crucified man was not prayed for. He was regarded as accursed of God. His name was excluded from the family register— his body from the family tomb. To this punishment was the Lord subjected, between two of the vilest of men, to make his death as vile as theirs.

3. It was instituted as a memento of the time, manner, and purpose of his death. "In remembrance of me"—"ye do show forth the Lord's death"—not his life, nor acts, nor miracles. These, great, valuable, miraculous as they were, were only auxiliary to the great purpose of his mission—merely incidental, for which no memorials were given, and no ordinances instituted. The Supper is a memento of his death, in shame, in ignominy, in woe—a broken body—blood shed by the spear, and oozing from the wounds torn and lacerated by the nails.

How soon the memory of the dearest and fondest fades! It is one of the kind provisions of the Father of mercies: else, brooding and sighing perpetually over the memory of the past, our duty to the present and to the living would be left undone, and the soul would weep itself away at the grave of the departed. When we stand at the death-bed of those dear to us, we feel that our hearts are broken—that our eyes will never cease to weep—the sun will never shine brightly again, and the heart be never more glad. But time, the great healer of many of the woes of life, stops the pulsation of sorrow with his rigid finger—tears are dried up in the fountain—healing voices soothe the sorrow—an unseen hand binds up the lacerated affections—the merry laugh echoes where death trod—the chiseled marble or glowing canvas are needed to call back the almost forgotten dead. Well did the compassionate Redeemer know that. So he instituted the Supper, that, through its simple but expressive symbols, those who loved him could recall his death in expiation.

4. It was instituted as a perpetual monument to his love for the Church. Men have a strange desire to live in the memory of coming generations. The best things and the worst that men have done, have been done that they may live in the future. The resources of nations have been wasted and exhausted —millions of lives have been sacrificed—the world turned into a gory battle-field—that base men might live after death in some fitting monument. But the records perish, the brass corrodes, the marble crumbles. Who knows the name of the builder of the Pyramids, or that of the incendiary who flung the torch into the great temple of the Ephesians? The monument that the Redeemer erected stands to-day,

with the sunlight of immortality gilding its summit. It was created by his own hand—severely simple, but imperishable. It was builded by his own might. It cost no tears, no sacrifice, no blood but his own. The emblems of the Supper are found in all climes— in the desert, on the sea, in every land. How well adapted to the end! The aged pilgrim, with joy, communes with his Lord, whom he expects to see; trembling, and scarcely believing for joy, the young Christian, for the first time, obeys the divine command, with thanksgiving, "Eat, O friends—drink, beloved." The believer for a moment turns away from guilt, worldliness, ingratitude, to the fullness of love in the Lamb of God. Blessed table, laden with the memorials of the Saviour's passion and love.

Amid shame, treachery, darkness, ignominy, and the prospect of a shameful death, the first Supper was celebrated. The magnitude of sin—the awful cost of a sinner's redemption—the worth of the soul —are inscribed on each particle of the broken bread, and sparkles in each drop of sacramental wine.

Peculiarities of the Last Supper.

It is thus promised by the Lord: "I will not drink henceforth of this fruit of the vine, until that day when I drink it new with you in my Father's kingdom." In the book of Revelation allusion is made to this heavenly feast: "Write, blessed are they that are called unto the marriage supper of the Lamb."

1. It will supersede the first, which was to "show forth the Lord's death till he come." Eighteen centuries have passed since the solemn consecration of bread and wine took place in that upper room on Mount Zion. But the memorials are as fresh and as precious as on the day of their consecration. He that appointed the mystic symbols gave them immortal vigor. In the Church will they be held in all honor till time shall end. In all lands, and among all nations, will the Saviour be remembered. Son will succeed sire, and the daughter succeed mother at the communion of the body and blood of our Lord. The millennium will come and go, nations rise and fall, but the Supper will remain till the kingdoms of this world and the glory of them shall be given to the Lord of the Supper, who is the King of kings and the Lord of lords. And when the purposes for which the Communion was given shall have been answered, the Communion on earth will cease to be observed.

But the end will be worthy of its Author, and worthy of the Church, the bride, the Lamb's wife, which has been redeemed by his precious blood. Once more will the table be spread. The Lamb of God will again gird himself to keep the feast with his elect. Not, as now, a man of sorrows, but reinstated with the "glory he had with the Father before the world was," having laid aside the form of man and reinvested himself with that form of God he had when "he thought it not robbery to be equal with God." Gathered out of all nations, the ransomed of the Lord, coming to Zion, will know the fullness of that promise: "I will drink it new with you in the kingdom of my Father."

2. It will be celebrated in the brightest hour of the Church. Her foes put under her feet—without stain, spot, or any such thing, she will stand in the presence of her exalted head, who loved her, from the foundation of the world, with an eternal love. She shall behold the dawn of the celestial day that shall know no close, whose brightness shall never be dimmed. She will see the King in his beauty, arrayed in his royal apparel, glimpses of which Peter and John saw "when they were with him in the mount," the brightness of which filled John with awe, on Patmos, as he fell at his feet as dead. Now he is the King invisible; then the saints shall bask in his presence, which is fullness of joy.

3. It will be a token that Jesus will never again leave his Church. Where he is, "there shall they be also." The Church shall be as angels, and "they do always behold the face of God." "Before the throne they shall serve him day and night." "He that sitteth on the throne shall dwell among them." "The Lamb shall lead them to living fountains." "God shall wipe away all tears from their eyes." "In his presence is fullness of joy."

4. It will not be celebrated by a feeble band, but by an innumerable multitude, that no man can number. The mass of the world die young. How blessed are the promises to little children! A child dead is a child in heaven. How many millions of those little ones, redeemed by the blood of Christ, will join their voices with the elder spirits in praise

of the Lamb! All these will be welcome to the marriage supper of the Lamb. Here will meet the noble spirits of every age who have borne testimony for Jesus. All nations, tongues, and languages will be represented—patriarchs, prophets, apostles, martyrs. They will come from the east and from the west, from the north and from the south, and sit down in the kingdom with Abraham, Isaac, and Jacob. Moses, Aaron, and the Church in the wilderness will unite with those redeemed under the better covenant. In our Father's house are many mansions—and all will be full. No more conflict, temptations, or sin; all will be safe in the haven of endless love. "There the wicked cease from troubling, and the weary are at rest."

5. The last Supper will usher in the bliss of heaven. The first Supper led to awful peril and conflict, to banishment and death. The last will usher those who have slept in Jesus into that rest that remaineth for the people of God. The panting runner will have touched the goal and borne off the prize. The warrior, with the dust and sweat on his brow, will take off his armor, having fought the good fight and gotten his crown. His home will be blessed. He will dwell near cool fountains, amid groves, fanned by spicy and balmy winds; delicious music shall fall on his ear, and fruits of exquisite flavor gratify his taste. The sun shall not smite, nor rude winds annoy. In the presence of God the blessed ones shall rest in love. With all their powers attuned to melody, gifted with angelic execution, the children of heaven shall sing the song of Moses, closed with the song of the

Lamb, singing, "Blessed and holy are they who are called to the marriage supper of the Lamb."

6. It will be celebrated amid the endless confusion of the enemies of the Church. "I never knew you," will be the answer to many who boast that Jesus had taught in their streets. In the day of the Church's triumph, the decree will go forth from her exalted head: "Bring hither my enemies that would not I should reign over them, and slay them before me." They who would enjoy the glory must share the shame. Those who would wear the crown must bear the cross.

Before the mystery of God will be finished, painful separations will take place—in many cases, where least expected. Here the wheat and the tares grow in the same field, and the sheep and the goats graze on the same hillside. In the same Church one will be taken and another left. The pious husband and the ungodly wife, the ungodly father and the holy mother—those who have walked hand in hand, arm in arm, through the vicissitudes of life, and borne common griefs and toil, will close their communion sweet. Youth's brilliant circle will be broken, and neighbors who have lived in peace or mingled tears together in hours of woe must bid each other a final adieu. There will be joy in heaven at the last Supper. There will be woe in hell.

It is so on earth. At the communion families separate and households divide; brothers and sisters part at the table of the Lord on earth. Some do not feel worthy, some the Bible excludes, some love sin too well to come to the Saviour. All do not eat at the table of the Lord below. Above, they are holy as well as blessed who sit down to the marriage supper of the Lamb, and their names are all in the Book of Life. Now men exclude themselves; then they will be excluded. Now they lack the disposition; then the opportunity. Beyond the tomb there are no Sabbaths of mercy; no repeated calls to repentance; no reopening of the book of life, that one's name may be written therein; once closed, he that is unjust will be unjust still. "Blessed are they which are called unto the marriage supper of the Lamb."

THE END.

NEW BOOKS

And New Editions Recently Issued by
CARLETON, PUBLISHER,
NEW YORK,
413 *BROADWAY, CORNER OF LISPENARD STREET.*

N.B.—The Publisher, upon receipt of the price in advance, will send any of the following Books by mail, POSTAGE FREE, to any part of the United States. This convenient and very safe mode may be adopted when the neighboring Booksellers are not supplied with the desired work. State name and address in full.

Victor Hugo.

LES MISÉRABLES.—*The best edition*, two elegant 8vo. vols., beautifully bound in cloth, $5.50; half calf, $10.00
LES MISÉRABLES.—*The popular edition*, one large octavo volume, paper covers, $2.00; cloth bound, $2.50
LES MISÉRABLES.—In the Spanish language. Fine 8vo. edition, two vols., paper covers, $4.00; cloth bound, $5.00
JARGAL.—A new novel. Illustrated. . 12mo. cloth, $1.75
THE LIFE OF VICTOR HUGO.—By himself. 8vo. cloth, $1.75

Miss Muloch.

JOHN HALIFAX.—A novel. With illustration. 12mo. cloth, $1.75
A LIFE FOR A LIFE.— . do. do. $1.75

Charlotte Bronte (Currer Bell).

JANE EYRE.—A novel. With illustration. 12mo., cloth, $1.75
THE PROFESSOR. —do. . do. . do. $1.75
SHIRLEY.— . do. . do. . do. $1.75
VILLETTE.— . do. . do. . do. $1.75

Hand-Books of Society.

THE HABITS OF GOOD SOCIETY; with thoughts, hints, and anecdotes, concerning nice points of taste, good manners, and the art of making oneself agreeable. The most entertaining work of the kind ever published. 12mo. cloth, $1.75
THE ART OF CONVERSATION.—With directions for self-culture. A sensible and instructive work, that ought to be in the hands of every one who wishes to be either an agreeable talker or listener. . . . . 12mo. cloth, $1.50

New English Novels.

RECOMMENDED TO MERCY.— . . . 12mo. cloth, $1.75
TAKEN UPON TRUST.— *In press.* . do. $1.75
THE GOLDEN RULE.— do. . do. $1.75

Mrs. Mary J. Holmes' Works.

'LENA RIVERS.— . . . A novel. 12mo. cloth, $1.50
DARKNESS AND DAYLIGHT.— . do. do. $1.50
TEMPEST AND SUNSHINE.— . do. do. $1.50
MARIAN GREY.— . . . do. do. $1.50
MEADOW BROOK.— . . . do. do. $1.50
ENGLISH ORPHANS.— . . . do. do. $1.50
DORA DEANE.— . . . . do. do. $1.50
COUSIN MAUDE.— . . . do. do. $1.50
HOMESTEAD ON THE HILLSIDE.— do. do. $1.50
HUGH WORTHINGTON.— . . do. do. $1.50

Artemus Ward.

HIS BOOK.—The first collection of humorous writings by A. Ward. Full of comic illustrations. 12mo. cloth, $1.50
HIS TRAVELS.—A comic volume of Indian and Mormon adventures. With laughable illustrations. 12mo. cloth, $1.50

Miss Augusta J. Evans.

BEULAH.—A novel of great power. . 12mo. cloth, $1.75
MACARIA.— do. do. . do. $1.75
A NEW NOVEL.—*In press.* . . . do. $1.75

By the Author of "Rutledge."

RUTLEDGE.—A deeply interesting novel. 12mo. cloth, $1.75
THE SUTHERLANDS.— do. . . do. $1.75
FRANK WARRINGTON.— do. . . do. $1.75
ST. PHILIP'S.— . . do. . . do. $1.75
LOUIE'S LAST TERM AT ST. MARY'S. . . do. $1.75

Josh Billings.

HIS BOOK.—All the rich comic sayings of this celebrated humorist. With comic illustrations. . 12mo. cloth, $1.50

Mrs. Ritchie (Anna Cora Mowatt).

FAIRY FINGERS.—A capital new novel. . 12mo. cloth, $1.75
THE MUTE SINGER.— do. . . . do. $1.75
A NEW BOOK.—*In press.* . . . do. $1.75

New English Novels.

BEYMINSTRE.—A very interesting novel. 12mo. cloth, $1.75
THE SILENT WOMAN.—*In press.* . . do. $1.75

Geo. W. Carleton.

OUR ARTIST IN CUBA.—A humorous volume of travels; with fifty comic illustrations by the author. 12mo. cloth, $1.50
OUR ARTIST IN PERU.—*In press.* $1.00

Pulpit Pungencies.

A new comic book of immense fun. 12mo. cloth, $1.50

www.ingramcontent.com/pod-product-compliance
Lightning Source LLC
Chambersburg PA
CBHW032010220426
43664CB00006B/197